BEYOND THE BAMBOO CURTAIN:

UNDERSTANDING AMERICA'S INVISIBLE MINORITY

DR. MICHAEL SOON LEE

where words connect

BEYOND THE BAMBOO CURTAIN:

UNDERSTANDING AMERICA'S INVISIBLE MINORITY

DR. MICHAEL SOON LEE

BEYOND THE BAMBOO CURTAIN: Understanding America's Invisible Minority

ISBN: 978-1-959811-14-5 (Paperback)
ISBN 978-1-959811-15-2 (eBook)

Library of Congress Control Number: 2023914493

Cover Design: Okomota
Interior Design: Amit Dey

Twitter: wordeeeupdates X (formerly Twitter)
Facebook: facebook.com/wordeee
E-mail: contact@wordeee.com
Website: www.wordeee.com

Published by Wordeee Beacon, NY 2023

Printed in the USA

DEDICATION

To my wife Miriam, our sons Chris and Ryan, my brother Daniel, and our extended family. I thank you for all your support and patience in making this book possible.

I especially want to thank my editor, Evi-Irena Ioannidou, for helping to bring order to the chaos that is the story of my life.

And to you, Dear Reader, I hope my story will fill you with hope and optimism in a world that is fraught with divisiveness and a fear of differences.

TABLE OF CONTENTS

AUTHOR'S NOTE

I was a lonely Chinese kid in an all-white neighborhood in 1950s Oakland, California, who could not wait to start school. When I stepped onto the playground my first day of school that I'd so longed for, some of the kids made fun of me and called me names because I was the only Asian in sight. That was the first time I realized I was different and that being different wasn't good.

Growing up, I felt more and more suffocated by the stereotypes in people's minds, movies, and TV—wimpy Asian guys who are quiet, good at math, and not virile enough to attract girls. I cringed at my father's accent because when he mispronounced words, I knew people were laughing at him behind his back. That was not going to be me! I went to great lengths to fit in, purging any trace of an accent and trying to peroxide my hair, believing the famous Clairol® slogan of the day, "Is it true…blondes have more fun?"

Thankfully, in my teens, the feeling of being invisible started to shift when Bruce Lee, the quintessential Asian alpha male, and hero, rose to superstardom. He was a role model whom I could identify with, so I learned martial arts, played in a rock band, and started building some confidence.

When my number came up for the Vietnam War draft, it brought into focus for me America's relationship not only with Asia, but also with Asian Americans and other minorities, since this was also the time of the Civil Rights movement and Flower Power. All I had experienced and witnessed in my short life was compelling me to raise my voice and make a difference. Realizing the power of the media in shaping perceptions, I wanted to become a television producer.

To give myself an edge in this extremely competitive field, I took advantage of an affirmative action program, and have always wondered whether I would have gotten my foot in the door if I hadn't fulfilled the company's quota. After a couple of weeks in my entry-level job, I was diagnosed with arthritis of the spine, which could have confined me to a wheelchair for the rest of my life. From that point forward, I have been racing against the clock to accomplish as much as I can in my life.

I have worked in TV and film behind the camera and in front. I loved acting but the only roles I was given were "martial artist" and "Asian gangster." At some point, unable to stomach the typecasting and discrimination any longer, I quit acting and started teaching, selling real estate, writing, and public speaking, presenting over 1,000 times to Fortune 100 and 500 companies around the world on topics of diversity.

I have been "the rebellious one," according to my parents, but I am not a natural-born fighter. Yet, I have had to sue for rights that non-minorities take for granted and stand against discrimination, regardless of considerable personal and professional cost. But I think my greatest battle has been against the stereotypes and expectations that I, unwittingly, took on as an Asian male in this country. I am not ashamed to say that it all took its toll. I have struggled with depression but survived and thrived, always motivated to make a difference by teaching about diversity.

For me, it has been a long and painful process coming to terms with how Asians are viewed in this country, the only home I have ever known as a fifth-generation American. I spent years questioning my cultural identity, whether "to be or not to be Asian," and to what degree. I have tried to understand the reasons for the bias against Asians by taking classes in college and researching the socio-historical context. Learning about the contributions of Asians to this country helped me feel proud to be Asian American. It also quieted my cultural identity questions somewhat because I finally knew where I have come from and who I am; an Asian American who belongs in this country and has every right to be here!

INTRODUCTION

What began as a memoir was quickly overtaken by my desire to help readers better understand what it's like to be Asian in America. It's a sad fact that, according to Pew Research, only 24% of Asian Americans consider themselves extremely or very informed about the history of Asian people in the United States. Since the Asian American experience cannot be understood outside of the historical context, my memoir incorporates the social, political, and historical background that defined our lives from the 1800s to the present. Because this material is dispersed throughout the book, I have added a chronology of milestones as a reference in the Appendix.

I also wanted the book to be more than just about my life, so I included other Asian American voices through interviews with Hollywood actors Kelly Hu, Peter Shinkoda, and Tzi Ma, talent agent Ray Moheet, and quotes from academics and researchers like Jeff Adachi, Evelyn Yoshimura, Chester Cheng, Nicole Ja, Derald Wing Sue, Jin Li, Lianqin Wang, Amy Chua, and Luis A. Sánchez. I also compiled a list of "who's who" to inspire Asian Americans and inform non-Asian readers that we have been involved in every aspect of life in the United States.

Beyond the Bamboo Curtain then explores the following topics pertaining to Asian Americans:

- Systemic racism and discrimination.
- Stereotypes from the 1800s to the present.
- The model-minority myth.
- The history of Chinese migration to America and of Chinatowns.

- Asian attitudes about money, status, and career.
- The anti-Asian sentiment and crime due to the COVID-19 pandemic, and so much more.

I hope that this book and my story will help non-Asians look past the stereotypes and see us as human beings like themselves. I hope that they will become more aware of the challenges we face that are like those of other minority groups, along with our distinctly unique roadblocks. I am certain that if they expand their awareness, they will enhance their own opportunities by relating to Asians better, whether they are their bosses, clients, or coworkers.

The book is meant to help Asian Americans as well as new immigrant Asians understand the unique challenges they face here in "the land of opportunity." Questions such as, why is it so difficult to get promoted despite working harder than anyone? Why is it tough to be accepted into a top-level university despite having stellar grades? Why are they stereotyped for what they are not? These questions are addressed in this narrative. I hope that the lessons I've learned will help them navigate the path more easily.

My greatest hope is that this book will help create awareness so that Asian American children won't face the discrimination that generations before them experienced. I believe in a cross-cultural world where familiarity does not breed contempt, but rather engenders empathy and understanding.

The title *Beyond the Bamboo Curtain: Understanding America's Invisible Minority* captures the main message that I wish to convey. The word "beyond" suggests getting past the differences, stereotypes, and preconceptions that make up the "curtain," to see how similar we all are on the inside. A symbol of tenacity, modesty, and integrity, bamboo is instantly associated with Asia. A strong and resilient plant, it is often considered a foreign, invasive species, much like the early Asians were thought of in America. Bamboo is used in a vast variety of ways, including for curtains and screens. Being an impermanent barrier that hides things from view, a "bamboo curtain" can be opened easily, if you take some action. Asians are often described as too different to fit in or be understood. The reality is that, in this country we have always been observed through "screens" that make us appear inscrutable. It is time to acknowledge that the bamboo curtain exists; lift it and view Asian Americans in a totally different light.

My story is only one of the of millions of Asians who have lived and are living today behind the bamboo curtain—a curtain that needs to be torn down.

STICKS AND STONES

Like so many American kids, I grew up with a lot of television. *Bugs Bunny* and *Road Runner* cartoons when I was around four years old were my window to the world, and the trajectory for my career in media.

I was born on December 30, 1950, at Children's Hospital in San Francisco. My father, John Git Wong, a second-generation Chinese American, was rather shy because his parents had migrated from China, and he still had a slight Chinese accent. He served in World War II as an aircraft mechanic in the United States Army Air Forces in China and Burma, supporting General Chennault's famous Flying Tigers squadron. After the war, he got a job at the Alameda Naval Air Station in the San Francisco Bay Area as a sheet metal worker, where he stayed for 50 years.

My mother, Ruth Wong, was a fourth-generation Chinese American whose ancestors survived a three-month journey from China to come over in the 1860s and ended up working in the fishing industry in Monterey, California. Her English was perfect, and she was as American as apple pie, with one exception, she was Asian. She supported the war effort by working in an armory factory in a San Francisco shipyard. After the war, my parents married, and she took business classes at a community college. She worked as a medical transcriptionist until I was born.

A year and a half later, my brother Timothy was born but died at six months of sudden infant death syndrome (SIDS), which basically meant that the doctors had no explanation for his death. My mother never got over losing "Timmy," as she referred to him, even though my brother Daniel was born happy and healthy two years later. After Timmy passed, I think she always kept her emotional distance from us to avoid being disloyal to his memory or maybe to protect herself from further heartbreak should anything happen to any of us.

In the 1950s, we were the only Asian family in our neighborhood in Oakland, California, and despite my mother being an outgoing and very social person, my parents kept to themselves because they felt somewhat uncomfortable around Caucasians. Only later did I learn about their experiences with discrimination, especially during World War II. As a result of our isolation, I was a lonely kid who never developed many social skills.

I remember how much I looked forward to my first day at Fruitvale Grammar School, which was literally two doors away from our house. I loved watching kids going to school in the morning, laughing and talking, and I couldn't wait to be one of them. Since I was born in December, the school gave my parents the choice of having me start kindergarten at five or six years old. I was rather small, so my mother was afraid that I would get picked on and decided to wait a year, so I could start at six.

After what seemed like an eternity, my first day of school finally arrived. I vividly remember my crisp, stiff new off-brand jeans, a red flannel shirt, and the Superman lunch pail with a thermos of milk to go with my peanut butter and jelly sandwich. My mother tearfully hugged me goodbye, and I skipped down the street to the school. I looked around at the sea of faces on the playground, hoping to find someone to talk to or play with, when I heard a very loud, harsh voice holler, "Hey, look at the chink!" I swung my head around to look at this obviously distasteful creature he was pointing at, only to realize that everyone was looking at me!

For the first time in my life, I felt singled out, rejected, and unloved. Without understanding why, I felt ashamed, inferior, and embarrassed to even exist. Until that moment, I had no idea that I was different, or that being different was a bad thing. The few kids I played with on my block were white, so, of course, I thought I was just one of them.

Despite the whirlwind of activity on my first day—being given a seat assignment, coloring books, and some homework —I could not forget the schoolyard incident because my face stayed beet red from embarrassment the entire day. I was a bad thing, a chink—whatever that meant.

After school, I impatiently waited for my father to come home. Since my mother was always so positive about everything, I instinctively knew that an honest answer about my experience could only come from him. The moment he stepped through the door, I asked, "Hey, Dad, what's a chink?" His face immediately showed disappointment that I knew this racial epithet at such a young age. Then he explained, "Some people make fun of us because we are Chinese." He saw that I didn't understand why, so he pulled me close and continued, "others are afraid of us because we are different from them. When you hear words like this, show no emotion. Otherwise, the other kids will call you a 'baby' in addition to calling you a chink." Then he said, "sticks and stones may break your bones, but words will never hurt you."

What a lesson to deliver to a six-year-old and, oh, how wrong he was! That word, and all the others I was called, like "slant eye" and "Ching Chong Chinaman," still sting many decades later. They served as reminders that I was an outcast, setting the stage for the rest of my life. Desperately wanting to belong, I became the ultimate people-pleaser. Whatever I could do to make others happy, I did, so they would like me and overlook my differences.

One of only two Asians at Fruitvale Grammar School for the next six years, I felt very alone. Sarah Wong was the only other Asian, and she was fighting her own battles with discrimination in her own quiet way. Every time I saw her, she looked like a beaten puppy, and I didn't want to add to her troubles by sharing my problems.

I became the designated outcast. Every day, I had to eat by myself at lunch. I was never asked to play tetherball or four squares with other kids, and no one wanted to sit near or talk to the chink for fear of becoming an outcast themselves. I would hear girls say things like, "Don't go near him. He has cooties." No one wanted to come to my house after school, and I wasn't invited to my classmates' birthday parties like all the other kids. I got very few Valentine's Day cards even though our teachers said we had to give one to everyone in our class.

To escape my daily torment, I buried myself in the pages of adventure novels like *Huckleberry Finn*. I loved reading about how people escaped miserable situations, hoping to find a way out of mine. Through such books, I learned about slavery, and how African Americans were sometimes called "niggers," just like I was called a "chink." Still, I could not understand why anyone should be treated with less respect just because of the color of their skin and ethnic heritage. My little brother Dan became my main companion during my early years.

By second grade, I had read so much that I was already reading at a fourth-grade level. So, they advanced me to third grade. By fifth grade, my bookworm life led to winning a national essay contest set by an author who was promoting his book. He even came to the school and gave me, during assembly in front of the whole school, an original drawing from his book.

You would think I would have felt proud. I didn't. I was terribly embarrassed to be the center of attention. Worse still, the following year, I was named class valedictorian. The last thing I wanted was to have the spotlight on me because my parents, who lived in fear of being placed in an incarceration camp like the Japanese during WWII, always reminded me that "the nail that sticks up gets hammered down." Ouch.

Being constantly on display because I was the only Asian was very hard on me. At the time, the only other Chinese people I knew ran the local grocery store. There was also our extended family and our weekly visit to Chinatown in San Francisco, of course, but the sense of being "oddities" seemed to follow us everywhere. I hated my parents for being Asian and different. I always wished they had been white so I would be white, the same as everyone else in our neighborhood.

Our summer vacations were spent camping, most often with my cousins, because my father planned the trips with his two brothers, Henry, and Chester. The thirteen of us went to places like Yellowstone and Pinnacles National Park because that was all we could afford. In the 1950s and 60s, gasoline cost about 23 cents a gallon (I know it's hard to believe!), and the parks charged two dollars a car. We brought our own tents, propane gas stoves, and food. The men set up shelter while the women cooked "traditional" meals, which for us Chinese Americans were hot dogs and chili.

Camping was uncommon for Asians at the time. On these trips, I could not help but notice the strange looks we were getting from other campers. I guess it was unusual to see so many Chinese people together, often outnumbering the area's total Asian population.

I also didn't realize that it had only been a decade since Japanese Americans were incarcerated during WWII, and there was still a great deal of animosity against Asians. I remember my mother telling me that during the war she had to wear a big yellow button that said, "I am Chinese," so she wouldn't get hassled about her race on the bus to and from work. There was violence against Asians in America then, much like there has always been, but which escalated following the Coronavirus pandemic.

Around that time, I noticed that the people who treated us most decently were minorities and gay people. Could it be that when you suffer discrimination, you become more sensitive to how others are treated? While I was somewhat aware of the history of African Americans, I knew very little about Hispanics, other than kids in my school calling them "spics" and "beaners."

I had almost no experience with gay people, who were the only group considered lower on the status scale than blacks. One boy in my school was very effeminate, and kids constantly called him "fag" and "homo" and sometimes beat him up. While I felt very badly for him, I was secretly glad that someone was more of a target than I was. I knew only too well that sticks and stones can break your bones and words can wound your soul.

"CHINKTOWNS"—
A SAD HISTORY

The racist slur "Chinktown," by which New York's famous Chinatown was sometimes referred to, is a poignant reminder of the sad history of America's Chinatowns.

While gold was being discovered in California in 1848, crop failures brought famine to Southern China. Chinese men, like my great-grandfather, sailed west to seek their fortunes, only to find themselves in a very hostile land. Considered not only odd, but also competitors to whites for jobs, California in 1850 imposed the Foreign Miner's Tax, aimed mainly at the Chinese. Unable to afford this tax, many were recruited to build the Transcontinental Railroad. Others were forced to cook or do laundry for miners since there were few women out west. Doing "women's work" gave rise to the notion that Asian men were not masculine and would not fight back if attacked.

Like European immigrants, who gathered in neighborhoods in communities of their own people, the first Chinatowns sprang up on the West Coast. But the Chinese were targeted even there. Since they were paid less than whites, they were blamed for driving down wages and taking their jobs. After the railroad was completed and white laborers feared for their livelihoods, anti-Chinese attacks increased, including beatings, arson, and murder. For example, in 1885 in Rock Springs, Wyoming, 150 armed white miners drove Chinese immigrants out of town by setting fire to their homes and businesses and murdering 28 people. No one was ever charged for the massacre. This was hardly an isolated incident; over 150 anti-Chinese riots erupted in the 1870s and 1880s, with some of the worst violence in Denver, Los Angeles, Seattle, and Tacoma. In 1871, a mob of 500 whites and

Hispanics hung 19 Chinese immigrants in one of the largest mass lynchings of the time. As a result, many fled East, which is how East Coast Chinatowns were formed.

On the West Coast, the Chinese sought safety in numbers, while discriminatory housing and labor laws prevented them from living and working outside of Chinatowns. They were prohibited from owning property and barred from most industries, aside from hand-laundry and restaurants. Most sustained themselves by selling goods and services to other Chinese in the Chinatowns.

Due to the 1882 Chinese Exclusion Act, Chinese men could neither bring their families to America nor afford the passage home because of the kinds of jobs they were allowed to perform. As a result, Chinatowns were mostly "bachelor quarters" where these Chinese men often lived and died alone. Adding insult to injury, Chinatowns were considered "depraved colonies of prostitutes, gamblers, and opium addicts bereft of decency." In 1885, the city of San Francisco formed a committee to investigate depravity in its Chinatown. The report is full of moral panic about crime, poor sanitation, and "white women living and cohabitating with Chinamen."

"The streets and habitations were filthy in the extreme, and so long as they remained in that condition, so long would they stand as a constant menace to the welfare of society as a slumbering pest, likely to generate and spread disease should the city be visited by an epidemic in any virulent form," the report stated and went on to say that Chinatown "is a continued source of danger of this character, and probably always will, so long as it is inhabited by people of the Mongolian race." Another passage whips up anxiety about it as a lawless zone: "Not only does the cunning and utter unscrupulousness of Chinamen enable them to evade our laws, but the evidence is conclusive that they have well-organized tribunals of their own which punish offenders against themselves when it is in their interest to punish, but which never punish those who violate the laws of the city or the State."

This extremely negative image continued until World War II. But as the U.S. fought wars abroad in the name of freedom and democracy, liberals worried that the Chinese Exclusion Act would make the country appear hypocritical. In fact, Japanese propaganda during this period called out the open racism of U.S. laws against Asian Americans. At the same time U.S. government leaders felt it complicated America's alliance with China against Japan, opponents of the Exclusion Act tried to re-brand Chinatowns as friendly, welcoming places. American writers like Pearl Buck wrote stories of Chinatowns as enclaves where law-abiding families thrived. This tension resulted in the Magnuson Act of 1943, which ended the Exclusion Act, allowing 105 Chinese to enter each year.

When American teens began to act out due to wartime social changes, fears about a juvenile delinquency crisis became so strong that FBI Director J. Edgar Hoover appeared in newsreels, exhorting parents to provide moral guidance for their children. Journalists started to point to Chinese families as virtuous exceptions. In 1956, Chinatown leaders across the country advanced the "model citizen" image, hoping it would protect them from physical and legal attacks, even hiring public relations specialists to promote a positive, friendly image of Chinatowns. And it worked, as publications like Reader's Digest painted the Chinese family as a model for solving the delinquency "crisis."

These contradictory images of Chinese Americans—constructed and disseminated in the interest of different sociopolitical agendas— persist to this day through media stereotypes, which can be traced back to the history of America's Chinatowns. Next time you visit a Chinatown for dim sum or cheap souvenirs, let's not forget these were also refuges where Chinese immigrants could share their culture and language in a very hostile country.

SIMILAR BUT DIFFERENT

In the seventh grade, I went to a junior high school where I finally came across kids who, like me, were different. Earl Dornan, whose family had just migrated from Ireland, had a very thick Irish accent, and was made fun of more than I, despite that he looked like most of the other white kids. As fellow outcasts, we bonded immediately and did everything together, from studying to doing gymnastics.

Around that time, I started becoming aware of the Asian stereotype that we were all supposed to be quiet, good at math, and never complained. On TV and in the movies, I noticed that most Asians were portrayed as being "fresh off the boat," and therefore didn't speak English well. When my father said certain words, like pronouncing "third" as "turd," I would cringe. I knew that people were laughing at him behind his back. The last thing I wanted was to be the butt of jokes, so I determined that I would have absolutely no accent. Even at that age, I instinctively knew that there were "good" and "bad" accents. Probably from watching so much television, it was clear to me that a French accent was considered romantic or sexy while a British one made people sound intelligent and sophisticated. A Chinese accent signaled that you were an uneducated foreigner, stuck in a menial job, like Hop Sing, the cook on the Bonanza television series of the 1960s, played by Victor Sen Yung.

Many years later, I learned the term "accent bias." Whether the bias is conscious or unconscious, studies show that people evaluate others based on how they look and sound. For example, white research subjects tend to rate people who speak "Black English" as the lowest in education, intelligence, and communication skills. Identical answers are deemed inferior when given by Black as opposed to white students. Hispanics with less Spanish-influenced accents receive higher ratings on education, wealth, success, and intelligence.[1] It's not surprising that many Asians feel that they are treated unfairly because of their accents, with the ones from Southeast Asia rated the least positive. Some people claim to feel uneasy listening to Asian-accented speakers, despite the general stereotype that Asians are intelligent and hardworking.

Knowing that the first step to "fitting in" was overcoming any bias because of my accent, I bought an inexpensive reel-to-reel recorder and taped myself reading the newspaper. I then compared my recordings with the newscasters on TV who had perfect Midwestern accents, the standard of the day. I kept at it for a year until no hint of my accent remained. Unconsciously, I began avoiding Asians with accents and—I'm ashamed to admit—sometimes joined in with other kids to make fun of them. One poor victim was a new immigrant kid named Bing Dong, who spoke very poor English. Every time we saw him, we made a doorbell sound, saying "bing-dong" instead of "ding-dong." Kids can be cruel, especially when they feel inferior; they will do anything to feel better than someone else. In fact, studies show that wanting to feel superior is the root of racism, white supremacy, and why minorities discriminate against other minorities, including their own people.

Despite purging the accent, my struggle with cultural identity and labels continued. In high school, I found almost all classes easy except for math. Not only was it frustrating trying to understand the abstract concepts of algebra and trigonometry, but when I failed a math test, all the kids said things like, "I thought Chinese people were supposed to be smart!" Suddenly, I seemed to be responsible for the image of the entire Chinese culture, which seemed totally unfair. Whereas grammar school

---

[1] P. McGrady and J. Reynolds, "Racial Mismatch in the Classroom: Beyond Black-White Differences," *American Sociological Association*, 86 (2012).

had been easy I started to have some difficulty in junior high because the American educational system is based on reading textbooks. Most new Asian immigrants tend to be visual learners because their native languages are based on pictures and though I was not 'new', I found I was an auditory learner. So, I resorted to reading my lessons into my tape recorder and listening to them—that helped my grades immensely. Many African Americans tend to prefer auditory learning because the information was passed down in Africa through oral storytelling. His-panics tend to prefer kinesthetic learning by demonstrating and trying things out physically.[2] No one knew about different learning styles in those days.

My cultural conflict made everything in my life feel like a burden. I began to rebel, cutting classes, and pretending I was sick because hardly a day went by without experiencing humiliation in one form or another. I couldn't even blend in by wearing the latest hairstyle because my hair was too thick and straight. So, I pretty much gave up and only did the bare minimum to get through school. One day, my math teacher took me aside and said, "I thought you were cheating because you paid so little attention in class, yet you passed every test. So, I checked your records, and your IQ's higher than mine. What's your problem?" I replied, "I just don't see any practical use for what you're teaching me." She said, "You might need trigonometry if you want to be an engineer or other professional." And I said, "I'm not going to be an engineer, and I know enough math to balance a checkbook, so what else do I need?" Yes, I was quite the smart-ass, but that conversation captured my atti-tude toward education, especially as it related to the "Asian" aptitudes and professions.

When I got to high school, which was very close to Oakland's Chi-natown, I no longer stood out like a sore thumb and made a few Asian friends. I began to notice the differences and similarities between my

---

[2] C. Malvik, "4 Types of Learning Styles: How to Accommodate a Diverse Group of Students," Rasmussen University (2020).

family and those of my non-Asian friends. In terms of food, there was no difference between my family and my white friends' families. We regularly ate Kraft macaroni and cheese made from a box, beef stew, and hamburgers. The only difference was that we had rice with every meal, no matter what the entrée was. One time, I made my parents a quiche for dinner, and my father insisted I make rice to go with it!

The biggest difference was in how we were raised. While my white friends were much more adventurous and outgoing, my brother and I were expected to abide by all our parents' requests and demands. I was told to respect all authority figures like policemen and teachers. Questioning them would be disrespectful. Maybe this was why it was hard for me to ask questions in class. My non-Asian friends were more willing to challenge our teachers with questions and opinions, but I and other Asians would never consider doing so.

All the families I knew had dinner together, but while non-Asian families talked about every topic imaginable, my parents limited our conversation to work and school. We never talked about politics or social issues, even though the civil rights movement was constantly in the news. They considered this "the black people's problem" and none of our business, stressing that "we should keep our heads down and our noses to the grindstone." My friends' families discussed, sometimes in loud voices, the issues of the day with the children's opinions given equal weight as the parents'. In our house my father's word was law and there was no debate. "That was a different time," one might say, but even today, Asian parents are very authoritarian, whereas white parents treat their children more as equals or friends. The only situation when the family dynamic shifted in Asian families, giving children greater authority and autonomy, was when the parents had to rely on the oldest son (or daughter if there were no male children). If the parents did not speak English well, they had to interpret conversations and documents. Among my Asian friends, I also noticed that the oldest son (like me) was expected to get a job to help support the family as soon as possible.

While I was taught by my parents to be conventional and follow traditions, my non-Asian friends were encouraged to be more independent and free-thinking. My Asian friends and I were steered towards traditionally expected Asian careers like medicine, engineering, or accounting, whereas my white friends, and to a lesser degree my Black and Hispanic friends were told they could be anything they wanted, including artists and musicians. My parents told me that, if you majored in the liberal arts, you were likely to starve and end up being taken care of by the government on welfare—this would be the biggest shame of all to them. My parents never encouraged me to play sports or get involved in school activities because they were afraid that it would distract me from my studies. They were very surprised when I tried out football in junior high school. I was cut because I was too fat, slow, and short. I just wanted to be accepted.

What I didn't realize was that I wasn't necessarily unathletic; I simply needed to find a sport that I enjoyed and could be decent at playing. While the chances of succeeding as a professional athlete are infinitesimally small (1.6% of college-level football players, 1.2% of collegiate basketball according to the NCAA), I did come to enjoy tennis and ice-skating. However, back in the 1950s and 60s, no Asian role models in professional sports existed. Back then there were no Kristi Yamaguchi, Yao Ming, or Michael Chang.

I don't think that we Asians were smarter than the other kids, but just more motivated and held to higher standards. My parents made it clear that getting a grade lower than an A would bring shame to them. "How are Michael's grades?" was one of the first topics of conversation at family gatherings. Rarely, if ever, did I receive any praise for my accomplishments. The only time I got an A in every class on my report card, my father said, "That's good, but you can do better." When my non-Asian friends got even one A, their parents would say, "Great job!" Talking with my Asian friends, I discovered that I wasn't the only one who didn't get positive reinforcement.

While hugging and displays of affection were common in non-Asian families, we never hugged, and I found that strange. What was wrong with me? Was I that unlovable? Were my grades not good enough? I think that one of the reasons my parents rarely showed affection or praised my efforts was that they were afraid that these acts might encourage me to become lazy.

Non-Asian parents treated their kids like they owed them a comfortable and happy life. They always got the latest toys, and all we got were second-hand games from the thrift store. I grew up feeling like I was a burden to my parents. I didn't feel like I mattered to them or that I was a source of joy for them, like white kids seemed to be for their parents. In fact, happiness was never talked about in our household because it was a "frivolous emotion." My father always said, "If you worked hard and provided for your family, you should be satisfied. Who needs happiness?" And that, of course, extended to romance and relationships.

At a time in my life when I felt like a total social failure, my mother sat me down for "the talk"—no, not the one about the birds and the bees— "Don't you ever bring a Japanese girl into this house!" she said sternly. I was shocked, "Why, Mom? They look just like us." She fired back, "No, they don't look anything like us, and during World War II, the Japanese were very cruel to the Chinese. Don't you ever bring a Japanese girl into this house!"

I fought her for years on this, not because I was a great social activist, but because there were way more Japanese girls in my high school than Chinese. If she cut the Japanese girls out of my dating pool, I was afraid that my odds of getting a girlfriend weren't going to be very good. That's when I became aware that Asians are not one big, happy family and that each group has a different language, religion, and food. Today, over twenty major groups are categorized as "Asian" in America, and as actor Kelly Hu told me in a recent interview, "We're not one monolithic group. Even if we are bunched together, there are so many different cultures, languages, and histories that make up this umbrella of Asian Americans and Pacific Islanders (AAPI). I think it's difficult sometimes for us to even find common ground, but we are very, very different in our cultures, and we all celebrate that."

I noticed the differences and similarities between Chinese and other Asian cuisines. My Japanese friends ate soba noodles, which were like Chinese thick chow mein, but also ate raw fish they called "sushi" and "sashimi," and which took me a long time to appreciate. My Korean friends had their own version of noodles and loved a spicy cabbage called "kimchi," which burned my lips and tongue. My Filipino friends had noodles, too, called "pancit," and they loved to fry everything. I also discovered that food was a great bridge between cultures.

In time, I realized that my mother was correct in that each group looked different. I noticed that Japanese people tend to have more round faces than Chinese, while Koreans' faces are even more round, while Filipinos look more Latin than Asian. Eventually, I was able to differentiate between Chinese, Koreans, Japanese, Vietnamese, Filipinos, and others at a glance, as well as whether they were new immigrants or Asian Americans. Since distinguishing between the different groups was a matter of dating survival for me, I became hyper-aware of who was Chinese and who was not.

LOVE YOU LONGTIME

L ike every teenage boy, I desperately wanted a girlfriend. However, my desire was much deeper than a natural sexual awakening. I hoped that having a girlfriend would be the answer to the incredible loneliness and rejection I felt. Unfortunately, my social clumsiness only led to more of the same. Not only did I have no clue how to begin a relationship, but girls also scared me to death because they were so different, so special. They looked and smelled good, unlike boys that reeked of stale gym lockers.

Asian American girls were particularly special to me because I believed they would understand how I felt inside, fitting neither into the white world nor the Asian world. One day I met a Chinese girl named Arlene and walked her home. She asked me in, and after we had sodas, as I was about to leave, she French-kissed me. The shock of my life! And with that, I was instantly in love. But she never returned my calls or impassioned love letters. Apparently, my clumsy first kiss was such a disappointment that she wanted nothing to do with me.

Between the restrictions that my mother had imposed on my dating pool and my social awkwardness, meeting girls was not easy. The thought did cross my mind to pursue non-Asian girls, assuming that they would be less threatening because they didn't seem so rare and unique. I also assumed that a relationship would have been less complicated because I wouldn't have had to deal with Asian cultural issues. Unfortunately, my initial feeble attempts were unsuccessful because it seemed that white girls didn't consider Asian guys as serious dating material. In fact, they seemed to look right through me as if I were invisible, so I quickly abandoned that idea.

Comparing notes with my Asian American male friends, we concluded that white girls were just not interested in us. They thought Asian boys were "wimpy" and not "cool." Little did we know how right our assessment was! Even today, some fifty years later, research shows that Asian American males are systematically excluded from romantic relationships during adolescence and young adulthood by white, and even some Asian women. Even as adults, socioeconomic success and higher education do not bring additional dating or marriage opportunities.

In sharp contrast, Asian women are sought-after by men of all other races because they are generally considered docile, great at domestic tasks, and eager to please men. The fetishization and exotification of Asian women have given rise to the social phenomenon referred to as "yellow fever," whereby many men see them as geishas, sexually suggestive but silent women with "magical slanted vaginas;" not as fully formed individuals. Regrettably, this predilection, which can go as far as Asiaphilia (a Caucasian male with a sexual interest only in Asian women) is supported by the statistics. On online dating sites, 90% of non-Asian, and 40% of Asian women said they would not date an Asian man. Only 9% of all women said that they had dated an Asian man, compared to 28% of all men who said that they had dated Asian women. Men of all races (except Asian men) prefer Asian women, who marry outside of their race at much higher rates than Asian men.[3]

In high school, we referred to white guys that preferred Asian girls as "rice lovers." To me, it seemed that they were using them as trophies or that they couldn't get white women to date them. But it still made me mad because there were already not enough Asian girls for the Asian guys, making dating even more difficult for me. Years later, I learned that the slang term "rice queen" is used for a gay man, usually white,

[3] G. Kao, K.S. Balistreri and K. Joyne, "Asian American Men in Romantic Dating Markets," *Contexts*, 17(4), 48–53. (2018).

who prefers Asian men. When I have been approached by gay white men, I have been complimented in ways that imply that I was attractive simply because I was Asian, echoing Asian women's experience of being racially depersonalized.

Being viewed as an object which can be easily replaced by someone with a similar appearance can erode one's self-worth. After decades of contending with these stereotypes, Asian American women are more suspicious and cautious when they are approached. One young woman was so fed up with the flurry of fetishizing messages white men were sending her on the Tinder dating app that she created an Instagram account, posting messages she received, like "I want to try my first Asian woman," or "I need my yellow fever cured."

Of course, these sexual stereotypes are not only reflected in culture but also reinforced by the media. Jeff Adachi's documentary, *The Slanted Screen* (2009), provides an overview of the portrayal of Asian American men in Hollywood films. He argues that Asian American men are usually absent, but when they appear, they are almost never portrayed as having any sexual desire. When romantic relationships involve Asian Americans, they are typically between a white man and an Asian woman and—until not so long ago—a prostitute, as exemplified by the well-known quote, "Me so horny. Me love you a longtime," from Stanley Kubrick's *Full Metal Jacket* (1987).

Asian women have been painted as hypersexual since the late 1800s. In the U.S., the Page Act of 1875 banned the importation of Asian women, who were believed to be engaging in prostitution, whether they were or not. By early 20th century, Asian women were beginning to be featured in plays like *The Good Woman of Szechuan* about a Chinese prostitute, and *Madame Butterfly* in 1904 about a Japanese girl who falls in love with an American military officer with devastating consequences. In 1922, *Toll of the Sea*, one of the first movies starring an Asian, Anna May Wong, an American man falls in love with a young Chinese woman while visiting China but abandons her because she has no value to him. In 1989, the play *Miss Saigon*, which was based on

Madame Butterfly, told the story of an Asian woman who loves a white man so much that she would kill herself and give her child to him.

In America, Asian women have often been thought of as exotic and subservient, dainty, and beautiful, with an implied absence of autonomy. In recent iterations, they are additionally infantilized as schoolgirls, "Asian Baby Girls," a stereotype defined by looks and mannerisms.

As traditional male roles are increasingly being challenged; men feel they are competing with women for jobs, even fearing them since the #MeToo era. Arguably, if they feel emasculated, they may seek out submissive women, which is how they may perceive Asian women. A 2013 study found that Asian women are the most desirable racial group among white men and other races, especially in regions with an extensive history of colonization, violence, and imperialism from Western countries, like the Vietnam War, the Indochina Conflict, and the Philippine-American War.

The defeat of imperial Japan in World War II allowed the United States to build an extensive military presence across East Asia, where it remains entrenched to this day. In these areas, the situation was doubly difficult and dangerous for women. Dehumanized both as "gooks" and sexual objects, "slant-eyed chicks" had no right to refuse the men who were there to "protect" them. As an ex-soldier described, "You've got an M-16, what do you need to pay a lady for? You go down to the village, and you take what you want." Veterans' accounts are full of examples of rape, torture, and murder of women and girls. Brutality was justified by the perceived alien-ness. As Evelyn Yoshimura wrote for *Gidra* in 1971, "The image of a people with slanted eyes and slanted vaginas enhances the feeling that Asians are other than human, and therefore much easier to kill."

Dehumanization was part of the desensitization campaign run by the military, which sought to ease any moral compunctions that U.S. soldiers might have had about killing Asians during WWII, the Korean conflict, and the Vietnam War, while dangling local women like carrots. During their tours, soldiers learned to expect Asian women as part of their deployment. After all, they were told that this was their "Rest & Relaxation." One of the most popular cartoons for men serving in Japan and Korea was Navy officer Bill Hume's *Babysan*, a series of pinups detailing Babysan's charms, instructing soldiers on "how to be occupied while occupying."

It is estimated that of the $185 million spent by U.S. troops in occupied Japan, half went toward the sexual procurement of Asian women.[4] Make no mistake: Not all women procured were prostitutes by choice. Asian women were sexually assaulted, raped, and impregnated by white soldiers. The colonization of the female body is an important part of the history of the fetishization of Asian women that affects Asian Americans to this day. The long-cultivated mentality, which keeps *Suzy Wong*, *Madam Butterfly*, and *Lookism* alive, not only turns human beings into racist, murdering soldiers, but also maintains the sexual stereotypes to which Asian Americans continue to be subjected.

[4] Jessie Kindig, "The Violent Embrace," *The Boston Review* (2021).

KELLY HU & PETER SHINKODA
ON SEXUAL STEREOTYPES

Asian American men are typically portrayed on screen as eunuchs or corrupters of white women. In *Showdown in Little Tokyo,* the Asian villain forces himself on a white woman before murdering her. He is killed by the white hero, who "wins" the Asian woman, while the hero's Amerasian sidekick is given no love life. "China doll," "geisha girl," or "lotus blossom," the Asian woman—regardless of ethnicity—is exotic, subservient, and eager to please men. Plots revolve around her needing the white man to romance and save her, as in *The World of Suzie Wong, Mean Girls,* and *Memoirs of a Geisha*. On the flipside of this stereotype is the scheming and back-stabbing "dragon lady," who uses her sexuality to accomplish some evil goal, like in *Daughter of the Dragon* and *Kill Bill*. The "Asian Baby Girl" is defined as an Asian female "gangster," who wears skimpy clothing and heavy makeup, enjoys partying, and has a taste for expensive brand names.

Negative portrayals and storylines have a real-life impact on Asian Americans' experiences. For example, American media has always implied that all that Asian women are interested in is sex, whether they are legitimate masseuses or manicurists. In 2021, a shooting spree at spas and massage parlors in Atlanta left eight dead, including six Asian women. The shooter told police that he had a "sex addiction" and that the spas were a "temptation he wanted to eliminate."

In recent television series and movies, there seems to be a concerted effort to move away from the older stereotypes, although Asian characters are still mostly peripheral and tokenistic. While Asian women are frequently cast as expert martial artists and sociopathic killers, fortunately, actors, like Sandra Oh, have been cast as "real people" in a variety of roles. Asian men are beginning to be cast in sexualized roles, like Simu Liu, star of Marvel's *Shang-Chi*, was cast as the "hot Korean," dating a white woman in the Canadian sitcom *Kim's Convenience.* In the series *Falling Water*, Will Yun Lee is also in a relationship with a white woman.

Kelly Ann Hu is an American actress, former model, and beauty queen (Miss Teen USA 1985, Miss Hawaii USA 1993). She has starred in the soap opera *Sunset Beach* and the police drama *Nash Bridges*, as well as *Cradle 2 the Grave, X2, The Tournament*, and *White Frog.* In *The Scorpion King,* she played a scantily clad evil sorceress.

Michael: How do you feel about a role when your appearance is as a stereotypical sexy "dragon lady"?

Kelly: Well, when I was younger, I just wanted to work. I didn't think about stereotypes. It didn't occur to me that these things could be harmful. I was less educated. Also, I grew up in Hawaii, and being a part of a majority there, I'd never really understood the plight of Asian Americans on the mainland. When people talked about "the cause or discrimination or racism," I had not experienced it. Coming to Los Angeles as an actor, I was working right away. So, I didn't really feel like I was being discriminated against; it wasn't until I was much older and started understanding what was going on and what other people were experiencing, and it made it much more real for me then.

Michael: When you look back on your career and perhaps your role in something like *Scorpion King*, do you have any regrets?

Kelly: I actually did a post about that on Instagram, where there was a woman who made claims about us being fetishized, and the kinds of roles that were given, or how we are viewed in film and television led to some of the shootings. Like those Atlanta shootings, and perhaps she has a point. However, there are a lot of prostitutes and women who are fetishized that are not Asians, who are not getting gunned down. So, I'm not sure how much of it is true. I mean, we can only guess at how these crazy people think, right?

Michael: Right.

Kelly: So, yeah, there are times when I feel like I am responsible for some of these stereotypical views of Asians, but as an actor, I didn't have a lot of other opportunities. Now that we have more producers, writers, creators who are the gate-keepers of the entertainment industry, we can start making better decisions and maybe understanding what stereotypical roles did to our community and work our way out of that. And I think that's definitely being addressed at the moment. We finally got an Asian Marvel hero (in Simu Liu), and we'll see what it does. It just took decades for that to happen.

Michael: Why do you think it's taken so long?

Kelly: From what I understand, these Asian characters have always been there, but the entertainment industry was never willing to invest in them. And we as a community really need to sup-port one another because the success of things like *Crazy Rich Asians* really helped us. People in the industry need to see that Asian stars and leads can pay off because really to them it's all money, right? They're not trying to make social commentary; to them, it's all about the bottom line, and if we can support our community, maybe we'll be able to get more opportunities in the long run.

Peter Shinkoda is a Japanese Canadian actor who stars in the science fiction series *Falling Skies* and the Warner Brothers web series *Mortal Kombat: Legacy,* and in the *films Midway, Predator,* and *I, Robot.*

Peter: I have appeared in 60 film and TV projects. In almost every case, my character was unable to express any sexual or romantic desire.

Michael: Do you see any changes?

Peter: Things have changed in the last year (2020), but I'm always getting the typical roles. I feel that, for Asian males, I can see that it's going to be harder to find any kind of mobility.

Michael: You mean in contrast to Asian women. What are the stereotypical roles for them?

Peter: For Asian females, they're the exotic oriental flower love interest or object of desire in a white man's fantasy. So, for a hundred years, it's been white American men writing what they think they know about the Asians but only derived from the very limited scope of imagination.

Michael: What are the male stereotypes?

Peter: Well, the wise old Asian man is probably the most respected version on screen. There's obviously the martial arts villain, or the Yakuza organized crime villain. Then there's the plethora of supporting roles like doctors, teachers, small roles that don't necessarily move the plot forward. We're usually relegated to those roles. Yet, by glorious chance, you might get a big role, and some of mine are big, but typically they're not. Ten years ago, I got lucky enough to be cast in Steven Spielberg's *Falling Skies* as an alpha male soldier, but I didn't last too long.

Michael: You mean your character was killed off early, as per the usual treatment of non-white characters. How do you feel the portrayal of Asian men impacts Asian men in real life?

Peter: Hollywood, I believe, [it]is the biggest culprit in spreading the racism that we experience as a community in the West, and I've seen it happening all throughout my life.

Michael: They tend to portray us as meek and not very manly.

Peter: Absolutely. Hollywood reinforces the same stereotypes and clichés of Asian men, so it is believed by the American public, or possibly the globe. It absolutely makes us look like the weakest link in society, and that's why we're getting beat up on the streets, and they're getting away with it. People are completely not afraid or intimidated by Asians to a point where we're laughed at, beaten up, and laughed at again. Stereotypes hurt our morale. The whole purpose of racism is to break you down so much that it's not even worth it to fight back. Well, that's what Hollywood has done. It made us so discouraged, so questioning of our own self-worth. It's absolutely psychologically and emotionally damaging.

Michael: Does how we're portrayed impact how white women view Asian men?

Peter: One thousand percent. I've heard countless times girls say, "I'm not into Asian guys." Why? Because a lot of people watch Hollywood, it lays out the rules of society. To avoid embarrassment in real life, you will adhere to the same societal rules you see in Hollywood products. Media is very powerful, as we've seen in the last couple of years. It can convince people that something is harmful, no matter that you show them they're wrong in a million ways they will still believe in the most incredible ideas.

TO BE OR NOT TO BE...ASIAN

When I was about eight years old, my parents sent me to a Chinese school to learn Cantonese. I had no idea how challenging it would be. Not only do Chinese words have no relationship to English, but you must also say them in the correct pitch, or they mean something completely different. Learning to write was even harder as there is no alphabet, only thousands of pictures that represent objects and ideas. I did not have an ear for the language and had difficulty drawing the characters because I always sucked in art class! To make matters worse, when I tried speaking Cantonese at home, my parents laughed at my pronunciation, even though they spoke only a smattering of Cantonese themselves.

How was I supposed to learn? Growing up, my contact with the Chinese culture and language was limited to extended family and Chinatown. My parents felt an obligation to attend the Chinese Presbyterian Church in San Francisco's Chinatown because it sponsored the camp where they met. Almost every Sunday, we went to the Chinese language service even though they had another one in English. Why is beyond me, because neither my brother nor I spoke the language. Our parents were probably hoping that we would somehow learn Chinese while earning the right to go to heaven if we endured an hour of this torture each week, sitting there in our little suits and dress shoes. Eventually, we only learned one Chinese phrase, *Yen naw mun kay tao*" ("Let us pray,") because it meant the sermon had come to an end.

The only thing that made this ritual bearable was that afterward, we went out to eat dim sum. In addition to chow mein, each of us was allowed to choose one dish to be shared. It was such fun watching all the different foods—chicken feet, fish heads, and sea slugs—that we usually didn't see roll by on metal carts pushed by Chinese women who yelled out what they had in Cantonese. My favorite was shrimp balls wrapped in wonton paper. My brother liked a similar dish with beef. Dad's favorite was stinky fish with rice, and Mom always chose tofu with vegetables. Invariably, there was an argument between my parents about how to pronounce this or that dish. It would've been hilarious if it weren't so embarrassing. The locals gave us funny looks because it was obvious that none of us spoke the language well enough to even place an order!

Sometimes, after lunch, we went to the oriental trading store where my brother and I were allowed to select a small toy. So many fascinating items like "Chinese handcuffs" made of bamboo—once you put your fingers in them, you couldn't get them off without knowing the trick. The first time I asked Dan to try them, he ran around the store screaming in panic. Because of our three-and-a-half-year difference, I teased him to feel better about myself, regrettably, adding to his life challenges.

It was at one of these lunches that our parents—to their horror—realized that he was left-handed. They said that you never use your left hand for writing or eating because it's "disrespectful" to others. They tried everything to stop him from using his left hand, including tying it behind his back at dinner at home. Later, I learned that, in Asia and other parts of the world, you never use your left hand for anything except wiping yourself after going to the bathroom. What started as a good hygiene practice, which made sense in ancient times, is totally unnecessary in the age of toilet paper. This prohibition was not just limited to Asians; in the Middle East, one punishment for theft was to cut off the thief's right hand so they could only use their "unclean" hand for the rest of their life. To this day, my brother still eats and writes with his left hand. I guess "old habits" in his case brain wiring are hard to break!

This was one of a million beliefs that my parents had that made no sense to my logical mind, like my father's firmness that we display no emotion in public because it disturbs the "feng shui," the good energy and brings bad luck. To me, all these fragments of language, beliefs, customs, and traditions were like a disjointed jigsaw puzzle of what it meant to be Chinese. They felt foreign, even absurd at times because the only cultural context I had was American. In our weekly visits to Chinatown, I was dropped into the Chinese culture with no appreciation or understanding of millennia of tradition. Sadly, my Chinese identity consisted of just being different—literally, the odd man out. Non-Asian people were always a little uneasy when they met me, probably because they didn't know how to find common ground with me. I wished I had had the courage to say to them, "Just treat me like anyone else."

In high school, I became aware that my Asian friends also struggled with cultural identity. Like me, they felt pulled in different directions, as if always asking, "To be or not to be Asian?" I had no idea that this inner conflict and dichotomy would shape the rest of my life. All through childhood and adolescence, desperate to fit in, I wanted to distance myself as much as possible from the stereotypical Asian image. I worked very hard and succeeded in purging any trace of a Chinese accent. Although I had tried to learn Chinese, not speaking the language made me an outsider to Chinese people who often called me "jook sing," which means "empty head" in Cantonese, because I couldn't speak the language. I was often told, in no uncertain terms, that not speaking the language meant I had lost my Asian culture and was not truly Chinese. At the same time, it was clear that white people in this country did not accept me as American because I looked different from them.

I was horrified! If I didn't belong to either culture, then who would accept me? Who would love me? More importantly, who was I? It was not simply a question of choosing one identity over the other but being rejected by both. As tough as my predicament was as a fifth-generation Asian American, it seems to be even more challenging for second-generation children of immigrants. They are forced to choose between two cultures, making either their parents or American friends unhappy, something that—I'm sure—causes them a great deal of angst.

In my senior year of high school, in 1968, I began to entertain the possibility that being Asian was something I could be proud of instead of ashamed. These were the days when the term "Asian American" began being used by students at the University of California at Berkeley when they founded the Asian American Political Alliance—an effort to unite students of Japanese, Chinese, and Filipino descent to fight for political and social recognition. I stopped feeling so alone and hopeless, identifying with their efforts to fight the system and with the empowerment they felt from working together. It brought to mind the term "Black Power," which was first used by Stokely Carmichael in 1966 during a civil rights march in Mississippi. I may have also been influenced by James Brown's hit song, "Say It Loud, I'm Black and I'm Proud."

For my family, during this time, seeing an Asian on TV was quite an event because it meant that we were becoming part of the mainstream, no longer invisible and ignored. The first Asian character I remember, who wasn't a cook or servant, was in 1966 when Bruce Lee played the sidekick to the crime-fighting hero on the *Green Hornet* TV show. My mother would call our friends and relatives to remind them that the show was on because you could not record shows in those days. If you missed it, you had to wait for the reruns, sometimes years later. Bruce Lee had very few speaking lines, but we all enthusiastically waited until the end, when he would kick the bad guy's butt (usually a white person).

That same year, the original *Star Trek* series premiered with George Takei as Helmsman Sulu. Although he rarely had much of a role, it was refreshing to see an Asian American actor who didn't do martial arts. In 1968, the TV show *Hawaii Five-O* also premiered; it was about a special division of the Hawaii police tasked with bringing down organized crime, especially an evil Chinese kingpin named Wo Fat. Despite being set in Hawaii, the main characters were both white, Head Detective Steve McGarrett (played by Jack Lord), and Officer Daniel Williams (played by Scott Caan), seconded by Chin Ho Kelly (played initially by Kam Fong and later by Daniel Dae Kim). However, the show did have many Asian actors in minor roles and in the background.

1968 was also the first time an African American was featured on a weekly television show when *Julia* premiered, starring Diahann Carroll. It was criticized for not reflecting the lives of most African Americans but gave minorities hope for more roles in the future. I understood that black folks also called each other to inform their community of this momentous event.

While minorities celebrate their differences to let whites know they aren't better than us, and that we are special, too, I believe that most would probably want to be white, not because they do not appreciate their own culture and race, but because this is the standard against which people are judged in this country. As a child, I always wanted to be white so I wouldn't be made fun of, discriminated against, and made to feel different. No one wants to have their differences constantly pointed out, to be worried about being treated unfairly, concerned about their physical safety, and more.

Minorities often envy those among their group who are more acculturated into mainstream American society and do not conform to the typical Asian culture, often disparaging them as "bananas" (yellow on the outside and white on the inside, "coconuts" (darker-skinned Asians like Filipinos and Hawaiians), or African American "Oreos" (black on the outside and white on the inside). While the extent of this assimilation is based on sociocultural factors, it can also extend to appearance. In mainstream America, people who have light skin, large round eyes, and straight hair tend to be considered attractive. Some members of minority groups will even modify their features to appear more white by lightening their skin, straightening their hair, and even undergoing surgery. One popular cosmetic procedure for Asian Americans is the double-fold eyelid surgery, which allows more of the upper lid to show and the eyes to appear larger. Another is nose reshaping to achieve a higher nasal bridge like that of white people.

Make no mistake—The United States legal system has clearly stated that Asians are not White. In 1922, a Japanese man named Takao Ozawa was technically qualified for naturalization and citizenship, but his application was rejected because the court ruled that, "The appellant...is clearly of a race which is not Caucasian" (Takao Ozawa v. US, (1922). In 1923, Bhagat Singh Thind claimed he was qualified for citizenship because, as an Asian Indian, he was categorized as Aryan or Caucasian according to the prevailing racial science of the time. Even so, the Supreme Court found that he would not be considered "White" in the eyes of the "common man," despite scientific race categories, and was therefore also ineligible for citizenship (US v. Bhagat Singh Thind, 1923). In 1927, Gong Lum's nine-year-old Martha, a native-born citizen, was notified that she must attend a "colored" school because "she was of Chinese descent, and not a member of the White or Caucasian race." Although Martha's father subsequently sued and won, the Supreme Court of Mississippi reversed the lower court's ruling, holding that Martha was of "the Mongolian or Yellow race" and could not be considered White (Gong Lum v. Rice, 1927).

FROM SHAME TO ACCEPTANCE

Since my first day of school, as a six-year-old, I lived a life of shame for being the repulsive "chink" that everyone mocked. I felt insignificant, ugly, unlovable, and ashamed of whom I was, always comparing myself to kids who were popular, better-looking, and—not Asian—the one thing that I could never change.

Shame pervaded my thoughts and feelings, even at home. My parents' mantra was, "Never bring shame to our family!" and that included not "losing face," the shame resulting from impulsive or emotional behavior, and why I was told to never express my feelings in public, or anywhere, for that matter. As if all that weren't enough, my parents would put me to bed with stories from China where criminals, who were placed in cages or in rectangular collars made of wood, were put on display at the city gates to shame them publicly and educate onlookers about the consequences of immoral misbehavior.

Chinese culture is heavily invested in concepts of shame. A study examined Chinese shame concepts and collected 113 terms that they had for the notion.[5] How did this cultural preoccupation develop? Two thousand five hundred years ago, Confucius taught that, in the interest of a harmonious family and society, the individual should submit to the collective good and that doing so honored oneself and others. The idea spread from China to Japan, Korea, and much of Asia. Over time,

---

[5] J. Li, L. Wang and K. Fischer, "The Organization of Chinese Shame Concepts. Cognition & Emotion" (2010) https://www.tandfonline.com/doi/abs/10.1080/02699930341000202..

other philosophical, educational, political, and religious viewpoints converged, reinforcing the need to preserve honor. As a result, Asian cultures are collectivist in nature, meaning they hold the core belief that your family, ancestors, town, and country are all affected by your actions.

Bringing honor to yourself extends to all those connected to you and so does shame via any means (academic, professional, behavioral, etc.). The Chinese have a saying, "I am so ashamed that my ancestors of eight generations can even feel it." Suicide, which is viewed very differently in the West, is viewed in the East as a way of re-establishing one's honor. In Japan, for example, rather than fall into the hands of the victorious enemy, the samurai warriors would commit ritual suicide by disembowelment with a sword when they disgraced themselves by losing a battle. Present-day Asians, regardless of differences in ethnicities, languages, and religions are still rooted in the shared values of collectivism, saving face, honor, and loyalty to one's family and culture. Therefore, one who feels they have shamed the family tends to suffer in silence, develop mental health issues, or even kill themselves to restore honor to their family and cultural group.

Compelled by this constant preoccupation with preserving honor, Asian parents tend to cultivate shame in their children. Chinese parents are masters of this motivational technique. Psychologists say that feeling inferior can drive you to eliminate weaknesses and perform better. The problem is that some children, like me, develop such strong feelings of inadequacy that lead to an inferiority complex. I was haunted by a deep sense of shame over my inability to excel scholastically in certain subjects, particularly math—this pressure was compounded by my white classmates who made fun of me because I didn't fit the stereotype of the smart Asian who's good at math. I had trouble sleeping and constant dreams of falling, which any psychologist will tell you usually indicates feelings of loss of control. As a result, at the age of twelve, I became addicted to over-the-counter sleeping pills so that I could escape my pain, if only for a short while.

I became submissive, passive, and shy. I did not dare look people in the eye; I was afraid to speak up, and always spoke in a quiet voice. I was ultra-sensitive to any criticism or slight. When a teacher told me to write, "I will be quiet," ten times on a piece of paper, I wrote it over 200 times. When I thought my parents were being discriminated against at a store or restaurant, I got really angry. They would try to calm me down by saying things like, "They're just busy," or "They probably didn't see us," but the underlying humiliation and fury festered and repressed since I was not allowed to show any emotion.

I also became a people-pleaser, caring about what others thought to an extreme. I worried about how I dressed, how I talked, and how neatly my hair was combed. When I learned to drive, I was extra careful because I didn't want to bring shame to our race by substantiating the jokes that circulated at the time— "Asians are so bad at driving, I'm starting to think Pearl Harbor was an accident."

On the other hand, I also became extremely competitive and driven. Early on, what helped me deal with my feelings of inferiority were a few victories that started to build my self-confidence. In junior high, I developed techniques to increase my efficiency for my paper route by putting butterfly handlebars on my bike so that I could sling my bag across it, reach in and throw the papers to each house without losing a beat. I learned to fold papers quickly so they could be thrown with great accuracy. I was so fast that I added other kids' routes to mine, more than doubling my income.

Even as I grew older and successful by society's standards, I still felt incomplete and unacceptable as a person no matter what I achieved. I thought that winning awards, making a lot of money, and winning the affection of women would make me feel worthy and accepted. They did not. I still felt powerless to control my life and future. Big or small, my victories could not resolve my deep-seated insecurities. Maybe that's why I always related to the sensitive but ugly monster in the *Frankenstein* movies, or to the runt of the litter when choosing a puppy.

As an adult, after seven years in a relationship with a white woman, whom I considered my ideal mate, I was unhappier than I had ever been in my life. Was I playing the role of the successful Asian man with a blonde on his arm as a trophy, perhaps? Success only temporarily placated my insecurities because I still felt like a fraud. The conflict between the external image we project and how we really feel inside inevitably takes its toll. I was always looking for the next mountain to climb, and it was exhausting. Things got so bad that I regularly contemplated suicide. No matter what I achieved, I was not fulfilled. Was there any hope for me?

Thankfully, yes. Out of sheer desperation, I put my ego aside and, at fifty years old, decided that I needed help. I signed up for a personal growth class, which forced me to examine my insecurities and the silent control that my father and others still had over my life choices. I realized that the reason I worked so hard was to prove worthy of his love. Nothing I did was good enough. I got my doctorate degree in business to prove that I'm not a "knucklehead," as he used to call me, although I didn't need the degree—I became dean of a university business school with just an MBA. The first time I made $75,000 in one month in real estate in 1980 (the equivalent of over $250,000 today) I felt good because that was more than he had ever made in a year! Even today, when I should and could be retired, I am still working harder than ever. Of course, this is not unique to me. Every Asian I know, especially the oldest male child, feels the same pressure to succeed. I'm sure that my father felt the same need to support his mother when his father passed away when he was young, despite not being the oldest son.

While doing my inner work, I came to see that I was taught to feel shame and unworthiness in my home, school, and society at large, and that racism greatly contributed to this emotional propensity. I learned that the solution is NOT to care what people think, but to care about what you think of yourself. I started learning to love myself for who I am, realizing that the only person I am ever in competition with is me. All I need to do is to be the best me I can be—that's what gets me up in the morning these days.

I also learned not to identify myself by my race despite the fact that it's the first thing most people notice when they meet me. I am a human being like everyone else, a sensitive person who cares deeply about others and does not want anyone else to feel the sting of discrimination. In fact, I address these issues as a speaker, coach, and author, always striving to create the change I wish to see in the world.

I no longer care how other people treat me and treat others with the respect that I wish to be given. I have been able to take back my personal power by living the profound truth expressed by Eleanor Roosevelt in her compelling statement, "No one can make you feel inferior without your consent."

While I was undergoing this emotional shift, I found it quite comforting that people like Abraham Lincoln, George Eliot, and John F. Kennedy also suffered from feelings of inferiority and self-doubt. Hey, if we can make lemonade with the lemons that life gives us that matters! Last, but not least, in my adolescence as a Chinese American male, a small starting point in releasing some of those feelings was Bruce Lee. His philosophy, "Always be yourself, express yourself, have faith in yourself, do not go out and look for a successful personality and duplicate it," helped me to begin accepting myself for who I am and seeing differences as positive, not negative.

BRUCE LEE—
KICK-STARTING CONFIDENCE

It's safe to say that the Asian martial artist stereotype originated with Bruce Lee and the popularity of his famous films of the 1970s. Although the typecasting that ensued has limited Asian American actors, Bruce delivered a lethal blow to the Asian screen stereotypes of cook, cleaner, or coolie. He became an emblem of pride and power for Asian American men, who had been saddled with negative portrayals since they arrived in America in the 1880s—asexual, effeminate, unattractive, meek, nerdy, and more.

"Unhappy the land that is in need of heroes," writes Bertolt Brecht. Without a doubt, Asians in America had few heroes we could identify with until the gods of cinema granted us, Bruce Lee. He embodied, and arguably still does, the quintessential Asian alpha male. He was handsome, exuded virile sexuality, and had romantic scenes in films in a society where Asian men were considered eunuchs.

Also, Bruce got angry! He challenged verbally and physically those who insulted or wronged him, while his ability to cry manly tears defied Chinese social norms—that was quite impactful on boys like me whose shame-training forbade any display of emotion. In this sense, Bruce was truly Asian American because he blended the demonstrative American disposition with the restrained Chinese. He even combined these two cultural norms in his fighting style by unleashing the fury in calculated, focused strikes.

Before every other movie featured a superhero, Bruce fought evil and social injustice with his bare hands. In his 1971 film, *The Big Boss*, he sided with laborers against a crime boss, while in *Fist of Fury*, he fought Japanese colonialism and discrimination against Chinese people. In *Enter the Dragon*, which he also wrote, produced, and directed, Lee exposed the intimate relationship between colonialism and racism. He also included direct references to police harassment of Black people and to the Black martial arts movement. This was the era of Black Power and its emphasis on self-determination and resistance in the face of a white supremacist society. Many Black activists and organizers began to recognize him as a kindred spirit.

Bruce defied the stereotype of the apolitical and compliant Asian only interested in academics and financial success, as per the model minority myth that had been established by that time. He was a leader, powerful and fair. As a populist philosopher, he also showed that the might of the mind should balance the might of the fist.

While Bruce's frame was average for an Asian male, he molded it into a positive body image for Asian Americans, highlighting that martial arts are about skill, not physical strength, and empowering everyone, regardless of their physique. "With Bruce, the body and its muscles are displayed as weapons. You always know when Bruce is really angry and means business because that's when his shirt comes off," says Mike Moh, the actor who portrayed Bruce Lee in the 2019 film *Once Upon a Time...in Hollywood*. Bruce's confidence was mesmerizing and made me consider that maybe I could be that self-assured someday.

Unconventional in all areas of life, Bruce also punched through other stereotypes and cultural norms. He reclaimed sex appeal and virility for the Asian American male, and not just on the screen. He married Linda Caldwell at a time when Asian men dating white women was frowned upon and even illegal in some states. Matthew Polly's book *Bruce Lee: A Life* explores Lee's sexual exploits, painting him as a playboy and adulterer, like all other stars of his time. The biography claims that beyond his chiseled body, magnetism, and lovemaking prowess,

Bruce impressed women by showing off his kung fu moves and cha-cha dancing, and even underwent circumcision to be more "American." Even so, "His goal all his life was to show the beauty of the Chinese culture to the world, so he started with me," his wife Linda is quoted as saying of the star who refused roles that featured Chinese people in a negative light, losing career opportunities. When he was up for the Asian lead in the 1970s television series *Kung Fu*, he was passed over for a white actor, David Carradine. He then moved to Hong Kong partly due to the difficulty in finding appropriate roles in the United States.

I believe what Bruce stood for, and meant to, Asian Americans is incalculable. His famous quote, "Defeat is a state of mind," spoke directly to Asian males, especially the young, affirming that we could be proud and powerful men, no longer invisible underdogs if we decided to be. For me, Bruce meant that I was no longer predetermined to be a wimpy bookworm; I could be a badass too, cool, confident, and sexy. My hero was only 5'7" and 135 pounds, very much like me. I figured if he could do martial arts, so could I!

Immediately after watching the first *Green Hornet* episode in 1966, using money from my paper route, I signed up for karate lessons with Master Sid Campbell in Oakland. I learned that martial arts are more than fighting. They instill a life of discipline, teaching you to use your fighting skills only when all other options have failed. Sensei Campbell taught me that a good defense is more important than a good offense. When we, his new students, complained one day about only learning how to block instead of punch, he invited all fifteen of us to attack him at the same time. He promised not to throw one punch or kick. He blocked every blow and attacking him was so painful that we all ended up on the mat, writhing in agony. Lesson learned, and we never asked him for punching lessons again!

Besides doing basic calisthenics, Sensei Campbell made us run a mile in the street around the dojo (studio) in bare feet before every class. I was pudgy from sitting around watching television and reading books, so I started dieting. My body had been a huge source of embarrassment for some time. The first time I had physical education classes in school, we had to change into gray shorts and white tee shirts in the locker room. I was mortified having to show the big roll of fat on my stomach from eating macaroni and cheese (my favorite meal) and the hamburgers my mother made from cheap, fatty meat. When "Buddha" was added to my epithets at school, I resorted to obsessive behavior. After a four-week diet of just Jell-O, which I didn't realize was nothing but sugar, my parents took me to the doctor for a lecture on nutrition. I also started extreme exercising, three hours in a sweat suit with the heat in my room turned up to 105 degrees.

Looking back at that dark time in my life, I shudder to think of the harm the crazy diets and over-exercise could have had on my health. However, by the time I got to high school, I had lost my excess weight. Modeling myself after Bruce, I bought an old-fashioned set of steel barbells and dumbbells at Sears. I built and toned my muscles to a point where no one made fun of me anymore. Then, my outer transformation began to fire up my inner self-confidence. I bought enough horsehair-filled 4-inch-thick mats to cover the floor of our garage and started teaching the neighborhood kids judo, which I had learned from books. This was the first time I was looked up to for knowing something others didn't.

Would I have embarked on that transformation without Bruce Lee as a role model? Not sure. All I know is that, at the right time in my life, he showed me what was possible. I followed his philosophy, "Be like water," which teaches that we should not let ourselves be trapped in one mindset and behavior. I vowed to go with the flow, not to be pigeonholed by others or to pigeonhole myself.

And then, overnight, my undefeatable hero was gone! Six days before the initial release of *Enter the Dragon* on July 26, 1973, in Hong Kong and one month before its premier in Los Angeles, Bruce Lee died of cerebral edema; there were rumors that the Chinese mafia had him killed or that he had been poisoned by a rival. A huge hit, *Enter the Dragon* elevated the image of the Asian American male in a way that has not been duplicated since. I and people all around the world were devastated because his legacy extended across borders, race, and color lines.

Bruce Lee showed me that I did not have to live by the stereotypes and cultural norms imposed on me by society and at home. Like so many other Asian parents, mine held rigid in their worldviews that were too narrow for me. Yes, I had a tough time resisting, and becoming wounded in the process, but, ultimately, the civil rights movement, the Vietnam War, and Bruce Lee were showing me new ways to be Asian in America. Because of Bruce, people no longer looked at me as someone they could automatically push around because "he might know karate." Even recently, on a crowded bus, a bunch of rowdy teenagers came on board looking for trouble. I just gave them that confident Bruce Lee smile, and they backed off. I didn't have to say a word, but they didn't want to mess with me because of the self-confidence that I had developed deep inside.

Thanks for everything, Bruce. I owe you!

NOT SO CRAZY-RICH ASIANS

My father often told the story of how he had given cigars to his friends wrapped in a paper that said, "It's a tax deduction!" instead of "It's a boy!" It seems my arrival, a first-born son, was viewed from a very practical perspective. I arrived on December 30th, just in time to give my parents a tax break for that year. Hearing your dad repeating that story as a child even in jest, you can't help but wonder whether his excitement about saving a few bucks trumped your birth.

One of my earliest realizations was that many Chinese are frugal, or what some people call "cheap," and that included my parents. Some people assumed that my parents were thrifty because they had experienced the Great Depression (1929-1933) in the U.S., but I always felt it was a cultural trait, especially after I learned that Chinese people's relationship to money is fundamentally different from what it is in America.

A main pillar of Chinese thought, the Tao Te Ching, considers frugality as one of the three greatest virtues, making it the first money principle in Chinese culture for centuries. But frugality is not just about money; it's the prudent consumption of all resources, the avoidance of waste and overindulgence—timeless wisdom that begets the mindsets of "Save as much as you can," and "Always get a bargain," which is a way of life in China. Another money attitude is "Cash gifts are best" because recipients can use it as they like. While cash-stuffed red envelopes are the standard gift for any celebration for the Chinese, in America, money is considered less thoughtful as a gift. The principle "Pay for things in cash" is smart money management by anyone's standards. The Chinese are wary of debt, but in the West, we are programmed to live on credit—money we do not have or cannot afford to spend. I understand that even today, the average person in China saves about 50% of their income![6]

Like many immigrant families of all races and cultures, in our home, there was no shortage of stories about how difficult our ancestors' lives were back in the "old country," and for good reason. The most recent of a long list of famines that haunt the collective consciousness was the Great Chinese Famine (1958-1961), believed to have claimed 55 million lives. One of the reasons my mother's ancestors came to the United States was to escape starvation in 1868, so having enough money to eat was always a concern for her. I cannot remember a time when she didn't have a discount coupon or bought something that wasn't on sale. Thanks to her coupon planning, a couple of times not only did she manage to take a whole bag of groceries home for free, but also get a cash rebate from the store. I've never seen her happier!

Cheap cuts of meat, second-hand items, thrift-store toys, off-brand clothes, lowest-cost holidays—we never got any of the "good" stuff, and not because my parents could not afford them. Worse still, they were so focused on saving that when money had to be spent on me, I felt guilty. I don't think they ever said that I was a financial burden, but they sure acted like it. I always felt that I owed my parents a debt of gratitude and that I was a disagreeable cost to them. It got so bad that, when I was a teenager, I had my dentist give me three fillings without Novocain to save my father money. Yeah, it hurt like hell, but —at least—the physical pain was temporary; the feeling of being unworthy was deep.

Looking back now, I see that my parents must have also felt undeserving. Mom wore the same old pink bathrobe until there was almost not one original thread left in it, and Dad wore tee shirts riddled with stains and holes. For Christmas, my brother and I would buy them new clothes, but they never wore them, saving them for "later." After they

[6] China Gross Savings Rate | Economic Indicators | CEIC (ceicdata.com). *CeicData*. (2021).

had passed away, we found dozens of packages of brand-new tee shirts and bathrobes in their closet.

I can only ascribe my parents' behavior to poverty consciousness, the mindset that there is not enough and that you are not entitled to everything you want. Sound familiar? This core belief keeps you living in fear, hoarding, and saving material things and, of course, money. It includes fearing change, fighting for "what's mine," being pessimistic, critical, skeptical, and a "know-it-all" —all central dynamics of how I was raised.

Poverty consciousness can be created by a traumatic scarcity experience, but often it has nothing to do with one's bank balance. It is an inherited mindset. Many middle-class families, like mine, believe that they cannot afford certain luxuries and, by extension, that they are not deserving of them. Have the Taoist teachings on frugality fixed this outlook, albeit in an imbalanced way, into the collective consciousness of Asians? Perhaps, but things have been shifting in recent years.

In sharp contrast to poverty consciousness, a new consumer class has arisen in Asia, the so-called "mass affluent," a market of 57 million people whose purchasing power affords them a wide variety of premium goods and services.[7] Today, these individuals make up 4% of the population, but the percentage is expected to grow exponentially. These are the ultra-rich who are depicted in the movie *Crazy Rich Asians* and represent a minuscule minority of the mass affluent nouveau riche who spend ostentatiously, buying products for the status they convey, albeit making sure they are worth the price.

As for me, growing up, I wanted nicer things, not necessarily to stand out but to fit in. My parents didn't buy me the Levis jeans that almost everyone wore at school—this meant that not only did I look different, being Asian, but that I also dressed differently. To save a few

---

[7] A. Bharadwaj, J. Tasiaux and V. Rastogi, "Beyond the "Crazy Rich" The Mass Affluent of Southeast Asia," *Boston Consulting Group* (2018), https://www.bcg.com/publications/2018/beyond-crazy-rich-mass-affluent-southeast-asia

dollars, they found an off brand, Foremost, which immediately branded me as poor. How could I explain to anyone that my parents were just cheap? How I hated them for that!

The need to distance myself from how my parents' viewed money and work extended to how I envisioned my future. Day in, and day out, I watched my father tolerate being a sheet metal worker at the Alameda Naval Air Station. Despite his work ethic and dedication, which I respected, I felt that he was an example to avoid, not imitate. When I told him that I wanted a job that was fulfilling, he could not understand because, to him, a job was just a way to support your family. I believed there was more to life than working to live. When I expressed that to him, he said, "What are you talking about, you knucklehead? You work to feed your family, not to feel fulfilled!"

Refusing to limit my life to such narrow parameters, after high school, I enrolled at the local community college and took every class that I had any interest in, from electronics to psychology to music. I explored my options. That was not what was expected of me. Since I was little, my parents had wanted me to be a doctor. After I failed all my biology and chemistry classes, it was clear that it was not in the cards. Besides, I couldn't stand the sight of blood. Looking for a fulfilling career outside of the most prestigious professions meant going against the wishes of my family and community. It was tough on me, especially since I had no specific professional goal at first. As an Asian who does not abide by social expectations, you are a disappointment, period. Asian parents place great importance on material success and career. About six in ten say that most American parents don't place enough pressure on their children to do well in school, while only 9% say the same about parents from their own Asian group.

Growing up, I learned that there were three classes of jobs for Asians. The first are doctors and lawyers that are regarded as the top professions in most societies because they are the "smartest" people. These professions not only require the most education but also tend to pay the most. This causes Asians to gravitate towards these jobs resulting in nearly 20% of all doctors being Asian according to the Association of American Medical Colleges. Unfortunately, there is still discrimination in the medical field. For example, while Asian Americans make up 13% of orthopedics faculty at U.S. medical schools just 5% hold chair positions. Also, of family medicine and OB-GYN faculty less than 11% are chairs.[8]

The second class is science-based jobs, like engineers, dentists, optometrists, pharmacists, psychologists, and architects. These don't require as much schooling but pay better than average. This class also includes jobs in finance, accounting, and economics.

Working in the high-tech industry falls between the second and third class of jobs for Asians. According to the Equal Opportunity Employment Commission, Asian Americans make up around 19.5 percent of professionals in this field but only 10.5 percent of its executives. Ironically, Pew Research says that Asians workers face the highest risk of job displacement due to artificial intelligence because so many work in tech.

The third class of jobs is everything else, teachers, artists, journalists, salespeople, technicians, etc. Most Asian parents would say that these are jobs anyone can do well at if they work hard. They have little value in Asian culture other than the fact that you're not homeless.

For young Asian Americans, even today, this very narrow definition of success comes at a high price. If they don't "make it" into one of the upper two classes, they are subtly or not-so-subtly made to feel like failures at family gatherings. When I settled on my first career as a television producer, my parents never understood what I did for a living. One time, I heard them telling their friends that my job was to "fix TVs."

Every parent wants a good education and financial security for their children—this is fairly universal. So, why do Asian parents place such

---

[8] A.M. Meadows, "Racial, Ethnic, and Gender Diversity in Academic Orthopaedic Surgery Leadership," *The Journal of Bone and Joint Surgery,* 104(13) p 1157-1165, (6 July 2022.)

an extra high value on education? Well, most come from countries where education is among the few paths to a better life. They believe that careers in writing, acting, fashion, and art are too risky because these professions involve subjective evaluation, thereby making their children unable to defend themselves against bias. Instead, they push them into medicine, engineering, law, or pharmacy, believing that advanced degrees protect them from the usual types of discrimination.

Is the anticipated discrimination a ghost of the past like famine? Unfortunately, it is real and present, as both the statistics and my personal experience show. As an Asian in a non-traditional profession, it's not enough to be good; you need to be great. Even as I advanced in my career, I knew that I could never have a bad day, no matter how tired or sick I may have been. I had often heard people say, "See, I told you Asians couldn't be…." You can fill in the blank with any job that people would consider non-traditional. For instance, as a professional speaker, I often had to fly from the West to the East Coast to present a morning keynote, leave home at 6 a.m. Pacific time, fly for eight hours, and present at 8:30 a.m. (5:30 a.m. Pacific Time) the next morning. I had to give a sensational program no matter how jet lagged I was, otherwise, people would say, "I told you that Asians can't speak in public!" I did this hundreds of times, sometimes internationally. I never missed a presentation and almost all attendees' evaluations said that I was sensational. Asian American exceptionalism? Based on stereotypes, we are expected to be exceptional in some areas and forced to be exceptional to be considered "as good as" whites in other areas.

Although the accomplishments of some Asian Americans, like tennis and gymnastics stars, are highly visible, the discrimination and challenges remain unnoticed. Many of the allegedly positive stereotypes, such as being smart, good at science, and hardworking, are just as insidious. In universities, for example, Asian Americans are included in diversity statistics but not in affirmative action programs. While a significant proportion of Asian Americans have attained success through higher education, a 2019 Pew Research survey found a great diversity among the groups: those of Indian (75%), Malaysian (65%), Mongolian (60%), or Sri Lankan (60%) origin were more likely than other Asian origin groups to have at least a bachelor's degree. By comparison, fewer than one-in-five Laotians (18%) and Bhutanese (15%) have at least a bachelor's degree. Roughly 33% of all Americans ages 25 and older had a bachelor's degree or more education in 2019.

Asian households in the U.S. had a median annual income of $85,800 in 2019, higher than the $61,800 among all U.S. households. But only two Asian-origin groups had household incomes that exceeded the median for Asian Americans overall: Indians ($119,000) and Filipinos ($90,400). Most of the other groups were well below the national median for Asian Americans, including the two with the lowest median household incomes—Burmese ($44,400) and Nepalese ($55,000). At the same time, 12.3% of Asian Americans live below the federal poverty level, ranging from 6.8% of Filipino Americans to 39.4% of Burmese Americans, according to the 2018 American Community Survey.

While it's great to see the success of blockbusters like *Crazy Rich Asians* (2013), the film reinforced the notion that Asians are well-off and do not have to deal with the stereotypes and racism that negatively impact 'real' minorities like Hispanics, Blacks, etc. In short, Asian Americans are pigeonholed into two diametrically opposed stereotypes—the cheap ones who haggle to save pennies and live in multiple-person homes, and the rich ones who frivolously flaunt their wealth or quietly squirrel away mountains of money. I love getting a bargain every chance I get, even though I don't really need to do so. Is frugality part of my Asian heritage or just me? This question is an example of what it's like to be an Asian American: You never truly know whether you are programmed by thousands of years of tradition encoded into your DNA or if it's just a personal preference.

Our culture is all about excelling and knowing exactly where you stand in society. Therefore, Chinese people, in particular, will ask anyone very personal questions such as, "How much money do you make?" In a Netflix special, comedian Ronny Chieng hilariously sums it all up:

"It's such a weird stereotype to have associated with your ethnicity: Asian parents wanting their kids to be doctors. It was like this obsession. And it's insidious as well because helping people is at the bottom of the list of reasons. It's about money and prestige, right? Because if you're a first-generation immigrant, your children becoming doctors is the quickest way you can turn it around in one generation. Instant credibility, instant respectability, instant money. Boom! Started from the bottom, and now we're doctors! Because Chinese people love money. We love that shit. Chinese people love money so much, we have a God of Money, Caishenye, we pray to him...for more money! Even during Chinese New Year, the biggest holiday for Chinese people, the way we greet each other is we say, *gong xi fa cai*, or *gong hei fat choy* in Cantonese. It means, "Hope you get rich!" That's not saying, "Happy New Year!"

RAY MOHEET ON NON-TRADITIONAL ASIAN CAREERS

Ray Moheet is a talent manager of Iranian descent at Mainstay Entertainment who manages the careers of clients like actress Kelly Hu and comedian Maz Jobrani. In our conversation, he reflected on traditional Asian careers in real life, as well as Asians in the entertainment industry both on the screen and behind the scenes.

Ray: I remember my first job at a Talent Agency, literally all the agents were white. I don't remember a single diverse agent during that time.

Michael: Why do you think that is?

Ray: I think a lot of immigrant cultures value careers like doctor, attorney, engineer. Some don't understand what it means to be an agent. Surely, my parents didn't understand what an agent or a manager or a producer is. They just couldn't relate to it. Because of that, it just wasn't a cool thing to do. You know, from their point of view, right?

So, I think there's a little bit of that parents want the best for their children, and obviously brought them to this wonderful country to have an amazing life and the opportunities that perhaps they didn't have access to. They are just not understanding this world that we call entertainment.

Michael: Why did you choose this line of work?

Ray: A big part of why I got into the industry was because when I was growing up, I didn't see people that looked like me on television. After doing my due diligence and some research, I figured out how I could play a role in changing that. I wanted to get into the representation business, and so that's what I did.

Michael: Do you see an increase in roles for minority actors compared to 10-15 years ago?

Ray: I think there's definitely been a gradual rise. It's certainly not enough; I mean, we all want to see more, but there's definitely been this gradual rise over the last five years that has paved the way for a lot of the movies that have had some great success. Whether it's *Crazy Rich Asians, Parasite, The Farewell, Minari*, and so forth.

Michael: Can you put your finger on something specific that caused that?

Ray: Well, I think a number of things. If I remember correctly, there was this campaign "Oscar's so white." It might have been five to seven years ago, (2015) but I think that really helped. Also, there's more and more first and second-generation immigrants, families, that are now in Hollywood. One way to impact this change is to have representation in all areas, right? Writers, show runners, directors, actors, managers, agents—you definitely see more today than you did when I got in the industry and more than five years ago.

Michael: What can be done to encourage casting directors to cast, let say Asians, in less stereotypical roles, just normal roles?

Ray: I think one of the biggest powers we have is to say no. If you want to stop perpetuating a stereotype, we all have a role to play in that. Stop saying yes to them.

Michael: But that could kill a career for an actor.

Ray: I don't think it would kill a career. Maybe it could slow growth. In one's early days, it can be hard because you've got to pay rent, you have bills, and those jobs mean everything when you're starting out, but when you're in more of a position to be picky, I think it's important that we all do our part.

MUSIC & FLOWER POWER

Except for Bruno Mars, who is of Filipino and Puerto Rican descent, and Nicole Scherzinger, a Native Hawaiian-Filipino, the absence of Asian American pop music stars is astonishing even today, compared to other areas of entertainment like actors, comedians, directors, and so on. Other than classical musicians and composers, it seems that mainstream America still cannot imagine Asian Americans in that role.

Things should be different because the music industry, which controlled everything the public heard and saw, all but collapsed with the advent of digital media. With the gatekeepers gone, shouldn't Asian American youth be seizing the opportunity to make music and promote it through social media? There are certainly artists like Japanese American Conan Gray; Korean American Sohmi and Tokimonsta; Indian American Raveena Aurora; and Arooj Atfab the first Pakistani American to win a Grammy, but they are far from being household names. Is there any room for them in the current market? The answer seems to be "maybe soon," since an Asian music revolution has been brewing for some time.

K-pop, short for South Korean popular music, combines genres like pop, hip-hop, R&B, and traditional Korean music. The K-pop sound originated with Seo Taiji and Boys in the early 1990s, but H.O.T. was the first K-pop idol group because it was highly manufactured. The members of so-called "idol groups" are formed and styled by entertainment professionals, just like "The Monkees" were in 1966, and many others such as the Spice Girls and the Backstreet Boys ever since.

K-pop appeals to teenagers and young adults and generates trillions in revenue. But what about artists from the United States? After 2006, K-pop artists started breaking into the American market. Se7en released an English-language single featuring Lil Kim. BoA became the first K-pop singer on the Billboard 200. The Wonder Girls charted on the Billboard Hot 100 at No. 79 and opened for the Jonas Brothers on tour. Rain sold out two nights at Madison Square Garden, starred in *Speed Racer* (2008) and *Ninja Assassin* (2009), and was named in one "100 Most Influential People That Shape Our World" by *Time* magazine.

Even so, K-pop remained mostly unknown until "Gangnam Style" by the artist PSY in 2012. PSY's YouTube video was viewed 3 billion times. Not only did it reach No. 2 on the Hot 100 but also compelled *Billboard* to consider YouTube views into their metrics. Most importantly, it introduced South Korean music, food, style, K-beauty, and K-drama to the world. Luxury brands like Chanel, Fendi, Dior, and Gucci collaborated with K-pop stars, while K-pop content on YouTube and Twitter expanded awareness further. In 2017, BTS won Top Social Artist at the *Billboard* Music Awards. Their U.S. success paved the way for others, including BLACKPINK, the first idol group to play at the Coachella Music Festival in California. With one billion views on one music video, -BLACKPINK's debut album zoomed to No. 2 on the *Billboard* 200, and their English-language collaboration with Selena Gomez, "Ice Cream," became a Top 20 radio hit.

By 2021, the likelihood of never having seen K-pop content was rare. Now, groups appear regularly in *Rolling Stone* and *Vogue*, and on *Good Morning America* and the late-night talk show circuit. In 2022, the Korean giant Hybe, which surpassed one trillion in annual sales, partnered with Universal Music Group's Geffen Records.

Perhaps K-pop's success will encourage Asian American musical artists to break out into the mainstream, helping Americans see Asians in a different light. This is important because music is, and has always been, an agent of change at the grassroots level. It captures the spirit of the time, conveying political and social messages. It can undermine racial bias because it's hard to idolize a musician if you hold strong contempt for their race. Simply by being in the public eye, minority entertainment stars indirectly cultivate acceptance. While I was growing up in the 1960s, there were already many Black musicians on television like Chuck Berry, James Brown, Marvin Gaye, and Stevie Wonder. There were even Hispanics like Carlos Santana, so I wondered why there were no Asians. So, I took up the guitar and formed a garage band with a group of other Asians from my high school.

My interest in music didn't happen overnight. When I was five years old, my mother decided it was time for me to start piano lessons. She had an upright piano in our living room, which she loved to play after dinner. I think she wanted me to learn music because she felt it would improve my chances of getting into college. Higher education was seen as the key to success in America, and neither she nor my father had graduated from college. Also, many Chinese believe that mastering an instrument requires self-discipline and determination—this is the same reason they put their kids into martial arts classes, not for self-defense, like most non-Asian parents.

Music has been an important part of Chinese culture for thousands of years. Playing an instrument has been considered a sign of refinement and skill only the wealthy could afford to acquire. This is the reason that even today, Asians are more often thought of as musical prodigies, not athletes. My mother used to say, "Learning the piano helps you use both sides of your brain and understand math and science concepts." Obviously, this didn't work for me because my math skills were nonexistent, and I got thrown out of chemistry class for nearly blowing up the lab!

The hours I spent with my piano teacher and practicing every week were absolute torture. Learning to keep my fingers curved and my wrists off the keys was not fun for a five-year-old. Also, I was only allowed to play scales and the song "Chopsticks." How ironic! However, being able to read music was a valuable skill because, in grammar school, I took up the violin, which led to playing in the orchestra. It was fun being part of a collaborative effort. In junior high school, I started playing the clarinet and eventually the saxophone, which I thought was way cooler. I become skilled at all the saxes—from alto to tenor to baritone—because they use the same fingering but different breathing techniques. It was then that my individualistic, rebellious side began to show. It started to bother me that in the orchestra, unless I had a solo, no one would notice if I stopped playing.

When rock 'n' roll burst onto the scene, it was the coolest thing to me. My parents hated it, which was an extra bonus! Elvis Presley was one of my first favorites, quickly followed by Janis Joplin, Jefferson Airplane, Santana, and many other San Francisco bands. I bought a cheap acoustic guitar at Sears and taught myself how to play using chord chart books. I would listen to rock songs and imitate them. This is when I bought a Fender electric guitar and amplifier and decided to form a band with some friends who played drums and bass guitar. We practiced in my parent's garage, which was behind our house but visible from the street, so the neighborhood kids came to watch. They were a small but supportive group that gave me a taste of what it felt like to be in front of an audience. I was hooked!

We played local high school dances for around $100 a night. When we first got on stage, there were always confused looks because the kids thought we were going to play some kind of Chinese music. But when we played songs like Creedence Clearwater's "Proud Mary," they would immediately start dancing. For the next two hours, I felt like any white kid would feel—no different. More importantly, being on stage not as part of an orchestra, I was taking another step toward owning my personal power. I was no longer the boy who did not want to stand out; a new me was emerging, informed by "the golden age of rock" and the anti-war and civil rights movements that all were gathering steam.

I loved rock 'n' roll because not only was it the tempo and energy of my generation, but the lyrics also expressed things I didn't know how to say otherwise. From ballads to Bob Dylan's protest songs, it helped me express what I was feeling in a deep and meaningful way. I also loved how they made fun of the police who were assaulting Blacks for protesting peacefully. Also, as a teen with a lot on my plate, music was a great way to let off steam. I just wish I had embraced my differences and written songs that expressed some of my feelings and challenges. Most bands make it because they write original music. Few become well known for playing "covers," their own renditions of famous songs. That's why being unique is a good thing!

To improve my skills, I started taking lessons on both the guitar and the organ from people in the rock scene in San Francisco. Some played with Carlos Santana and other rock stars. While my parents appreciated my continuing interest in music, they didn't care for rock 'n' roll, so they never came out to see me play in public. In fact, they never even saw me speak in public until 2000 when my father came along to help me sell my books at a National Association of Realtors convention at San Francisco's Moscone Convention Center. I spoke to almost 1,000 people, who then lined up outside the auditorium to have me sign my books that they had purchased. Afterward, when I asked my dad what he thought, in typical fashion, he said, "Not bad. Why did all those people want to buy your book?" His inability to acknowledge any of my accomplishments still stung at the age of fifty.

In my late teens, on weekends, I would take the bus to San Francisco to see rock bands at the Masonic Auditorium and free concerts at Golden Gate Park. I loved hanging out in the Haight-Ashbury district—the main center of the Hippie Movement of the mid-1960s, a hub of counterculture ideals, drugs, and music. The neighborhood's fame peaked when it became home to psychedelic rock superstars like Janis Joplin, Jefferson Airplane, and The Grateful Dead.

I dreamed of moving to Haight-Ashbury, began wearing bellbottoms, paisley shirts, a bandana, and grew my hair long just like everyone else to protest conformity—another irony of the times. I tried marijuana, which felt great. Being allergic to alcohol, there was no other way for me to get high and relax. During this period, I felt tremendous pressure from my parents to succeed at school. I was struggling in

English and math classes to the point where I was extremely frustrated. Sometimes, I even felt like ending it all because I didn't know how to relieve the pressure of school, while also struggling with my identity and the incredible loneliness I felt. I didn't try LSD or other strong drugs because I was afraid of what they might do to me. I didn't like being out of control. When offered hard drugs, I would decline by saying, "I'm high on life!"

There were many Asian hippies. When I went to college, one of my roommates, David Fong, had long hair and was a very laid-back guy who smoked a lot of grass in our apartment. Despite the social turmoil of the era, that was a wonderfully innocent time, not only in San Francisco but also in America in general. We could even safely hitchhike wherever and whenever we wanted. Can you imagine doing that today?

My parents didn't care for the people I hung out with, especially those with long hair. They considered them lazy and a bad influence. They constantly discouraged me from hanging out with them, and that only drove me to spend more time with them. But that was not just youthful rebellion; I thought the Hippies were the coolest people. Blacks, whites, Asians, and Hispanics living together—race, color, and creed didn't matter to them. Flower Power truly spoke to my values of humanity, racial equality, freedom, and individuality. It was a far cry from everything I had experienced as a young Asian American saddled with the experience of discrimination and the preconceptions and expectations of both cultures. The Hippies did what they wanted as if the rules of the establishment meant nothing to them; they even peacefully protested the Vietnam War.

NO VIETNAMESE EVER CALLED
ME CHINK

Being Asian, our country's involvement in Vietnam during the 1960s was of great interest to me because I couldn't understand why we were militarily involved in a place so far away. At first, I had bought into the "domino theory," the reason our government gave for why we were there. The theory said that if one country in Southeast Asia fell to communism, others would follow, eventually becoming a threat to the United States.

In August 1964, when I read in the newspapers that North Vietnamese torpedo boats attacked two U.S. destroyers in the Gulf of Tonkin, like most of the country, I felt that President Johnson was justified in ordering retaliatory strikes on military targets in North Vietnam. It wasn't until 2005 that declassified documents revealed that the incident never happened, and Secretary of Defense McNamara knew it.[9] The story was a lie told to declare war.

The war machine went into full swing when Congress passed the Gulf of Tonkin Resolution, giving the president broad war-making powers, after which U.S. planes began regular bombing raids in Vietnam and Laos. The plan was to disrupt the flow of supplies across the Ho Chi Minh Trail into Vietnam to "stem the tide of communism."

As early as 1965, when U.S. combat forces were sent into Vietnam, I began to feel uneasy about our involvement. I questioned the narrative.

---

[9] P. Paterson, "The Truth About Tonkin," *Naval History Magazine.* 22(3) (2008).

It didn't make sense to me when we had so many problems to solve here in America, like racism and poverty. Yet, we were going to spend millions of dollars and lose lives in a place most Americans couldn't point out on a map. Also, being three years away from draft age, I could foresee being sent to Vietnam to fight against Asians with whom I had no quarrel. However, believing in the military superiority of the United States, I assumed that the fighting would be over before then. I vividly remember General William Westmoreland repeating, "American victory in Vietnam is imminent." As time went on, I wondered if he had a different definition of 'victory' from the rest of us.

The anti-war movement began gathering momentum by 1967 when the number of American troops in Vietnam reached 500,000. My support of the war waned when it came to light that U.S. soldiers had slaughtered over 400 unarmed Vietnamese civilians in the village of My Lai in March 1968. I was horrified that Americans could do this to innocent Asian people.

Protests continued to increase until November of 1969, when 250,000 Americans gathered peacefully in Washington, DC, to call for the withdrawal of all American troops. Days later, on December 1, 1969, a lottery draft was televised from Washington, DC, to determine which able-bodied young men between the ages of 20 and 26 would be called up for induction in 1970. I turned twenty in 1970, so this draft included me. Our old television set had barely warmed up before my birthday, December 30th, was picked in seventh place out of 365 possible dates. How ironic, since this was the only time, I can remember winning anything!

According to the draft rules, attending college would not keep me out of the draft. I never liked violence and had always been able to talk my way out of trouble. The prospect of killing and being killed in some Asian country terrified me. Since Americans knew virtually nothing about us Chinese, I doubted soldiers would know the difference between a North Vietnamese and myself. And my fears were well-founded. I learned that the army had formed a team of Chinese, Filipino, Japanese, and Native American rangers called "Team Hawaii" to conduct long-range reconnaissance because they could "pass" for Vietnamese. I heard that the loyalty of Asian American soldiers was constantly questioned, and some were fired upon when mistaken for Viet Cong. Worse still, the communist Viet Cong especially targeted Asian American servicemen, sometimes putting a price on their heads.[10] While, proportionally, Asian Americans suffered fewer casualties compared to other ethnic groups in Vietnam, 139 Asian American servicemen died during the conflict according to the National Archives. I just never felt very lucky.

Among the 8.7 million Americans who served, approximately 35,000 were Asian Americans who faced unique racial challenges. In 1971, former Marine Mike Nakayama, a Japanese American, testified at the Winter Soldier Investigation that, during basic training, his drill instructor told him, "Stand up! Turn around so everybody can see you!" Then he announced to his platoon, "This is what a gook looks like!" Within a year, Nakayama was awarded a Bronze Star and wounded twice. The second time, he lay untreated in a dirty cot in a military hospital with an open chest wound and shrapnel in his skull. Seeing other U.S. soldiers with less severe wounds receiving medical care, he managed to utter, "Hey man, when are you going to deal with me?" The doctor answered: "Oh, you can speak English? Why didn't you tell us you were an American? We thought you were a gook."

During the war, we all looked like "gooks"—the subhuman enemy—to Americans. Until Vietnam and the cultural revolution of the 1960s, the term "Asian Americans" didn't exist. We were referred to mostly as "Orientals"—a word that reinforced the idea of us as foreigners despite that, by 1975, almost 80% of Japanese Americans and roughly 50% of Chinese and Filipino Americans had been born in the United States. The opposition to the Vietnam War was a key component of the newly formed Asian American Movement, which was heavily influenced by Black Liberation. Japanese American activists

---

[10] R. Jaleco, "Excluded Fil-Vets Now Eligible for Lump-Sum Money," *Balitang America* (2010).

Yuri Kochiyama, a confidant of Malcolm X, and Kazu Iijima founded Asian Americans for Action to oppose the Vietnam War and build solidarity among Asian Americans. Asian Americans turned Black Power into a Yellow Power anti-war movement, declaring, "No Vietnamese ever called me chink."

Having been on the receiving end of more than a century's worth of anti-Asian exclusion and violence in the United States, for Asian Americans, the war was personal. Silently, many of us empathized with the Vietnamese and recognized the threat of "gookism" (the lumping of all Asians into one subhuman group so they could be killed without feelings of guilt). Linking the Japanese incarceration and Hiroshima-Nagasaki atomic bombings to the race extermination in Vietnam, Laos, and Cambodia, Chester Cheng said: "We are able to unleash the most terrifying, vicious, and horrible weapons devised by man in this war because yellow people are as expendable as the buffalo and the American Indian. We are gooks in the eyes of White Americans."[11] The Vietnam War, which lasted nearly twenty years, cost the lives of over 58,000 Americans and more than three million Vietnamese, Cambodian, and Lao soldiers, and civilians.

Asian Americans, including service members, struggled with our complicated status as victims, witnesses, and reluctant perpetrators of U.S. imperialism. Living in America afforded us certain superficial and conditional privileges, and it was not our families being killed, maimed, and displaced in Southeast Asia. When the war started, for older Asian Americans, speaking out against it was out of the question because they were afraid of being charged with disloyalty and put in concentration camps as the Japanese had been during WWII. The loyalty of Asians has always been questioned in this country: Would we feel more alliance to the U.S. or to the Vietnamese who looked more like us?

Until my number came up in 1969, Vietnam had been mostly a distant concern for me, as it had been for many other people—perhaps

---

[11] C. Cheng, "Hiroshima—Lest We Forget," *Gidra*, 2:11 (1970).

I was too young to grasp the situation or just burying my head in the sand. But being almost sure to be drafted certainly changed my perspective. I did everything I could to avoid conscription. As patriotic Americans, my parents supported anything the United States did. Initially, I would try to reason with them by saying that I was afraid that I would get shot by both sides. We argued a lot about my position on the war, but there was no debate with my father. He was proud of his service during WWII and wanted me to do the same.

My mother was less eager for me to go to Vietnam because she shared my concern about being mistaken for the enemy. At the same time, she was worried about us being viewed as disloyal to the U.S. She would often say, "If the Japanese were put in internment camps it could happen to us." While she didn't want me to openly protest the war, she also didn't want me to get killed in Vietnam.

Seeing no way out of the draft, Raymond Lowe, a Chinese American friend, and I decided to enlist in the U.S. Air Force because that would give us the lowest chance of facing North Vietnamese on the ground. To be proactive, I decided to get a physical exam from my personal physician. He discovered that I had a serious hernia condition, which made me unfit to serve. Raymond eventually got a desk job with the Air Force. After my rejection from service, I became an ardent opponent of the war—this was my political awakening.

When I got to college, I realized there was a concerted anti-war movement that included many Asian American students as well as veterans—that got me thinking about race in more global and geopolitical terms. I started to recognize the racist and imperialistic roots of the war. I didn't buy the argument that communism would come knocking on our door if we didn't stop it in Vietnam. My thinking was, "If they want to be communist, let them. If they want an open and free society, they should be willing to fight for it themselves. Why should we intervene in an internal political and economic struggle?" I felt compelled to join the marches. Extremely uncomfortable at my first march, I just mouthed the protest words and held my sign low. Over time, I gained more confidence, and my anger made me more outspoken. Also, hearing people calling the Vietnamese "gooks" affected me, especially since they began to call me that, too. Not only was it as dehumanizing as being called "chink," but I was also incensed by people's ignorance of the vast differences in race, culture, food, and language between Chinese and Vietnamese people.

The more the anti-war movement grew and service members, including Asian Americans, spoke out after returning from their tours of duty, my parents' support for the war softened, but not to a point where they would actively protest. At least they began to understand my position. Vietnam was unlike WWII, where there was a real threat to world freedom. Also, my father did not have to kill Japanese soldiers face-to-face, serving as ground support for General Chennault's famous Flying Tigers in China, Burma, and India in an all-Chinese squadron behind the front lines. Had I found myself in Nam's jungles, would I have been able to kill another Asian? I don't know...but I'm thankful that I never had to make that choice.

THE ASSIMILATION OF PERPETUAL FOREIGNERS

In the 1800s, single young men from Southern China started coming to the U.S. to work as miners, railroad builders, farmers, factory workers, and fishermen. "They are among the most industrious, quiet, patient people among us. Perhaps the citizens of no nation except the Germans are quieter and more valuable," wrote the *Daily Alta California* in 1852. Railroad officials were pleased by their work ethic. The Chinese "prove nearly equal to white men, in the amount of labor they perform, and are far more reliable," one executive stated.

Despite having proved themselves valuable as a work force, and far more profitable, since they had no choice but to accept much longer hours and lower wages, they were not considered equal to white Americans. In 1853, the *Daily Alta* published an editorial on the question of whether the Chinese should be permitted to become citizens. It conceded that "many of them it is true are nearly as white as Europeans" but "they are not white persons in the sense of the law. They are not of our people and never will be."

By 1870, the Chinese represented 20% of California's labor force, but only .002% of the entire U.S. population. With the depression of 1876, amidst cries of "They're taking away our jobs" and slogans like that of the Workingmen's Party, "The Chinese must go," anti-Chinese legislation and violence raged on the West Coast. With the Chinese Exclusion Act (1882), by 1924, all immigration from Asia had been completely banned, and Asians were considered "aliens ineligible for citizenship" under the law. Until the legislation was removed in 1952, Asian Americans tended to be restricted to segregated neighborhoods and schools and banned from certain kinds of employment either by law or by custom. They were treated—albeit not as brutally—much like African Americans.

After been forced into segregation and stereotyped as perpetual foreigners for two centuries, Asian Americans are still considered by many Americans as clannish, alien, and unassimilable. There is still a notion that we do not fit the definition of an American, meaning someone who embraces the culture of competition, individualism, outspokenness, freedom of speech, and speaks English. Sixty percent of Asian immigrants to the U.S. speak other languages in addition to English, prefer cooperation over competition and silence over outspokenness, value community and family over individuals, defer to authority as opposed to speaking our minds, and look to tradition to guide our actions. However, this does not make us bad Americans, just different. In fact, we adopt more American characteristics the longer we live here. Even so, whites feel they have things in common with us only 62% of the time. The only group they feel they have less in common with are Muslims at 43%, while for Hispanics it's at 71% of the time and African Americans 73% of the time.

Between 1940 and 1970, something remarkable happened to Asian Americans. Not only did they surpass African Americans in average household earnings but also closed the wage gap with whites. Many credit this to education but a recent study by Brown University economist Nathaniel Hilger shows that schooling rates among Asian Americans hadn't changed significantly during those three decades. Instead, Hilger's research suggests that Asian Americans started to earn more because their fellow Americans became less racist toward them. How did this happen? The political rhetoric began to change!

In the 1960s, with the rising anxiety felt by white Americans due to the civil rights movement, it became politically convenient to promote Asians as a "model minority." It was less threatening to give the small population of Asian Americans (0.5% at the time) some upward mobility rather than to recognize the rights of African Americans (10.5%). "If Asians could find success within the system," politicians asked, "why couldn't African Americans? It's because they don't work hard." Gookism, which had been created to dehumanize Asians during the Vietnam War, had deepened the general anti-Asian sentiment in the U.S., but it was superseded by a more pressing political agenda: neutralizing the "black threat."

The propaganda machine continued to paint Blacks as lazy, violent, ne'er-do-wells, but changed the previous image of Asians from filthy, opium-smoking degenerate foreigners to a hardworking race with strong family values. The rhetoric became, "If we must tolerate non-white minorities in this country, they ought to be like the Asians." The pro-Asian public relations campaign worked so well that even Asians believed that we had become successful in America because of our hard work and education. For the first time, we were painted in a positive light and offered a clear path to assimilation, perhaps even to acceptance: Learn English, excel in school, get a good job, have a family, buy a home in a good neighborhood, and you have achieved the American dream.

Nevertheless, the view that we were foreigners persisted, and to the collection of other century-long stereotypes, one more was added. The humanitarian crisis of the "boat people" (refugees who fled Vietnam after the end of the Vietnam War in 1975) was at its highest in 1978-1979, but continued into the early 1990s, reinforcing the perception that Asians are literally "off the boat." Of course, gookism hadn't vanished into thin air just because the political narrative changed. Many Americans were not, and still are not, able to differentiate between Asians, nor do they know our contributions and long history in this country. There is no education in this matter. Because of the impression that all Asians just got here, I am often subjected to questions and remarks like, "Where are you from?" and "You speak good English"—microaggressions that erode my self-esteem and remind me that I am not considered an American despite being fifth generation.

Unfortunately, America's difficulty in seeing us as Americans is only rising. Up a staggering 20% from 2021, in 2022, one-third of Americans believed that Asians are more loyal to their country of origin than to the U.S. This concern has been exacerbated by our country's increasing tensions with China and yet, a 2023 Pew study showed that while 78% of Asian Americans viewed the U.S. favorably, only 20% view China favorably.

It's no surprise that we are the least likely racial group to feel accepted, even if we were born here, as 43% of us are. Being labeled a foreigner leads to 40% of the public saying that newcomers threaten traditional American customs and values. Also, according to a 2017 Public Religion Research Institute survey, most conservative Americans believe that immigrants are a burden because they take jobs, housing, and health care. "These foreigners believe they are superior to us because they are unwilling or unable to be like us," they may think, considering us not only as disloyal to the host country but also as parasites that drain it of resources.

Despite the prevalent perception that we are perpetual foreigners in America, there has been assimilation and upward mobility. Today, Asian Americans are the highest-income, best-educated, and fastest-growing racial group in the United States. We are more satisfied than the general public with our lives, finances, and the direction of the country. We also place more value than other Americans on marriage, parenthood, hard work, and success, according to the Pew Research Center.

Yet, there has been a price to pay for our success. For example, Asian American parents often put too much pressure on their children to do well in school, and the system ignores the specific problems of each group under the pan-ethnic "Asian American" banner, which now includes more than twenty different cultures and ethnicities. The purported success of the so-called "model minority" does not apply to all.

THE MODEL MINORITY

Sold as the way to assimilate and raise our socioeconomic status, many Asian Americans of previous generations, including my parents, bought into the political agenda that painted us as "the model minority" —invisible, silent, compliant, hardworking, studious, and family-oriented. While not all these characteristics are negative, they perpetuate stereotypes that have been used against us since we first came to America in the 1800s.

When I was growing up, Asians were all but absent from the media. If people were not making fun of us, they looked past us as if we were mannequins. There were moments when I felt so invisible that I wished that someone would call me "chink" because that would acknowledge my existence! Eventually, I realized that all Asian Americans felt neither seen nor heard to some degree—just the way society at large liked it.

Along with invisibility, our silence and compliance were expected. After Japanese Americans were released from the camps, scared of being rounded up again, they wanted to prove that they were good Americans by working hard and not complaining. Their tolerance implied that you could do anything to them, including taking their homes and businesses, and they could survive, and even thrive. With the scars of internment fresh and the threat of gookism ongoing, my mother always told me to never talk back to white people even if I felt we were being treated unfairly otherwise we might be put into a camp. She also told me never to speak Chinese in public because others might think we were talking about them, or worse, that we were Japanese.

A strong assimilationist movement aimed to prove that we were worthy of the rights and privileges of citizenship by keeping our mouths shut and our heads down, working hard, and making enough money to live like white people. Our standard of living was lower. In 1960, United States-born Japanese men earned 23% less, Chinese men earned 13% less, and Filipino men earned 39% less than white men in similar jobs. We were paid less than whites because employers knew we would never complain.

Asian Americans saw assimilation as the remedy to a century of discrimination. Yet, discrimination was not widely discussed. Even general conversations ended up in arguments in my home. Any time I brought up an instance of being mistreated or derided, my father's response was "sticks and stones!" It was an exercise in futility. The inability to express my frustration to my family compounded my feelings of neither being seen nor heard. When I shared my experiences with my Asian American friends, they relayed similar treatment.

The model minority myth may have been psychologically seeded by the internment experience, but its development was interwoven with the history of African Americans. After the abolition of slavery in the 1860s, for a short period of time, Black men voted and held political office. Despite their constitutional rights, they were increasingly subjected to discrimination and violence, especially in the South. For the next one hundred years, the Jim Crow "separate but equal" laws segregated public facilities into "white" and "colored." Asians were included in the definition of colored. In 1954, Jim Crow was weakened and eventually dismantled with the Supreme Court's Brown v. Board of Education decision and other rulings. This made many white Americans afraid of the growing rights of Blacks.

As a child in the 1950s and 60s, I watched the inhuman treatment of peaceful African American protesters on TV—sprayed by high-powered water hoses, attacked by police dogs, and shot. It was traumatic. For Asian Americans of my parent's generation, such scenes reinforced the fear that "tomorrow it might be us," even as things were improving for them in the United States. Thanks to the political activism of African Americans, the Civil Rights Act of 1964 banned discrimination based on race, color, religion, sex, or national origin in employment and prohibited racial segregation. The Voting Rights Act of 1965 restored and protected voting rights for minorities and the Fair Housing Act of 1968 banned discrimination in the sale or rental of housing.

While these gains benefited Asian Americans, they were but a drop in the bucket for African Americans after almost 200 years of brutal oppression. By the late 1960s, some Blacks demanded violent action to fight American white supremacy, and organizations like the Black Panther Party came to prominence. To counter the increasing threat by Blacks, *New York Times Magazine* in January of 1966, published an article entitled, "Success Story: Japanese American Style" by sociologist William Petersen, who proposed that Japanese Americans had succeeded because they have strong family values and focus on economic, not political progress. The author stated, "By any criterion of good citizenship that we choose, the Japanese Americans are better than any other group in our society, including native-born whites." Most historians point to this article as the start of the myth of the successful minority.

To cement this thinking, *U.S. News and World Report* published in December 1966, "Success Story of One Minority Group in U.S." It stated, "At a time when it is being proposed that hundreds of billions be spent on uplifting Negroes and other minorities, the nation's 300,000 Chinese Americans are moving ahead on their own with no help from anyone else. What you find, back of this remarkable group of Americans is a story of adversity and prejudice that would shock those now complaining about the hardships endured by today's Negroes." Clearly, the model minority myth was created not to congratulate Asian Americans but to tell African Americans and other minorities to stop protesting and start assimilating. Such public relations campaigns were, and still are, one of the most powerful tools of white supremacy to silence racial justice movements.

In the 1960s, the Asian American Movement was formed by a small number of Chinese American and Japanese American students, who wanted to mobilize under a pan-ethnic banner. Only by forging a new sociopolitical entity could the "Asian American," gain enough numbers. This resonated with Asians across the country who sought safety in numbers and political clout. But the pan-ethnic banner and the model minority myth created the illusion that all Asians do well and do not face the discrimination that impacts the "real" minorities, -resulting in the notion of "yellow privilege" (see Yellow Privilege chapter). Over half a century later, as a result of this politically convenient over-generalization and misperception, systemic racism is rarely addressed, while we Asians continue to uphold the model minority stereotype that wants us invisible, silent, and compliant. Who will fight for us if we do not fight for ourselves?

To my parents, assimilation meant both blending in and not making waves. Like most other Asian American parents, they saw education as the only road to upward mobility. Consequently, at present, about half of Asian Americans over the age of 25 hold college degrees, compared with only 28% of Americans overall.[12]. Yet, we earn 5% less than whites with the same level of education.[13]

In my career, I expected my efforts to be rewarded with automatic promotions and pay raises, as my mother had taught me. Unfortunately, other people took credit for my hard work. Yoked by the model minority myth, Asians do not advocate for ourselves and are often looked upon negatively when we do.

Regrettably, this mindset impacts more than our careers. In 2003, Shaquille O'Neal was asked on the radio about one of the first Chinese players in the NBA. He responded using a Chinese accent, "Tell Yao Ming, 'ching-chong-yang-wah-ah-soh.'" Host Tony Bruno not only laughed but also invited listeners to call in with jokes on the topic. To the minimal protest, mostly from the Asian American community, O'Neal responded that he was "only joking." Why does American society still find it acceptable to publicly make fun of an individual of Chinese descent? Well, because it can! Even today, in America's most

---

[12] J. Nam, "AANHPI in Higher Education: Facts and Statistics," *Best Colleges* (2023).
[13] J. Guo, "The Real Secret to Asian American Success was not Education," *The Washington Post*, 19 November 2016.

diverse cities, Asians of all backgrounds are fearful of being verbally harassed, spat on, pushed, punched, stabbed, or killed in the recent surge of racial violence by hateful people who believe we are easy targets.

And the insidiousness of the model minority myth does not stop there: We are driven to disprove the stereotypes we don't like and prove the ones we do. For most of my life, I have felt tremendous pressure not to get into trouble because it would bring shame not only to my family but also to the whole Asian culture, even in the most ridiculous ways, like having a mishap on the road that would prove that Chinese people can't drive. Has any white person ever considered themselves a representative of all Caucasians?

I believe that the cost of assimilation is high for Asians. With everything we do in life, we must choose our level of blending in which can range from: 1) Assimilation: when one abandons their own cultural habits and values to totally accept the cultural habits and values of the new country; 2) Integration: when a person holds onto some aspects of their culture and, at the same time, tries to blend into the new cultural environment; 3) Separation: when an immigrant focuses on maintaining their values and avoids contact with the majority culture as much as possible (such as in many Chinatowns); 4) Marginalization: when one neither holds on to their original culture nor joins the new culture—this can be the most stressful of all.

Obviously, the longer a family has been in the United States the more likely they are to assimilate. Even so, every Asian American faces the conundrum of exactly how much to integrate into the society, which can cause psychological issues in addition to the ordinary pressures of everyday living. When I was young, I felt compelled to reject everything Asian and adopt everything American. Trying to blend in made me ashamed of being different and hurt my self-esteem. My confusion and inner conflict did not start to ease up until much later in life when I understood that being different could be a benefit and I began accepting and appreciating myself as I am— a unique individual like every other person on this planet. By then, I had changed my name several times, with each change representing a step away from or closer to assimilation. Born Jonathan Lee Wong, which rang too Chinese and wimpy to me as a teen, I legally changed my name to Michael David Lee when I turned eighteen, believing that an obvious Asian name would not be helpful to my career. At some point, I realized that I was lost in the millions of other Michael Lees; Asians, whites, and blacks. So, to differentiate myself, I added my childhood nickname "Soon" to my professional name. When my father would ask me when I was going to do something like mow the lawn I would simply answer, "soon" and the name stuck.

"A lazy person will find many excuses to delay working," my parents reminded me daily, implying that procrastination is laziness, which is considered a sin in most world belief systems. Perhaps, this belief is taken to extremes in Chinese culture because it values the family over the individual, who is—in turn— 'worthless' if not productive. For hundreds of years, China practiced "9/9/6," working from 9 a.m. to 9 p.m. six days a week, but in recent years this has been ruled illegal. In 2021, a company in China faced backlash after it fined workers for taking a second toilet break during an eight-hour shift. They justified their actions by saying, "Frequent toilet use is the sign of a lazy worker."

"A lazy Chinaman does not exist," Mark Twain observed, but I don't believe a work gene has ever been discovered! Many Asians reinforce the hardworking, financially stable, and well-educated stereotype, which is among the most detrimental because it disregards racial inequality as a systemic issue. Believing that hard work pays off, we work harder; and it does pay off, especially in fields that are fact-based and not dependent on subjective opinions and trends like the arts. Our parents often push us into Science, Technology, Engineering, and Mathematics (STEM) because they are practical, high-paying, and in demand. While only 7% of all U.S. workers held STEM jobs in 2021, over 18.4% of all Asian American and Pacific Islander workers were in STEM.[14]

Hard work and studiousness are two sides of the same coin, which help to buy Asian Americans our model minority title and perceived success,

---

[14] "Examining Educational, Workforce, and Earning Divides in the Asian American and Pacific Islander Community," *New American Economy*, May 13, 2021.

which is often linked to educational attainment. As of 2021, while 54% of Asians hold a bachelor's degree, only 36% of whites, 23% of Blacks, and 16% of Hispanics earned this degree. While 21% of Asian Americans have earned advanced degrees, only 14% of whites have done so.[15]

What about money? As of 2020, Asian families had a median household income of $94,903; white families had $74,912; Hispanics averaged $55,321; and Blacks averaged $45,870.[16] While the numbers seem to support the "Asians are prosperous" piece of the model minority myth, from 1970 to 2016, income inequality between Asians went from being one of the most equal to the most unequal among America's major racial and ethnic groups. The percentage of new immigrants in low-skill occupations increased due to the surge in Asian immigration following the Immigration and Nationality Act in 1965 and the end of the Vietnam War. Meanwhile, concentration in the STEM fields and the reduction in discrimination against Asians led to higher-paying jobs through the model minority narrative and the gains of the civil rights movement.

"You can be anything you want if you study hard, even the president of the United States," my mother would tell me from my first day in school. For Chinese immigrants, education for their children is close to a religion. Families build their entire lives around providing the best they can afford. Relative to other minorities, more Asian Americans live in wealthier neighborhoods, which gives us access to better schools. While I was growing up, due to discriminatory housing laws, my parents could only buy a home in a lower-income area in Oakland, CA. My high school (Oakland High) was rated academically lower than Skyline High in the more affluent Oakland hills where actor Tom Hanks went to school.

Another trait of the model minority stereotype is being family oriented. While marriage and family are important to most Americans, in

---

[15] J. Nam, "AANHPI in Higher Education: Facts and Statistics," *Best Colleges* (2023)
[16] D. Waddington, "Census Bureau Statistics Measure Equity Gaps Across Demographic Groups," *Census.gov* (2021)

recent decades, social changes have resulted in fewer adults being married, more babies being born outside of marriage, and fewer children being raised by two married parents. In contrast, Asian Americans— particularly the foreign-born—are something of a throwback. We place the highest priority on being good parents with two-thirds saying it is "one of the most important things in life." According to U.S. Census Bureau data from 2017-2021, 80% of Asian American children are likely to grow up in a household with two married parents, compared to 66% of White children, 57% of Hispanic children, and 34% of black children.

Divorce can affect a family's finances, and is there any doubt that a stable home enables children to achieve more? My parents always reminded me of the benefits of being married. They claimed that divorced people are unhappy and struggling. As I grew, I noticed that they were not the happiest couple; they were not struggling, but not well-off either. It all seemed a bit hypocritical to me. Worse still, they always said, "Divorce brings shame on your family." When I got divorced, the stigma was very hard on me and on my parents.

What my parents didn't explain was that, in most Asian cultures, marriage is not just a relationship between spouses; it involves both extended families. That's a lot of people to please! Parents are often involved in many, if not all, aspects of their children's lives, and perhaps stiflingly so. Children are expected to perform in very specific ways and criticized if they do not excel academically. Rarely are they allowed to participate in extracurricular activities, like sports, for fear that it would take away time from studying. Asians generally frown on "participation trophies" and not keeping score in sports. Our culture is all about excelling.

Enter the "tiger parent" whose sole purpose in life is to make sure their children are the best, not just the best they can be. The term was coined by Yale Law School professor Amy Chua in her 2011 memoir *Battle Hymn of the Tiger Mother,* where she explains how she focused on her daughter's academic achievement over her happiness and self-esteem by using shame to motivate and discipline. University of Texas at Austin Associate Professor Su Yeong Kim tracked how the parenting practices of 444 Chinese American families affected their children's adjustment based on the four parenting styles: "supportive" (45%), "tiger" (28%), "easygoing" (20%) or" harsh" (7%). Kim found that the children of tiger parents had higher rates of depression, aggression, anxiety, illness, and alienation than those with easygoing or supportive parents. Children who do not meet their parents' often unrealistic expectations feel unworthy, unlovable, insignificant, and inherently flawed—this describes my childhood exactly! Not only can this have a serious and long-term impact on their physical and mental health but also can bring the opposite of the desired result. They often have more trouble academically, making friends, and finding life partners.

While Chinese tiger moms are notorious for driving their children to succeed, I believe that South Asian parents are more so; especially first- and second-generation. Today, there's a whole industry built around helping kids (mostly Asian) prepare to score high in college entrance exams, and this is not just for high schoolers. I know Indian parents who have enrolled their kids in supplemental math classes and grammar at three years old!

Instead of thriving, quite a few kids crack under the pressure. Children, as young as nine, contemplate suicide, believing that their parents will not want them if they do not achieve a certain academic standard. Asian American college students have a higher rate of suicidal thoughts than white students and, according to the Centers for Disease Control, suicide is the leading cause of death among Asian American young adults ages 15-24. According to the American Psychological Association, in 2017, suicide was the 8th leading cause of death for Asian Americans, compared to 11th for the general population, yet only 8.6% seek help for their mental health compared to 18% of the population. The statistics are worse for Asian American females. According to the University of Washington, almost 16% of all U.S.-born Asian American women have contemplated suicide, compared to 13% of all Americans, and they are also more likely to attempt suicide than other groups. Why? Because failure is not an option, and Asian women are under added pressure compared to men. The submissive, hyper-sexualized, or "dragon lady" stereotypes hurt their self-esteem. Add to this a constant battle against discrimination and trying to live up to the beauty standard set by white women in America, and you have a recipe for disaster. Worse still, mental health disorders are seen as failures in the Asian culture, and seeking treatment outside of the family is an even bigger failure. Consequently, few Asians enter the mental health field.

I experienced firsthand the lack of culturally competent mental health clinicians when I sought help. I could have been added to these suicide statistics. Throughout my adolescence, I struggled under the weight of my parents' expectations about my education and always felt inferior. I may have expected more of myself than they did of me, or perhaps they just accepted me as a disappointment when it became clear that I would not become a medical doctor. Dashing their hopes early on probably freed me to follow my path. Nevertheless, my suffering was intense. I often thought about how I would end it all. I heard about kids hanging themselves and jumping off buildings, but my choice would have been an overdose of sleeping pills, to which I had been addicted since the age of twelve. Just falling asleep forever seemed like a peaceful way to end all the pressure and pain I was feeling. Ironically, the only thing that kept me from swallowing a bottle of pills was that my suicide would have embarrassed my parents and family.

It wasn't until my brother decided to become a church missionary when he was in high school that the pressure diminished a little. I guess my parents figured that if they had a man of God in the family they were at least guaranteed to go to heaven! Nevertheless, I felt so alone. I couldn't talk to my Asian American friends because they were facing the same pressures. Their parents told them constantly, "Second place is no place," reminding them that there can only be one top student in any class, while the rest suffer in shame.

MODEL MINORITY
MYTHS & REALITIES

In the United States, there are over 22 million people of Asian descent, approximately 7% of the nation's population. Chinese, Indian, Filipino, Vietnamese, Korean, and Japanese accounted for 85% of all Asian Americans as of 2019. The other 15 Asian-origin groups make up about 2% or less of the nation's Asian population. The model minority myth that paints Asian Americans as invisible, mute, compliant, hardworking, studious, and family-oriented has concealed anti-Asian racism for too long by propagating the false picture of a uniformly successful group with no "real problems," overlooking the challenges of each subgroup within this diverse community. The most prevalent myths are:

Myth: Most Asian Americans are successful.

Reality: This generalization cannot be applied to all groups classified as Asian in America. For example, the Bhutanese, have the highest rate of poverty of any group in the country, including Blacks.

Myth: The perception that Asians are successful was created to highlight their work ethic and family values.

Reality: No, it was designed to chastise African Americans for demanding their civil rights.

Myth: Asian Americans are fairly, or overrepresented in senior positions in U.S. companies, politics, media, and other realms.

Reality: Asian Americans only hold about 3% of these positions despite composing 7% of the U.S. population. They have the lowest degree of representation in political office compared with other racial or ethnic groups. They are also underrepresented in management positions in all industries despite having the highest level of education of any group.

Myth: Asian Americans are fully accepted in American society.

Reality: 92% of Americans polled said they were comfortable with Asian Americans as doctors or friends, but only 85% said they were comfortable with an Asian American as a boss and 73% as a president of the United States.

Myth: Most Asians in the U.S. are new immigrants. They are not featured much in history books because they are relatively new to the United States.

Reality: 43% of Asian Americans were born in the U.S. with some families having migrated in the 1800s. Traditional American K-12 curriculum is taught from a Eurocentric point of view and the only thing that most students learn about Asians is Chinese New Year.

Myth: Asians never protest or fight for their civil rights.

Reality: Asians have had to sue for the rights that others take for granted. The first time Asian Americans brought a civil rights case to federal court was after a Chinese American man named Vincent Chin was beaten to death by two white men in 1982. The killers received a $3,000 fine each and zero prison time. The sentencing sparked national outrage and a pan-Asian American civil rights organization called American

Citizens for Justice (ACJ) was formed. The ACJ and other groups petitioned the U.S. Department of Justice to investigate Chin's murder as a civil rights violation. As a result, one defendant received a sentence of 25 years in prison, and both paid substantial fines.

Myth: All Asians excel academically.

Reality: Not all Asians excel academically. Southeast Asian, and Pacific Islander students, often underperform compared to all other racial and ethnic groups in the United States.

Myth: Asians are widely considered to be loyal Americans.

Reality: Most Americans believe that Asians are foreigners who are more likely to be loyal to their homeland no matter how long they've been in the U.S.

Myth: Asians are successful because they are "almost white."

Reality: No, Asians are allowed more freedoms and face less discrimination because they are not Black.

Myth: The model minority stereotype is positive for Asian Americans.

Reality: No, it creates tremendous unnecessary pressure, for example, to conform to the stereotype of working hard and never complaining. It also conceals the socio-economic, political, educational, and psychological needs of Asians.

TAKING AFFIRMATIVE ACTION

When America banned immigration from China in the late 1800s, the so-called "paper son" business thrived. Paper sons or daughters were Chinese people who were born in China and illegally immigrated to the United States and Canada by purchasing documentation that stated that they were blood relatives of Chinese people who had already received U.S. or Canadian citizenship or residency. To prove to the immigration officer that you were the child of a legal citizen you had to describe the home and town where you grew up and other pertinent details. If your description matched the one given by the "father," you were allowed into the country.

My paternal grandfather migrated as the paper son of a gentleman named Mr. Wong so he had to forgo our Lee surname. Growing up, I often told my parents that I wanted to honor him by reclaiming the family name but was not completely honest with them. I also wanted to "whiten" my name, and Lee certainly offered that advantage.

Even in adolescence, my instincts told me that some people might discriminate against those with ethnic names. Studies by Stanford University, Harvard Business School, and the University of Toronto found that—when applying for jobs—only 11.5% of Asians with identical qualifications as other applicants receive callbacks if their resumes included references to ethnicity or race. When resumes were whitened, 21% of Asians got calls. Such discriminatory practices are prevalent even in businesses that claim to value diversity. Of course, we now have more nuanced terms to describe the same thing, like "unconscious bias," and set percentages to determine the number of minority hires.

While my parents had ingrained in me the belief that success comes from hard work, it wasn't until I was exposed to African American history in college that I began to understand systemic racism. It became clear that when every aspect of the sociopolitical structure is stacked against you, no amount of hard work can create upward mobility for the vast majority of those who face discrimination. I saw, firsthand, from friends and coworkers how the system prevents you from getting ahead and demoralizes you. The few who succeed against all odds are often extolled in the media as examples of what you can achieve if you only work harder.

Systemic racism begins before a child is even born by disenfranchising the parents and then continues with education. In ethnic studies classes, I learned that from preschool, Black children are subject to harsher punishments than white kids. They also tend to be pushed more into vocational programs instead of universities and professional careers. Many live in poorer neighborhoods, so they do not have access to better schools, nor have the financial means to go to a university.

Many people are calling the awareness of systemic injustices "woke" and fighting to avoid any discussion about it at all costs. We don't need to make anyone feel guilty that it exists, but I believe that it's important to understand historical context if we are ever going to end white supremacy and violence against minorities in America. Florida Governor Ron DeSantis' administration has been the biggest opponent of "woke" which is defined as, "the belief that there are systemic injustices in American society and the need to address them." I agree that we all need to be alert to racial or social discrimination and then be willing to do something about it.

Facing less discrimination from the 1960s onward because of the model minority myth, Asian Americans were able to improve their standard of living. Asian parents spare no expense to purchase homes in the best school district they can afford, for tutors and classes after school and on weekends. They keep telling their children that they are guaranteed an Ivy League education if they get good grades, but this is not necessarily the case.

In 2014, a group called Students for Fair Admissions (SFFA) filed a lawsuit against Harvard University claiming that its race-conscious admissions policy discriminated against Asian American applicants. Like most universities, Harvard aims to expand opportunities for minority students who have been underrepresented in higher education. This policy has resulted in admitting fewer Asian Americans despite comparable, or higher, grades and scores than non-Asian applicants.

On June 29, 2023, the Supreme Court ruled that colleges and universities can no longer take race into consideration as an express factor in admissions.[17] While most AAPIs supported affirmative action they were divided on whether it should be applied to admissions to institutions of higher education. Many experts believe that the ruling will benefit white and AAPI applicants to the detriment of Black and Hispanic students. This is just another example of how AAPIs have been used to divide communities of color for the benefit of the majority. Only time will tell but history has proven that trying to right the wrongs of the past can be extremely complicated and fraught with unintended consequences.

Such considerations were not part of the Executive Order on Equal Opportunity Employment (1961) when I enrolled at a local community college in 1969. Just having been rejected for the Vietnam draft because I was deemed physically unfit to serve, I was trying to figure out what I wanted to do with my life. It had been years since I had shattered my parents' highest hope that I would be a doctor or follow any other highly valued STEM career. So, I was free to explore. I took every class at my local community college I was even remotely interested in—from psychology to electronics to auto shop—but remained at a loss until I came across a course catalog from San Francisco State University, describing their unique broadcast communications program. It combined everything I was interested in; it was creative, technical, and not traditionally Asian. Not only did it sound like fun, but I also thought I could make a difference in the world by producing television documentaries to correct wrongs, like discrimination.

---

[17] *Students for Fair Admissions, Inc. v. President and Fellows of Harvard College,* 20-1199 (2023)

I applied but was denied admission because there were so many people who wanted to get into television and radio at the time. The department chairman suggested that, if got into the university under another program it would be easier to transfer into broadcasting the following semester. I asked which majors were available, and he said that the music program always had plenty of openings. So, I dusted off my clarinet and was accepted. While I had always enjoyed playing music, I simply hated academic subjects like Music Appreciation and Music Theory.

After six months of torture as a music major, I was accepted into the broadcasting program. I enjoyed learning radio and television production, but in my first semester, I realized that I wasn't as creative as many of my fellow students, who were always coming up with clever ideas for scripts. So, I asked one of my professors if he thought I was in the right major. I explained despondently that I didn't have as much creativity as many of my classmates. He replied that there are many forms of creativity. Some people can write unique stories but have difficulty getting their scripts produced without someone like me. He said that he had noticed that I was very good at taking ideas and figuring out all the steps to bring them to life. He said writers needed producers, otherwise their great works would sit on a shelf gathering dust. That was a huge relief to me.

While the skillsets of a producer were within my comfort zone, I realized that the profession was incredibly competitive. For every television producer, there were dozens of technicians working behind the scenes, so as soon as I graduated, I set about studying for the three Federal Communications Commission licenses that I would need to become a broadcast technician so I could get my foot in the door. I passed all three in record time. Like most people in their twenties, I still wasn't sure what I wanted to do with my life.

While being a television producer sounded exciting, the barriers to entry seemed daunting. So, I toyed with the idea of becoming a California Highway Patrol (CHP) officer because I wanted to fly airplanes and helicopters, which were an integral part of the CHP. I passed all tests but was rejected because I didn't meet the minimum height requirement of 5'8". I was a quarter inch too short, but I just couldn't see how an arbitrary height limit would affect an officer's ability to do the job.

In fact, it seemed to me that this rule was discriminatory since Asians tended to be shorter than 5'8" on average; so, I reached out to the American Civil Liberties Union, and they threatened a lawsuit against CHP. As a result, the height requirement was quickly waived, and the Highway Patrol sent me a letter asking me to reapply but, by then, I could see that I didn't want to work in an organization with that kind of bureaucracy and mindset. However, I understand that as a result of my action, thousands of minorities, and women under 5'8" have since been able to serve in the Highway Patrol, not only in California but throughout the country.

So, I went back to pursuing a television career by registering with an affirmative action nonprofit organization called the San Francisco Minority Broadcast Skills Bank, where companies listed their available positions and mostly African Americans and Hispanics listed their skills. I had qualms about the registry because I had never taken advantage of the fact that I was a minority before. I had always earned everything I received without any special considerations. However, because the industry was so hard to get into, I felt I needed to use every opportunity available to me.

Growing up in the 1960s, I saw President Kennedy on television sign Executive Order 10925, which instructed federal contractors to take "affirmative action to ensure that applicants are treated equally without regard to race, color, religion, sex, or national origin." At that time, my parents were very much against affirmative action because their unshakable core belief was that if you work hard, you don't need any extra help.

My parents and I had also witnessed the signing into law of the Civil Rights Act of 1964 that prohibited employment discrimination and established the Equal Employment Opportunity Commission (EEOC). We also watched President Lyndon B. Johnson issue Executive Order 11246, requiring all government contractors and subcontractors to expand job opportunities for minorities. This sparked more discussion in my family about the pros and cons of affirmative action, especially when this Order was amended to include women. My mother never quite understood why this was necessary, as she always felt that women were treated equally where she had worked.

My mom wasn't aware that it was the Equal Pay Act, which passed on June 10, 1963, that made it illegal to pay women lower rates strictly based on sex for the same job. Demonstrable differences in seniority, merit, quality, or quantity of work, and other considerations might justify different pay, but sex could no longer be viewed as a drawback on one's resume. The U.S. Bureau of Labor Statistics reported that in 1963, women earned 59% of men's wages; in 2012, they earned 80.9% as much as men, and in 2020 women earned 89% of men's pay. It is estimated that it will take 40 years to achieve parity at the current rate of progress.

My father felt that accepting help of any kind, whether affirmative action or food stamps, brought shame and dishonor to the family—a feeling obviously shared by many other Asians. For example, in 2021, only 3% of Asians used food stamps compared to 37% of whites.[18] Despite my parents' disapproval, thanks to the Minority Broadcast Skills Bank, I was hired at a local ABC television affiliate as a broadcast technician. Yes, I often wonder whether I would have been hired had I not been a minority. This is one of the drawbacks of affirmative action; it makes you doubt your self-worth. Are you there because of your merit or just to fill the quota? This was the argument that former New York Mayor Ed Koch made when I had an opportunity to chat with him about this issue. It was a point that was hard to counter.

With that said, had it not been for affirmative action, I may have never gotten into broadcasting. It's impossible to know what my life path would have been instead. I would venture to say that it would have been very different. A great deal of what I have accomplished in traditionally non-Asian fields may have not been in the cards for me. Who knows?

[18] H. Hartline-Grafton and E. Vollinger, "New USDA Report Provides Picture of Who Participates in SNAP," *Food Research and Action Center,* (2019).

HISTORIES OF PAIN

In the mid-1970s, only reruns of old shows and news were broadcast on television during the summer months, so experienced TV engineers went on vacation and rookies, like me, kept things going. Thanks to affirmative action I was hired at the TV station as a "summer relief worker."

In true Asian fashion, I worked very hard to excel at my job. For instance, while the reruns were playing, I practiced threading film through the projectors because—in those days—the news was shot on film and after developing and editing it often wasn't ready for the 6 o'clock news. This is why newscasters would often read a story and then say, "Film at 11pm." I got so fast at threading film that the news director counted on me to get the film on the air at the last minute. What didn't dawn on me until later was that's why I was always assigned to the projection room instead of running cameras or audio, which I would've preferred.

A couple of weeks after I started working at the TV station, I woke up one morning and found I couldn't move. It felt like someone was jamming a hot poker up my back. I crawled to the phone and called for an ambulance. At the hospital, I was diagnosed with ankylosing spondylitis, more commonly known as arthritis of the spine. I refused to believe it because I was young and thought arthritis was only for old people. The doctors said that this form of arthritis targets young men in their prime and, if serious enough, could confine me to a wheelchair, or worse. After thinking about it long and hard, I decided that if I ended up in a wheelchair, I would commit suicide before that happened.

I was prescribed prednisone, an anti-inflammatory drug, which made me feel much better but can cause your bones to become extremely brittle, especially as you get older. So, I went to the library and did as much research as I could; unfortunately, there was almost no information about Asians and arthritis. Even today, despite that Asians are the fastest-growing minority population in the U.S. we are still underrepresented in medical research in areas like cardiovascular disease, mental health, cancer, and women's health. Many researchers ignore us due to our small numbers in the U.S. In addition, Asians are often less willing to participate in health research projects due to a lack of trust and experience with the healthcare system, discomfort with the English language, and other factors. So, we are lumped together with white people or placed in the rather useless category of "other." Even though the population has increased by 72% since 2000, clinical research efforts focused on Asian American, Native Hawaiian, and Pacific Islander populations have made up only 0.17% of the National Institutes of Health budget since 1992.[19]

Determined to find a better way to manage my health issues, I continued doing research. At the library, I came across *The Arthritic's Cookbook* by Dr. Collin H. Dong that suggested avoiding red meat because it can cause inflammation of the joints. Out of desperation, I became a strict vegetarian and immediately lost 15 pounds, along with much of the broadness in my chest and shoulders. But I felt better. I started exercising to keep my body strong and flexible. To this day, I still suffer from backaches and stiff fingers, but I'm able to stand upright and function fairly normally without medication. I also eat fish and poultry for protein, which doesn't seem to bother me.

Despite the pain, I was able to return to work. Eventually, I made friends with the production manager at the station and would periodically pitch him show ideas. After nine months of mastering all equipment

---

[19] L.N. Doàn et al., "Trends in Clinical Research Including Asian American, Native Hawaiian, and Pacific Islander Participants Funded by the US National Institutes of Health, 1992 to 2018," *JAMA Network Open*, 2:7 (2019).

as a broadcast technician, the station offered me a permanent position with a handsome salary, full union benefits, and a retirement plan. This was extremely tempting for a 23-year-old with back problems and no health insurance, but I decided to stay focused on becoming a producer. I knew that if I took the technician job, I could end up still pushing a camera at 60 years old, and I didn't want that. So, I not only turned down the offer but also packed my bags!

On my very first day at San Francisco State University, I met a girl named Bernice from Hawaii. We dated during college, and when I left the station, I decided to try living in Oahu for a while. It sounded like heaven, so I put all my summer clothes in a large duffel bag and got on a flight.

At first, Hawaii seemed like the island paradise I had seen in ads. A beautiful flower lei was placed around my neck as soon as I arrived at the airport. I was immediately told that visitors needed to respect the island culture, starting with the lei. You never take it off within sight of the person who gave it to you or put it in a trashcan in public because this disrespects the person and the Hawaiian culture.

Hawaii was an interesting experience—being in a place where Asians were the majority, I didn't get funny looks when I walked into a store or restaurant, and no one commented about how good my English was. There were Asians everywhere as bank tellers, store clerks, in hospitals, and even on television. For the first time in my life, I grasped how comfortable white people must feel being the majority on the U.S. mainland.

I stayed in a hotel for two weeks while I did some sightseeing and job-hunting at various television stations. I visited Bernice's family, and they were very concerned about me because jobs were hard to find, even for locals. The best most people could do was work in the tourist industry for extremely low wages. Fortunately, the local television station, KGMB-TV, had an opening for a broadcast engineer. I was hired and rented an apartment. My girlfriend's family was amazed at how lucky I was.

From my native Hawaiian coworkers at the station, I learned about the oppression of the indigenous people, the Polynesians who arrived over 1500 years ago after navigating the ocean with only the stars to guide them. In the 1820s, during the rule of the Kamehameha dynasty, the first white missionaries arrived. They quickly destroyed ancient altars and temples, replacing them with Christian churches. In 1835, the first sugar plantation opened on Kauai, and labor was recruited from China, Japan, Korea, the Philippines, and Portugal. Then came western law in the form of the Hawaiian Constitution in 1840, a supreme court, and a parliament.

By 1850, foreigners could buy land and did so in droves. In 1887, largely supported by the Hawaiian people, Queen Liliʻuokalani tried to restore the monarchy. She wanted to eliminate the voting privileges of European and American residents and businessmen. In 1893, the U.S. put the Hawaiian kingdom under martial law, the queen was placed under house arrest and forced to abdicate. On the 100th anniversary of the overthrow of the Hawaiian kingdom, Congress apologized to Native Hawaiians on behalf of the United States, but no reparations were given. This is why, if you talk to Native Hawaiians, there is still a lot of animosity against the "Haole," the non-Polynesian residents of Hawaii, especially the whites.

I had a great time in Hawaii, surfing in the morning, working from 2 p.m. until 10 p.m. and partying on the weekends. But this quickly became boring, so I reached out to the production manager at my old television station in San Francisco. He told me about a job opening as a summer relief production assistant and said the job was mine if I wanted it. While this wouldn't be as a producer, at least I would be in the production department instead of engineering. I packed my duffel bag and flew home. Within two weeks, I was performing "vital" tasks like cleaning the weather map and getting slides from the art department, but always going the extra mile. On one film shoot in an art gallery, I saved a very valuable painting from being torn by catching it just before it landed on a sharp statue. To show his appreciation, the artist gave me one of his paintings.

Around this time, things with Bernice had cooled. She was a wonderful woman, but she was ready to settle down. I was just starting my career, so we parted ways. At one of my acupuncture sessions for my back, I met a young lady named Elena, an assistant in the clinic. We started dating, and she encouraged me to attend Asian Studies classes at our local community college to increase my awareness of my cultural background. She called me a "banana" because she felt I looked yellow on the outside but was really white on the inside. I guess I deserved the epithet because my whole life I had tried to fit in with the majority by being as Caucasian as possible.

In class, I learned about the Asian American Movement, formed in the 1960s by students who organized campus coalitions known as the Third World Liberation Front. They demanded the establishment of departments of Asian American, African American, Hispanic, and Native-American Studies. I learned about the earliest experiences of Asians in this country. It was both fascinating and infuriating because I knew nothing about the history of discrimination against Asians, only of African Americans. This was history I could relate to because it was about people who looked like me—how and why we came to America.

As the story goes, Chum Ming was a merchant from Guangdong Province who sailed to America and ventured into the Sierra Nevada foothills where he struck it rich in 1848. He wrote to a friend back home, and the news began to spread through villages across the Pearl River Delta. At the time, it was illegal for Chinese citizens to leave the country, and Qing dynasty officials offered little protection for emigrants. Nevertheless, men throughout the region began booking passage on ships bound for what they called "Gum Shan" or Gold Mountain. They were just like other gold seekers from around the world: farmers, artisans, and merchants, who either paid their own way or borrowed money for the voyage to America. The trip across the ocean was frequently a dangerous journey. It generally took ten to twelve weeks to sail from Hong Kong to San Francisco. Shipmasters often stuffed the men into overcrowded, poorly ventilated, disease-ridden holds. One ship arrived in San Francisco Harbor having lost a hundred Chinese men, one-fifth of those on board. "There can be no excuse before God or man for the terrible mortality which has occurred on some of the vessels containing Chinese passengers," said William Speer, a Presbyterian missionary who treated many Chinese after they disembarked.

I was especially intrigued to learn that, shortly after the American Revolution (1776), the main trade route between the U.S. and China was from Boston to the port of Canton (Guangzhou) where my family was from—like other locals, my ancestors must have learned about the West from speaking with sailors and merchants. My mother had told me that her grandmother, Jennie Kwok, arrived on the only one of five wooden single-mast junks to survive the trip from Canton in 1868, but I had no idea why they came. Everyone knows that gold was discovered in California in 1848, but few are aware that 24,000 Chinese males, primarily from Canton, came at the same time with hopes of sending money back to their families or returning to China as rich men. The Chinese were facing economic hardship and famine because of the Taiping Rebellion and the growing British dominance over China, but that wasn't the only reason. For them, America also represented freedom from intolerance based on one's views, just like it did for the Pilgrims.

My Asian studies professor explained that after the gold rush ended in 1853, with so few women on the frontier, the Chinese took jobs like cooking and washing clothes because these jobs required very little ability to speak English. This explained why there are still so many Chinese restaurants and laundries in America today. Before then, I just thought we were naturally good at cooking and washing clothes!

In 1865, 15,000 Chinese were hired to build the Transcontinental Railroad, especially for the most difficult section through the Sierra Nevada Mountains. To cut through the granite rock, dangerous and unstable black powder and nitroglycerin were used. Many Chinese were assigned this job because, being smaller and lighter, they could more easily be hoisted in baskets up the rock faces and, possibly, because they were considered expendable. So many died that the phrase, "You don't have a Chinaman's chance" was coined.

After the railroad line was finished, the Chinese worked as small-time merchants, gardeners, domestics, laundry workers, and farmers but were hounded out of many railroad towns in Wyoming and Nevada because they were so different from the locals. In 1854, the California Supreme Court in People v. Hall, denied the Chinese the right to testify against whites, as was also the case for Native Americans and African Americans. They could be robbed, beaten, or killed without consequence. I can't imagine how helpless and vulnerable they felt after this ruling.

During the Civil War, Chinese workers kept the wool, cigar, shoe, and garment industries going. In school, only one history teacher even mentioned African American involvement in the Civil War, so I was surprised to learn that about seventy Asians (Chinese and Filipinos) enlisted in the Union Army and Navy. Smaller numbers also served in the Confederate forces.

We did learn in school that, in 1869, the Fourteenth Amendment to the Constitution gave full citizenship to every person born in the U.S., regardless of race. What was new to me was that, in 1877, Denis Kearney founded the Workingmen's Party of California to protest Chinese workers accepting lower wages, poorer conditions, and longer hours than white workers were willing to tolerate. They had little choice but to work for whatever wages since most had to support their families in China and repay loans for their passage to America.

It made me furious to learn that not only did many white people in America hate Asians, but the laws discriminated against us as well. In 1878, when a Chinese immigrant by the name of Ah Yup wanted to become naturalized, the Ninth Circuit Court in California ruled that Chinese are ineligible; only "free white persons, aliens of African nativity, and…persons of African descent" had the right to citizenship. In this respect, even Blacks had more rights than Asians.

By 1880, the 300,000 Chinese (10% of California's population) were condemned by newspapers and even church leaders. As a result of this Anti-Asian fervor, twenty-eight Chinese miners were massacred in Rock Springs, Wyoming, in 1886. In the following year, robbers killed

31 Chinese miners in Snake River, Oregon. Of course, many other acts of violence and killings went unreported. As a matter of survival, the Chinese retreated to isolated communities called "Chinatowns," where the tradition of small business ownership developed as many provided their services to other Chinese and, eventually, to non-Chinese.

The anti-Asian sentiment grew to such a degree that, in 1882, Congress passed the Chinese Exclusion Act prohibiting immigration from China for ten years. The law was extended for another ten years by the Geary Act in 1892 and made permanent in 1902. According to the Encyclopaedia Britannica, "The excluded Chinese did not passively accept unfair treatment but rather used all types of tools to challenge or circumvent the laws. One such tool was the American judicial system. Despite having come from a country without a litigious tradition, Chinese immigrants learned quickly to use courts as a venue to fight for their rights and won many cases in which ordinances aimed against the Chinese were declared unconstitutional by either the state or federal courts. They were aided in their legal battles by Frederick Bee, a white California entrepreneur and attorney who was one of the principal American advocates of the civil rights of Chinese immigrants and who represented many of them in court from 1882 to 1892. They also protested against racial discrimination through other venues, such as the media and petitions. Some Chinese simply evaded the laws altogether by immigrating illegally. One of these methods was the 'paper son.'"[20] Again, these were young Chinese men, like my grandfather, who paid to come to the country by falsely claiming to be the child of an American-born Chinese citizen. I never really understood the history and reasons behind this until the Asian American studies class.

Severe restrictions on female immigrants, young men migrating alone and laws prohibiting Chinese men from marrying white women led to a largely bachelor society. Many had to cohabit secretly with white women or marry African American women. The U.S. Census of Louisiana (1880)

[20] https://www.britannica.com/topic/Chinese-Exclusion-Act; accessed August 2023

showed that 57% Chinese American men were married to African American women, and 43% to European American women. The same census, according to Brittanica, showed that "there were 105,465 Chinese in the United States, compared with 89,863 by 1900 and 61,639 by 1920."[21] To further reduce the growth of the Asian population, the United States Immigration Act of 1924 banned almost all immigration from Asia. The quota for most Asian countries was zero. While the Immigration and Nationality Act of 1952 gave Asians the same rights as other immigrants, the quota system did not end until 1965.

Fascinated and angered by the history of Chinese Americans, I sought to learn more about the experience of other Asians. From my Japanese American friends, I learned that, from 1890 to 1907, Japanese arrived in large numbers, with many going to Hawaii to work in the sugar plantations. Since Hawaii was more multicultural, they didn't experience any more discrimination than other minority groups there. And in 1898, when Hawaii was annexed into the United States, anyone born after August 12th of that year was declared a citizen. Things were not as easy for Asians on the mainland. In California, Japanese immigrants ("Issei") were banned from buying land in 1913, so they purchased in the names of their U.S.-born children ("Nisei") who were citizens. But much worse hardships were to come.

As everyone knows, the Japanese navy attacked Hawaii's Pearl Harbor on December 7, 1941. What is less known is that, almost immediately after, the FBI arrested pro-Japanese community leaders in Hawaii and on the mainland. These were U.S. citizens. Then, over 120,000 people of Japanese descent, mostly U.S. citizens, were incarcerated. In a huge transfer of land and wealth, they were forced to sell their businesses and homes in a short amount of time, some only a month, at a great loss. One thing that shocked me was that even those who were as little as 1/16 Japanese could be placed in the camps.

---

[21] ibid

I was amazed to learn that while many of their families were in American concentration camps, Japanese American soldiers fought in Europe in the all-volunteer 442nd Regimental Combat Team, the most highly decorated military unit in United States history. Were they trying to prove their loyalty to the American people, or just incredibly brave?

The more I learned the angrier I became that our stories were not included in my American history classes. We were treated as invisible and insignificant. Even today, rarely is Chinese involvement in the building of the Transcontinental Railroad or the incarceration of Japanese Americans mentioned in school. I believe that this is one reason why Pew Research found that 75% of Asian Americans are unaware of our history or know our contributions to this country. I also came to realize that we were considered strange, dirty barbarians, almost not human, and unfit to become part of a land meant for whites.

The plunge into our long painful history became the groundwork for my activism and speaking career on diversity. Learning where I came from, and how my ancestors were treated was transformative for me. It gave purpose and meaning to my life.

EXTRA BENEFITS

At the television station I met Jerry, another Production Assistant, and we became the best of friends. He was Jewish and he helped me to understand why they were so persecuted even though they seemed white to me. He told me that Jews in America have always been considered white in that they were permitted to become naturalized citizens, a right reserved only for "free white persons;" even though they are of Eastern European descent. However, Judaism is a religion with a specific set of ideas about the world and the way Jews should live their lives; but many Jews are not religious. He explained that anti-Jewish sentiment has existed for centuries. Even before the rise of Christianity, anti-Jewish prejudice could be found within ancient Greek and Roman cultures, and certain interpretations of the Christian Bible's New Testament seemed to blame Jews for Jesus's crucifixion. Today, white supremacists see Jews as trying to supplant them as the superior race in America.

After a year in the production department of the TV station, I was offered one of two jobs. The first was as a permanent production assistant with union benefits that could lead to becoming a television director but only after one of them retired, or died, because these positions were highly paid and very prestigious. The second was as one of three producers of a live, weekly minority television show. It was 90 minutes long and roughly divided into one-third African American, one-third Hispanic, and one-third Asian. I really didn't want to do a minority show but felt it could lead to producing a non-ethnic program, so I accepted it. It also paid only half the salary of the union job and had no health benefits, but I felt it was worth the risk to become a producer. Gotta start somewhere, right?

While I was nervous about whether it was a wise decision, the Confucian philosophy about continuous progress kept me optimistic. It states that no matter how challenging a situation is, even the smallest step in the right direction is progress. And in my case, it certainly was! In 1975, when I took that position, Department of Labor statistics showed that 378 broadcasters in areas with 5% or greater minority populations employed no minority full-time employees, while 209 employed no minority persons whatsoever. With media jobs being so rare for Asians, a producing job was a big opportunity because producers make content decisions—they have a say in what ends up on the screen—as long as they remain within the parameters set by the executives. Producing a public affairs show on a local TV station was not a huge platform but it was my chance to bring my perspective to the airwaves.

Media is a window to, and a mirror of the ideas and beliefs of the era. At the time, it was very depressing to see that Asians were disproportionately depicted as Chinese restaurant workers, Korean grocers, Japanese drug lords, martial artists, gangsters, laundry workers, and prostitutes. In contrast, Asian parents were relentlessly driving their children into the STEM fields. In essence, we were being pigeonholed by both sides. "When Asians only see themselves in stereotypical jobs that's all they and their parents consider for careers. In order to make real change on the screen we need to change the makeup of the people who really control what the public sees. This is why I first opted to work behind the camera where I could help make changes in the industry rather than be subject to the whims of executives, many of whom never knew an Asian or other minority on a deep, human level. This is why I wanted to eventually produce non-minority programs to show the world that an Asian American could make general programming that would appeal to the whole country, not just a small segment that I should automatically be an expert at," writes Nancy Wang Yuen, professor of sociology at Biola

University, echoing my own reasons for accepting the minority show job despite my hesitations.

So, I dove in and subscribed to every Asian American newspaper and magazine I could find and began to make connections with Asian American leaders in the San Francisco Bay area. I was able to convince some very high-profile guests to appear on the show, which became very popular with minorities in the Bay Area, particularly Asians who were not used to seeing their issues covered on television. I also found myself in front of the camera, conducting interviews and acting as a substitute host for our show. Our Executive Producer auditioned me as a news-caster, but because the most popular newscasters were Asian women at the time, I wasn't considered.

Professor Yuen wrote, "One stereotype that I have particular aver-sion to, and experience with, is the Asian TV anchorwoman. The anchor gets the hard-hitting news stories about war and hurricanes while the co-anchor gets the stories about kittens and kids rescued from wells. During the 1970s, a few television stations tried to appease the civil rights movement by auditioning some male and female Asian news co-anchors. I was one of those. The women were extremely popular with audiences while men never caught on. I was not considered because it was said that I was seen as 'smart but not trustworthy' as is necessary when you're reading the news. These are two stereotypes commonly applied to Asian males. The older white male anchor paired with a younger Asian female co-anchor became the norm in many major mar-kets for almost two decades. Rarely was the woman the anchor, though."

It's safe to assume that this trend is rooted in the long-standing sexual stereotyping of Asian women as desirable. In 1976, when Connie Chung (the first Asian American and second female news anchor at a major network) became an anchor at the CBS affiliate in California, the station went from third to second place in ratings. Other stations took notice and soon, almost everyone had to have at least one appealing Asian female news co-anchor because they attracted male audiences and were considered good counterparts to white male anchors. The same was not true for Asian males who were generally only seen, if ever, as field reporters doing short news or public interest segments.

Having set my sights on jumping out of minority programming, while I worked on my show, I also volunteered on non-ethnic shows, learning different production techniques, and being exposed to new ideas. During the three years I was a producer, I worked 12 to 16 hours a day, seven days a week. Part of what drove me so hard was the fact that I never knew when my arthritis might flare up again and possibly end my career, so I was very focused on doing as much as I could with whatever time I had left. Also, I was motivated to keep learning and develop a "beginner's mind," also known as "Shoshin" in Zen Buddhism.

As I gained experience as a television producer, I became interested in film production. I realized that films have more longevity than TV because, once our show aired, we were off working on next week's program. Our weekly efforts produced temporary entertainment and, sometimes, cultural awareness, but a film takes months, sometimes years, to complete. It can be screened in theatres, on television, and then included in reruns, rented on VHS tape (at the time), and now streamed almost indefinitely.

It occurred to me that the best way to learn film production, in addition to reading a ton of books, was through experience and observation on the set. After some research, I discovered that many movies were filmed in San Francisco, like Clint Eastwood's *Dirty Harry*, and TV shows like *Streets of San Francisco* (starring Michael Douglas and Karl Malden).

I also learned from friends that you could get paid to be an "extra" while watching the crew set up lights and sound equipment and shoot the scenes. Extras are non-speaking players that populate a scene to make it look more realistic. Being part of the "background" seems simple enough, but some skills and experience are required. For example, one scene may be shot from different angles, and if the extra does not perform the on-screen action in exactly the same way every time, the editor would not be able to cut the shots seamlessly together. For example, if the extra ties his right shoe in one "take" and he ties the left shoe in the next, what is called "continuity" is ruined; this means that the scene may either have to be reshot or left on the cutting room floor. Obviously, if you caused this to happen, you would never get called back as an extra again. To get hired as an extra, all you had to do was phone the casting agency to see if they had any "calls" for the following day. Then they would give you a time and location at which to report. Being a television producer on a Saturday morning show afforded me a lot of flexibility. If I had my segments and guests lined up, no one cared where I was during the day.

During my breaks, I would slip into an empty studio with a telephone and manually dial the casting agency's number over and over, up to 200 times because there was no auto-redial in those days. My persistence paid off since I got to be on sets where people like Clint Eastwood and Chuck Norris were producing and directing—that was my world-class education in film production, and I was being paid to do it! In addition, I read books and magazines on film production.

After a few months of working as an extra, I developed an interest in acting. Realizing it was not an easy transition, I started taking classes at the Asian American Theater Company and acting in plays. My first experience was as one of the main actors in playwright Frank Chin's *The Year of the Dragon.* This play portrayed a Chinese American family in San Francisco's Chinatown during Chinese New Year. It was essentially a critique of the racism in American society and poked fun at American tourists who eroticized, objectified, and misunderstood the real meaning behind Chinatown and its residents. *The Year of the Dragon* was one of the first plays by an Asian American playwright to be produced. Eventually, it made its way to New York City, where it premiered in 1974 at the American Place Theatre, starring Randall Duk Kim, Pat Suzuki, and Tina Chen.

Having thoroughly enjoyed the experience, I was compelled to continue acting in other small theaters in the San Francisco Bay Area, as well as in industrial films and commercials. Although I had noticed that I kept getting cast as a scientist or engineer, it did not bother me because I was not fully aware of typecasting yet, despite having been exposed to it my entire life through Asian caricatures, yellowface, and whitewashing.

ASIAN STEREOTYPES THEN AND NOW

Learned, reinforced, and sustained through social influences, stereotypes are generalizations about a group of people. Not only can they vary but also contradict each other. Many have a long history and were created as a result of specific economic, political, or social circumstances. The argument that they are based on some kernel of truth is highly problematic because overgeneralizations are inaccurate and harmful. According to L. Rosenthal and N. Overstreet, in *Encyclopedia of Mental Health* (2016), they can lead to (1) stereotype threat; for instance, when an individual is worried that performing badly on a test will confirm people's beliefs about the intelligence of their race, gender, culture, ethnicity; (2) internalization, meaning that the stereotype compels the individual to define themselves within its narrow parameters; (3) discrimination by other people.

Evidence suggests that Asian Americans are frequently denied leadership opportunities and overlooked in research, clinical outreach, and advocacy efforts.[22] I believe that this is a result of stereotyping—a distortion, misrepresentation, and denigration of our humanity and individuality. It is often used to demean, denounce, dehumanize, and parody. The following are some of the stereotypes that have been used against Asians over the years:

GENERAL:

The Oriental—The term was widely used before the 1960s to imply that we were exotic and unknowable. Today, we are referred to as Asian Americans, and the term "Oriental" is only used for inanimate objects like furniture and rugs. In 2016 President Obama signed a bill eliminating the use of the term from federal law.

---

[22] "The Illusion of Asian Success," *Ascend.* (2017).

Inscrutable—From our earliest days in America, we have been called "inscrutable," which is commonly defined as "impossible to understand." Whites felt that our language, culture, foods, and beliefs were too different from theirs. Many would be happy to have us as neighbors because we would likely be quiet, but they could never conceive of having one of us as a friend.

Unassimilable/Perpetual Foreigners—One hundred and fifty years ago, Asians in the United States were perceived as illiterate, undesirable, full of "filth and disease" who would never become "good Americans." Considered "marginal members of the human race," we were denied the right to citizenship. Many people still feel this way about Asians in America. When cast in television shows or films, Asians often have a heavy accent and are made fun of because of the way they speak. This perpetuates the stereotype that all Asians are foreigners.

Yellow Peril—Russian sociologist Jacques Novikow coined the term in the essay "The Yellow Peril" (1897), and which Kaiser Wilhelm II used to encourage the European empires to invade and colonize China in order to neutralize the existential threat it posed to the West. As the pollutant stereotype, the term "yellow peril" began to take hold in 1890s California, Asians were viewed as alien and a threat to wage-earners, so a movement aiming to make California racially pure began. This concern has mostly been forgotten.

Coolie—In the 1850s, the lowest-paying unskilled jobs were called "coolie labor" or "nigger work." The term was applied to Chinese laborers as a means of preventing them from entering the skilled trades. This term has largely fallen out of use.

Deviant—This stereotype developed after Asians began moving away from their typical jobs in America as common laborers, household servants, and laundrymen following the Gold Rush. Based on a handful that operated opium dens and imported women for prostitution, all Asians were considered to follow deviant behaviors.

Gook—The term originated with the U.S. Military during the Korean War as a generic term for Asians and became more popular during the Vietnam War. A gook is an invisible and powerful inhuman enemy with extraordinary endurance and the ability to withstand punishment.

Asian Martial Artist—Before Bruce Lee, Asians in American films were portrayed as servants or unskilled laborers. By demonstrating his fighting skills, Lee wanted to show the world that Asians could do more. Unfortunately, this created a new cinema stereotype for Asians as martial arts experts. After Bruce Lee, Jackie Chan, and Jet Li solidified Hollywood's use of Asians as martial artists. Many people still believe that all Asians practice martial arts.

The Evil Genius - This is the Asian supervillain, the Dr. Fu-Manchu character, whose murderous plots involved members of secret societies as his agents, usually armed with knives, poisonous snakes, other peculiar animals, or natural chemical weapons. Unfortunately, this stereotype still exists in movies and TV shows.

The Model Minority—The myth assumes that all Asians are a uniformly high-achieving racial minority that has assimilated well into American society through hard work, obedience to social mores, and academic achievement. The stereotype denies discrimination and disregards the diversity among Asian communities as well as the need for everyone to be treated as an individual.

Competent But Cold—In a 2003 national random-sample survey, Princeton University psychologist Susan Fiske's research found that Asians, along with Jews, are consistently stereotyped as "competent but cold." This perception causes people to feel envy and resentment, which can lead to anger and violence. It also hurts the chances of Asians for promotion into leadership positions at work.

All Asians Have Yellow Skin—Asians have skin colors that range from pale ivory to yellow-tan to dark brown, depending on the region where they live, how much time they spend in the sun, and other factors.

All Asians Look Alike—This is a that myth stems from not paying attention or being aware of how one Asian person of descent differs from another. Within the different ethnic communities, there are vast differences in physical features. If it's any comfort, many Asians have difficulty differentiating between white people for the same reason.

All Asians Are Smart—Again, this is obviously not true because there are people at each end of the intelligence spectrum in every culture with most people being in the middle. This stereotype puts an undue burden on Asian students to excel academically.

Asians Can't Drive Well—I believe this stereotype started when many Chinese people immigrated to America from Taiwan in the late 1970s. Many were wealthy and highly educated, so they had drivers because labor was cheap in Taiwan. When they arrived in the U.S., they discovered that labor is expensive, so they had to learn to drive themselves. As a result, you had Taiwanese whose first language was not English learning to drive for the first time. Yes, they probably didn't drive very well. I can tell you that every Asian I know drives extremely carefully here, so they don't perpetuate this stereotype.

Cause of COVID—Since the COVID-19 virus originated in China, many blame the Chinese for sending the virus to the rest of the world. The pandemic has brought increased incidents of racism, discrimination, and violence against Asians, particularly in the United States, with reports of hate crimes of over 100 per day in 2022.

ASIAN MEN:

Eunuch/Asexual Male—The image of the nerdy Asian guy with thick glasses and an accent, who can't get a date, even with women from his own race, implies that these men are impotent and pose no sexual threat to other males. Asian American men have generally not been viewed as attractive or sexual by the mainstream culture and media, although many film and TV productions are now starting to cast Asian men as sexual beings and even as love interests. Nevertheless, these same productions almost always include dialogue that seeks to convince American women that Asian men are indeed "dateable" or sexy. A recent Buzzfeed article published, "17 Reasons Why Asian American Men (or Any Other Western Asian) Make The Best Boyfriends."

Asian Men Have Small Penises—Hand-in-hand with the Asexual Male/Eunuch stereotype, this myth has been in existence for decades. Only now are we seeing attempts to invalidate it in the media. In almost every film and television production that presents Asian men as dateable, penis size is included in the dialogue in an all-too-obvious effort to dispel the myth. "Chinese men have no reason to feel inferior about the size of their penises, according to a Hong Kong study which showed local men measured up 'below the belt,' to others elsewhere in the world," NBC recently reported.

Misogynist/Authoritarian Male—Another stereotype is that Asian men are insensitive and disrespectful towards women. This is seen in best-selling novels like Michael Crichton's *Rising Sun* in which Japanese businessmen mistreat and denigrate their white mistresses.

Even Amy Tan's *The Joy Luck Club* has been criticized for perpetuating racist stereotypes of Asian men.

Asian Baby Boy (ABB)—An extension of the term "Asian Baby Girl" (ABG) refers primarily to younger men who have adopted a gangster aesthetic or personality. Associated traits are being interested in partying, fashion, and sexual attractiveness.

South Asian Service Worker—Indian and Pakistani men are often portrayed in service-related occupations like motel owners, gas station owners, or cab drivers.

Pacific Island Men - Often shown as fat, happy, simple people who lack ambition and intellect, or as aggressive savages.

Southeast Asian American Men—Generally portrayed as lazy alcoholics or violent criminals.

South Asian American Scientist—Indian and Pakistani men are often portrayed in science-related occupations such as medicine, engineering, and computing.

ASIAN WOMEN:

Asian Prostitute/Masseuse - White men have fetishized Asian women since the early 20th century when many Chinese American women were considered to be prostitutes. This made white people fear that Asian women were coming to ruin their "pure" families and seduce white men, resulting in the 1875 Page Act, which barred Asian women from coming into the U.S. A modern iteration of this stereotype is the Asian masseuse, who is always eager to give the client a "happy ending."

Southeast Asian Women Service Workers—This is as an outcome of over-representation in low-paying occupations such as manicurists, aestheticians, cooks, and sewing-machine operators due to their lack of English skills.

Asian Women Have Slanted and Tighter Vaginas. Likely rooted in colonialism and the trafficking of Asian women during the Korean and Vietnam Wars, this myth is linked to the fetishization and exotification of Asian women. Comedian Amy Schumer once joked: "It doesn't matter what you do, ladies, every guy is going to leave you for an Asian woman... And how do they bring it on home for the win? Oh, the smallest vaginas in the game."

China Doll/Lotus Blossom/Geisha—These non-threatening and servile female stereotypes are sexually objectified and hyper-sexualized. They are the innocent, gentle, and obedient girls, or the damsels-in-distress—just perfect for fulfilling a white man's fetish. Dating sites show that many white men hold this stereotype of Asian women.

Exotic South Asian Woman—Indian and Pakistani women are often portrayed as mysterious and seductive.

Pacific Island Woman—In media, Hawaiian women are often shown as sexy hula dancers.

Harajuku Girl—Racialized fashion, like the outfits of Harajuku girls, is another way of codifying the fetishization of Asian femininity. This stereotype was introduced to the American mainstream by Gwen Stefani but had been part of Cosplay pornography for years. The infantilized girl links attractiveness with powerlessness and innocence. She does not challenge the pre-existing racial hierarchy and Western cultural dominance.

Asian Schoolgirl—The innocent schoolgirl who wears short skirts and is looking for her first sexual experience.

ABG or Asian Baby Girl/Gangsta—Asian Baby Girl culture originated in the 1990s with Chinese American youth gangs, especially in New York City. They wore black, lightened their hair, and presented themselves as a counterculture to the submissive "model minority" stereotype of Chinese American women. In the 2020s, the term resurfaced as a fashion trend. Asian American women created tutorials and transformation videos to showcase the look.

Asian Ninja Girl/Female Warrior (Kunoichi)—The Asian Ninja Girl is a popular anime character, who is a young martial arts expert. The adult version, the Japanese "kunoichi," has appeared in numerous novels, TV dramas, movies, and manga. The term was popularized by novelist Futuro Yamada's novel *Ninpō Hakkenden* (1964). The stereotype has made its way into the Western mainstream through movies and TV shows, like Maggie Q's character in *Nikita*.

Damaged Asian Girl—An Asian woman, usually young, who has experienced a lot of emotional damage and, as a result, inflicts suffering on others. This type appears in Western movies and television.

Asian Geek Girl—A popular anime character who is smart, tech-savvy, and sexy. In the media, Asian women are overrepresented as working in higher-wage technical fields like software development and computer programming.

Dragon Lady—Asian women have often been portrayed as cunning, aggressive, and opportunistic sexual beings, or as predatory gold diggers. This is still a very common image in the media.

Tiger Mom—While almost all stereotypes fetishize Asian women in some manner, their sexualization seems to stop when they have children and become "Tiger Moms." Highly controlling and authoritarian, these mothers drive their children to high levels of success at any cost.

CARICATURES, YELLOWFACE, WHITEWASHING

———

Seeing coolie hats, or Asian conical hats, in Chinatown souvenir shops has always bothered me. I wonder if the people wearing them know what they represent. Worn by rice field farmers in East, South, and Southeast Asia for protection from the sun, they originated with the so-called "coolies," a slang term for manual laborers and slaves. Add to the hat a long braid, the traditional Chinese garb, buckteeth, and a funny accent, and you have the well-known "Chinaman" caricature.

During the Vietnam War there was no shortage of caricatures of "gooks," but the first time I learned about the history of the century-old negative image was in my Asian Studies class in the 1970s. We were shown posters, ads, and handbills from the mid-1800s that either mocked the Chinese or promoted aggression toward them. I was embarrassed and hurt that white Americans would portray us that way.

The first time I saw white people playing Asians, known as "yellowface," was in 1961, in the film *Breakfast at Tiffany's*, when the White actor, Mickey Rooney was made up to play the buck-toothed Mr. Yunioshi with his eyes taped back in a slant and speaking "fortune cookie" English. I was only eleven years old, but it still struck me as wrong that a white guy was playing an Asian in a mocking way. I had been a big fan of Rooney but came to hate him for making fun of us.

It seemed to me that yellowface was a parody of our race even when it wasn't intended for comedic purposes.

One of the earliest known uses of yellowface was in 1767, when Arthur Murphy's *The Orphan of China*, based on a traditional Chinese play, was staged in Philadelphia with all white actors. At the time, very few Americans had seen an Asian. We were so rare that museums and circuses even featured the so-called "Oriental," among other exotic racial groups, for education and entertainment. A famous "'specimen" was Afong Moy, the first Chinese woman in America. This "Chinese Lady" with bound feet was put on display in P.T Barnum's, and others', sideshows in the 1830s.

By the beginning of the 20th century, California and Hawaii had substantial Asian populations but acting careers were not a priority for people who faced much bigger problems, like discrimination and violence. At some point, however, the use of yellowface was no longer a result of a lack of Asian actors. By 1910, Lee Tung Foo was known as "the most remarkable China man in the United States" due to his vaudeville performances. At the same time, Japanese American Sessue Hayakawa's roles in The *Wrath of the Gods* (1914) and *The Typhoon* (1914) had made him not only as famous as Charlie Chaplin and Douglas Fairbanks, but also one of the highest-paid stars of his time. He was making $5,000 a week in 1915 ($150,000 in today's money) for *The Cheat*, and $2,000,000 a year via his own production company. According to Wikipedia, "His 'broodingly handsome' good looks and typecasting as a sexually dominant villain made him a heartthrob among American women during a time of racial discrimination, and he became one of the first male sex symbols of Hollywood."[23] Today, he is best remembered for his Oscar-nominated role in *The Bridge on the River Kwai* (1957).

---

[23] "Sessue Hayakawa," Wikipedia, last modified August 14, 2023, https://en.wikipedia.org/wiki/Sessue_Hayakawa

Anna May Wong was arguably the first Chinese American female movie star and the first Asian to play opposite a white romantic lead in *Toll of the Sea* (1922). Among other films, she starred with Marlene Dietrich in Josef von Sternberg's *Shanghai Express* in 1932. Despite being internationally known, her roles were limited by stereotypes and prejudice. Things got worse after 1927 with the implementation of the Hays Code—a media industry guideline that continued until 1968. The Code prohibited interracial relationships from being shown on the screen and casting non-whites in roles where they may be perceived as love interests of a white character. One example of its impact was *The Good Earth* (1937), a film about a Chinese farmer's struggle to survive. The role of the wife should have gone to Anna May Wong. "She deserves consideration," said MGM producer Albert Lewin "but does not seem beautiful enough." So, opposite Paul Muni, German-born Luise Rainer was cast and then won an Academy Award for Best Actress for her portrayal. Needless to say; MGM could have abided by the Hays Code by casting two Asians. Almost certainly, the Hays Code was used to justify yellowface because the studios were concerned that audiences would not respond well to Asian actors. Had Sessue Hayakawa's phenomenal success not already proved this thinking wrong?

"That was a different time," one might argue, but even today Asians are often not deemed worthy enough to play themselves, despite their successes over the years. Merle Oberon was born in India in 1911 to a British father and Sri Lankan-Maori mother. She hid her ancestry to avoid discrimination and typecasting by claiming she was born in Tasmania and that her birth records were destroyed in a fire. Sessue Hayakawa's Japanese wife, Tsuru Aoki starred in over 45 motion pictures throughout the 1910s and 1920s, including many famous films of the silent era, like The *Dragon Painter, The Breath of the Gods, The Vigil,* and *The Geisha.* Keye Luke was the first Chinese American actor signed by RKO, Metro-Goldwyn-Mayer, and Universal Pictures, as well as one of the founding actors of the Screen Actors Guild. After his debut in *The Painted Veil* (1934), he was best known for playing Charlie Chan's son in the film franchise and for originating the role of Kato in *The Green Hornet*.

Japanese American actress Miyoshi Umeki was the first East Asian to win an Academy Award for her role as Katsumi in the 1957 film *Sayonara*. An accomplished singer, she was nominated for a Tony Award for Best Actress in a Leading Role during the Broadway production of *Flower Drum Song*. Born in Hawaii in 1929 to second-generation Japanese parents, James Shigeta's acting, and baritone voice won over audiences throughout the 1960s and beyond. He is most known for his roles in productions, such as *Flower Drum Song*, *The Crimson Kimono*, *Bridge to the Sun*, and newer favorites like *Die Hard* and *Mulan*. Nancy Kwan is still considered a pioneer for Asian representation in Hollywood. Her first role as the title character in *The World of Suzie Wong* made her an overnight sensation, even earning her the nickname the "Chinese Bardot." Other films, like *Flower Drum Song*, cemented her celebrity at just 22 years old in 1962.

Despite that American audiences have responded quite well to Asian American actors since the beginning of the 20th century, "meaty" roles are still rare. And since yellowface would be considered as offensive as blackface today, the industry has turned to whitewashing, where even Asian characters in books and comics are reinvented as white. Netflix's adaptation of a Japanese manga, *Death Note*, stirred controversy when a producer gave the excuse that they "couldn't find the right person," in large part because actors from Asia "didn't speak perfect English." Fearing commercial failure, producers still won't roll the dice, prolonging the minimization and misrepresentation of Asians.

The television series *Kung Fu* aired in 1972 with David Carradine as Kwai Chang Caine, a half-Asian Shaolin monk who travels through the American Old West, armed only with his spiritual training and martial arts skills. I was really torn. Each week for three years, I resented that a white actor pretended to be Chinese but cheered his use of martial arts because at least, one part of Asian culture was being promoted. Bruce Lee, an actual Eurasian, was rejected because they felt that the American television audience would not accept him. Was this fear based on prejudice or real? Unfortunately, we'll never know.

The first three Charlie Chan detective movies, which were financial failures, featured Asians as Chan, whose role was minimized to as little as ten minutes on the screen. When Swedish American Warner Oland taped back his eyelids, the franchise became a hit in 1929. Some sixteen films later, when Oland died, Sidney Toler (of Scottish descent) played Chan for eleven more movies. Then, he was succeeded by Roland Winters (of Austrian and German descent) for another six. Between 1932 and 1948, Charlie Chan was also a popular radio series with the sing-song voice provided by white actors. I love detective films but cannot stand to watch a Charlie Chan movie. That's why, in 1981, I turned down a role in *Charlie Chan and the Curse of the Dragon Queen* starring Peter Ustinov, Richard Hatch as his half-Chinese son, and Angie Dickinson as the Chinese villainess. As I had suspected, it was a terrible film, which would not have helped my acting career. It was certainly not worth adding myself to that demeaning history.

Caricatures, yellowface, and whitewashing have impacted me well beyond turning down one role. They caused me to ask deeper questions like, "Am I more American, or more Chinese? What should I sound like? What should I look like? By which culture's rules should I live my life? Whom should I marry? Where do I fit in?" They made me look at my efforts to pass as white as I possibly could—purging my accent, dying my hair blond, changing my name, and favoring my American identity over my Chinese. I've realized over the years that I'm not alone in this quandary; these are just some of the conundrums facing every Asian in America today.

YELLOWFACE & WHITEWASH IN MOVIES AND TELEVISION

One of the first appearances of yellowface in film was in D.W. Griffith's *The Chink at Golden Gulch* in 1910. It had no Chinese actors, and the hero was a laundryman. Others include:

Madam Butterfly (1915): Mary Pickford plays a submissive Asian woman who pines for the love of a white man.

The Charlie Chan detective series (1931-1981): Warner Oland, Sidney Toler, Roland Winters, and Peter Ustinov play the very smart, but accented, Chinese detective Charlie Chan.

Dr. Fu Manchu (1932): The evil doctor, literally a monster, was always played in yellowface by white actors, like Warner Oland, who also portrayed Charlie Chan. The most controversial incarnation of the character was MGM's *The Mask of Fu Manchu* (1932), starring Boris Karloff and Myrna Loy. At the time of its release, the film was considered racist and offensive by representatives of the Chinese government.

Dragon Seed (1944): Katharine Hepburn played a Chinese woman who resisted the takeover of her village by the Japanese.

The Conqueror (1956): John Wayne plays the 11th-century Mongolian warrior, Genghis Khan. This is considered among the worst films ever made.

The King and I (1956): Yul Brynner plays King Mongkut of Siam.

Breakfast at Tiffany's (1961): Mickey Rooney plays the bucktoothed Mr. Yunioshi.

Kung Fu (1972): David Carradine plays Kwai Chang Kaine a meek, martial arts master. He was chosen over Bruce Lee for this role.

Short Circuit 2 (1988): Fisher Stevens plays Benjamin Jahrvi a Southeast Asian Indian.

*21 (*2008): Jim Sturgess as Jeff Ma, who's part of an MIT blackjack team who beat Las Vegas casinos at their own game. In real life, the majority of the team members were of Asian descent but somehow Sturgess, Kevin Spacey, and Kate Bosworth ended up as the main members of the team. Ma has a small cameo role as a blackjack dealer.

Dragonball Evolution (2009): Justin Chatwin plays Goku whose character is based on the Monkey King from the classic Chinese novel *Journey to the West.*

The Last Airbender (2010): Noah Ringer plays Aang when the heroes in the TV series were Asian. It was awarded the Razzie for being the worst movie of 2010.

Star Trek: Into Darkness (2013): Benedict Cumberbatch plays the evil Indian villain, Khan Noonien Singh.

Edge of Tomorrow (2014): Tom Cruise plays Keiji Kiriya renamed Bill Cage.

Aloha (2015): Emma Stone plays Allison Ng who's a half-Asian Hawaiian woman.

The Martian (2015): Mackenzie Davis plays Mindy Park, a Korean NASA engineer.

Doctor Strange (2016): Tilda Swinton plays The Ancient One, who is an older Asian man in the original Marvel comic.

Ghost in the Shell (2017): Scarlett Johansson plays Motoko Kusanagi. While the casting choice raised eyebrows, the film got even more controversial when it was revealed that Paramount did tests to see if CGI could make white actors appear more Asian.

Alita: Battle Angel (2018): Rosa Salazar plays the title role of Alita.

STANDING UP, FALLING DOWN

One controversial topic I consistently covered as a television producer was the so-called "International Hotel occupation." On the outskirts of San Francisco's Chinatown, the run-down hotel was very affordable and important to the social integration and upward mobility of Filipino workers, many of whom only spoke their native Tagalog. Also, a hub of Asian American cultural expression, it was home to the Kearny Street Workshop, which brought together Chinese, Filipino, Japanese, and Korean playwrights Lane Nishikawa and Norman Jayo; artists like Jim Dong; photographers Crystal Huie and Leny Limjoco; silkscreen artists Leland Wong and Nancy Hom; and poets Luis Syquia, Al Robles, George Leong, Doug Yamamoto, Genny Lim, Russell Leong, Jeff Tagami, and Shirley Ancheta.

In 1968, Milton Meyer & Company purchased the International Hotel with a plan to re-develop the building. The residents fought eviction, and their struggle for housing rights galvanized community activists. In 1974, the Four Seas Investment Company bought the hotel and ordered the tenants to vacate. For the next three years, the International Hotel Tenants Association led a grassroots effort to stop the evictions. The issue became high profile in 1976 when Mayor George Moscone proposed that the law of eminent domain be used to keep the hotel out of the private real estate market, sparking a push to take the International Hotel public. Asian college students organized demonstrations, and when the eviction order was issued, the sheriff refused to serve the tenants.

During those last three years of the fight, I covered the developments almost every week on our television program, raising awareness about the real people behind the headlines, and the financial challenges faced by the hotel's mostly elderly Filipino and Chinese residents. When the courts rejected the appeal for eminent domain, on August 4 of 1977 at 3:00 a.m., a 3,000-member human shield resisted the intrusion of 400 riot police, capturing widespread local, national, and international support. To this day, the eviction is considered by many as the most offensive government action in San Francisco's history.

This was a huge story and one that impacted the local Asian community. When I produced a special segment chronicling the ten-year struggle, immediately, many of the station's advertisers threatened to pull their support from all its programs, not just ours, because of the controversial nature of the story. As a result, our station manager sent a memo prohibiting us three producers from presenting on our show social issues faced by minorities, limiting us to covering just ethnic music, art, and dance. I took issue with this gutting of the heart of our show, so I sent a letter to everyone at the station pointing out the underlying racism behind the decision, and I resigned.

I felt I had to quit my job, but was it really my choice, or was it encoded in my DNA? Was I acting on the Confucian belief about the social responsibility that you must always be ready to become selfless, stand for the wellbeing of the collective, and promote virtues like social harmony and empathy?

In any case, the platform I had been using to address social issues was gone. Before this, I had artists and authors talking about how being Asian in America affected their work, immigration lawyers discussing the challenges of Asians coming to this country, and people who grew up in the internment camps retelling their experiences—all to help viewers understand us as people. I had even interviewed Wendy Yoshimura, who had been involved with the radical Symbionese Liberation Army which had kidnapped newspaper heiress Patty Hearst and had been convicted of unlawful possession of explosives and firearms.

The focus of our interview was how the American legal system treated Asian Americans.

That memo from the general manager, which so casually discounted our humanity as minorities, was the last straw because I had recently also learned about an unwritten rule that producers of minority shows at our station would never be hired to work on non-minority programs. We were deemed incapable of developing the necessary skills to work on shows for a white audience. Obviously, the bias had nothing to do with skills, but with being too "alien" to reflect, represent, and appeal to the widest American audience. Finally, I understood why I never got hired on any other shows I applied for despite my extensive experience. It became clear that while I had worked hard to constantly improve my skills and knowledge as a producer, I was denied promotion simply because of the color of my skin. I immediately sued the station for discrimination, but at what cost?

I found myself in an expensive, protracted legal battle to obtain the rights that most people take for granted—being promoted on merit. I felt like David versus Goliath, my local attorney, and I against a staff of corporate New York lawyers with unlimited resources.

Walking away from my job was not easy. Being a TV producer was all I had focused on for the five years since I graduated from college. My career as a television producer was integral to my identity, and my self-worth was inextricably tied to my success—something that can be quite harmful to one's mental health, as any therapist will tell you. Worse still, I had given it all up to take a stand up for my community, but where was their support for me?

I guess I had hoped that there would be a public protest, like for the International Hotel, because I could no longer cover social issues like discrimination against Asians, especially after a front-page article was published about my firing in the largest community newspaper *Asian Week*. But after three years of giving my heart and soul to our community, the silence was deafening. There was no outcry, and although a few people did call to offer their condolences, no Asian producers or newscasters offered to help me find another job. Apparently, the lawsuit had made me toxic to anyone who claimed to be my friend. Even my parents didn't understand why I would quit and sue my former employer, but that was nothing new because their stance had always been to keep quiet and suffer in silence.

I felt alone and adrift. Having become a pariah for standing up for what I believed in, I fell into a deep depression. For a time, I was unable to get out of bed, not bothering to shave, shower, or eat. I confided in my parents, but they told me to "think happy thoughts" and stop openly talking about my mental health state because, if others found out, it would bring shame to our family. Again, nothing new; they had taught me never to display any emotion in public. "Creating bad feng shui" was the reason my father always gave, based on the traditional belief that emotional outbursts disrupt group harmony. In Chinese culture, talking about emotions is not encouraged, often considered irrelevant and meaningless, while strong emotional displays can even imply mental illness.

So, I kept my feelings bottled up, not wanting to lose face and disgrace my family. This made me feel even more isolated and unsupported. I began thinking again about suicide, just so the feelings of hopelessness and lack of direction would stop. As a last resort, I got a referral to a psychiatrist. He, a white male, who had probably never been discriminated against in his life, had a very difficult time understanding how cultural issues could affect my situation. None of my unique symptoms matched anything he had studied or encountered. Unfortunately, he was not the exception but the rule. Eventually, I learned that it's not unusual for mental health professionals not to be trained in culturally specific issues. This lack of awareness often results in the misdiagnosis and under-diagnosis of mental illness for Asian Americans and Pacific Islanders (AAPIs). Regrettably, this also extends to all health care.

Professor Vickie Mays of the UCLA Fielding School of Public Health says, "We now have decades of research showing that when people are chronically treated differently, unfairly, or badly, it can have effects ranging from low self-esteem to higher risk for developing stress-related disorders such as anxiety and depression.[24]

To compound my problems, I had no health insurance and could not afford therapy as often as it was recommended—this predicament is common, especially for first-generation AAPIs. Not that they would readily seek it out since they generally do not view mental health as integral to a person's overall well-being, or as something that can be treated. Many older Asian Americans describe their malaise in physical rather than psychological terms, neglecting their mental health for the same reasons as I did: the topic is strictly taboo. Speaking about it can result in stigmatization and shaming because mental illness is often attributed to poor parenting or a genetic flaw, labeling one as defective. When AAPIs do seek support, they tend to turn to friends, family, and religious community members rather than mental health experts; getting outside help conflicts with their cultural value of interdependence, which stresses that family or community can meet all needs.

We Asian Americans tend to suffer from similar stressors—social expectations, shaming, stigma, identity, and assimilation. While it's no surprise that first-generation immigrants experience trauma adapting to life in a foreign land, assimilation continues to be traumatic for second-generation immigrants and beyond. In fact, racist and xenophobic violence and discrimination can disrupt psychological functioning and alter the genetic code, even predisposing entire communities to self-harm. Again, according to the Centers for Disease Control, suicide is the number one leading cause of death among Asian American young adults ages 15-24. A major factor contributing to this alarming statistic is that suicide is seen in Asia as a way of preserving honor and atoning for disgrace, whereas in the West,

---

[24] D. Gordon, "Discrimination can be Harmful to your Mental Health," *UCLA Newsroom*, January 13, 2016.

religions like Christianity view it as a sin. Since Asian parents hold onto the centuries-old culture of shame and honor, their beliefs are passed down to the next generation.

As we've seen in previous chapters, Asian Americans are under added pressure to live up to the model minority myth. Since they place the utmost value on family and community, their self-value depends on how well they perform in those roles. Shame results from failing to meet expectations, (unacceptable grades and romantic relationships), or defying the wishes of their parents, who sometimes threaten to ostracize or disown their children. In addition to being confined to narrow roles, young Asian Americans feel that they are not allowed to experience setbacks, pain, and loss, and often consider their problems insignificant compared to the hardships their parents and grandparents endured.

The study "The Role of Guilt in Cross-Generations Conflicts in Asian American Families" explores themes like parents inducing guilt in children and denigrating acculturation, as well as the children's anger tied to fear of disappointing parents. [25] Adult children expressed survivor guilt towards their parents, while parents utilized guilt to motivate them to obey their wishes, "We came here for you." Made to feel like their parents sacrificed so they can have a better life, children may minimize their challenges, including their bicultural identity, torn as they are between their ancestral and American worldviews, which are diametrically opposed in many respects. They have difficulty navigating this inner conflict, which does not seem to lessen from generation to generation.

Even I, a fifth-generation Asian American, struggled with developing a bicultural sense of self. Finding myself out of a job, and possibly a career, for standing up against discrimination only amplified my inner

---

[25] T. Li et al, "The Role of Guilt in Cross-Generations Conflicts in Asian American Families," *The Wright Institute, Samford University, Graduate Theological Union, University of California-Berkeley*. Presented at the Annual Convention of the Western Psychological Association, Las Vegas, NV, April 30 – May 3, 2015.

struggle. Here I was, for the second time in my relatively short life, morally obligated to legally assert my birthright as an American citizen, first in the case of California Highway Patrol, and now in television.

Despite my willingness to accept outside help, without health insurance and culturally sensitive professional support, there was no way I could effectively address my emotional challenges. My psychiatrist prescribed some medication, which helped with the depression, and in true Asian style, I got busy looking for another job.

Easier said than done. Every time I applied for a broadcasting job, my calls went unanswered despite my breadth and depth of experience. When I was able to talk with a hiring manager, every position seemed to have "just been filled" the moment they heard my name. I don't know whether that was a coincidence or that I was blacklisted, but the situation certainly didn't help my mental state. When I mentioned it to my father, he said, "That's what happens when you speak up against authority, you knucklehead." Be that as it may, I believe that doing what's hard is what creates personal growth and social change.

Would I have done anything differently knowing the challenges I would face? No, because I could not, and still cannot, let discrimination in any form go unchallenged. Despite all the negativity and humiliation, I faced at this time, one pearl of Eastern wisdom sustained me. "Be like bamboo in the storm" means that we should be resilient and flexible in tough times so that we will bend, not break.

Eventually I did manage to pick up some freelance work, like working three months out of the year, producing the annual Bay Area Easter Seal Telethons. While my dream of making my mark as a television producer seemed to be vanishing in the rear-view window, little did I know that I was on a new trajectory that was perhaps even more ambitious and rewarding!

SILVER SCREEN DREAMS

In 1977, I auditioned for a sports TV anchor position at another local station. I was the number one candidate, but unfortunately, the existing anchor decided not to leave. Had I landed the job and been forced to choose, I probably would have left the minority show, which I had always seen as a stepping-stone.

Needless to say, my parents thought it was a total waste of time to pursue an acting career, thinking it was a frivolous job. I don't think they ever came to one play I was in, not even *Year of the Dragon* by Chinese playwright Frank Chin. Were they not interested, or embarrassed, or was it their way of showing their disapproval? Thinking that there were so many ways that I could be discriminated against without any recourse, they probably thought I was foolish expecting to be treated fairly in any of these "white" media professions. My depression, unemployment, and financial difficulties that resulted from quitting my producing job and suing the TV station did nothing to assure them that I was on the right path; even after I had dug myself out of the black hole and started working again.

I produced three consecutive San Francisco Bay Area Easter Seals Telethons in 1977, 1978, and 1979 with hosts like singer Pat Boone and actor George Takei. Around the same time, I met Robert Fiveson, who was in the process of producing and directing a science fiction film called *Parts: The Clonus Horror* (1979), starring Peter Graves, Keenan Wynn, Dick Sargent, and Tim Donnelly, about a group of healthy young people who were being unknowingly groomed as clones for rich people in case they needed any organs or limbs in the future. He asked me to co-produce the film, which turned out to be modestly successful by Hollywood standards grossing nearly $3 million but very successful for a low-budget movie that cost only $350,000 to make.

As exciting as that experience was, the hard reality was that I needed a decent income between film and TV projects to pay my mortgage. Thinking that selling real estate was an easy way to make money, I started working toward getting my license. I prepared taxes and taught television production part-time at a local college, but I barely covered the payments for the house that I had bought in San Francisco while I was working at the TV station. Things got so bad that I resorted to going to Happy Hour every night at various bars where I could eat their free food while drinking a Coke for one dollar. Yet, I clung to my silver screen dreams.

In 1980, I got a contract with the premier agency for Asian actors called the Bessie Loo Talent Agency. Bessie Loo was a Chinese American actress who started out in the 1930s mostly playing small parts. When she appeared in *The Good Earth* (1937), she began working with Central Casting because her bilingual language skills proved useful with the many Chinese-speaking extras. Later, she started her own agency, representing actors like Jack Ong, Keye Luke, Robert Ito, Beulah Quo, James Hong, Soon-Tek Oh, Mako, Lisa Lu, and Guy Lee. Thanks to Guy Lee, who took over the agency when Loo retired, I auditioned for roles in major motion pictures and landed a part in *Foul Play*, starring Chevy Chase and Goldie Hawn, as a limousine chauffeur with two Japanese tourists as passengers. The driver needed to be Asian to give a hint of what was to come. In the scene, Chevy and Goldie are driving madly through San Francisco in a pickup truck to save the Pope from an attempted assassination. When they crash, I drive up in a stretch limo and ask what happened. They tell me there's been an accident and that I need to help some people who had been injured. As I leave the car, Chevy and Goldie leap into the limo and continue their mission to prevent the Pontiff from being shot. Then they notice the terrified Japanese couple who didn't speak English in the back. Looking back at it now, the exchange was very stereotypical and somewhat racist, but at the time, audiences thought the scene was hilarious.

Even though my credit at the end of the film probably lasted longer on the screen than my performance, since *Foul Play* was a big hit in 1978, it led to other roles, including an audition for a film called *Die Laughing* with Robby Benson. The audition was rather interesting because the part was as a gang member who spoke a few lines in Chinese. All the actors auditioning for the part were young Asian Americans and none of us was fluent in Chinese. In true Asian collaborative style, we pieced together the few words we knew in broken Chinese so we could all phonetically read the script. It goes without saying that trying to emote while reading something akin to a Chinese restaurant menu did not make for a compelling audition. Fortunately, they also auditioned me for the part of an English-speaking sleazy strip club barker—and that reading I felt I had nailed!

Later that day, my agent Guy Lee called, "You know, they hated you for the part of the gang member," and I said, "Yeah, I know. It was very difficult doing that in Chinese." Then he said, "But they loved you for the role of the strip club manager."

"Great!" I responded, and he continued, "Do you play the drums by any chance?" Guy explained that I had to play the drums on camera because the part was for a member of Robby' rock and roll band. "I haven't played drums in a long time. How long before we shoot?" I asked, to which he replied, "About six months."

"No problem. I'll brush up on my drumming skills, and it'll be fine. Just have them send me the music tracks."

Little did Guy know that I had never played the drums in my life! However, I did have extensive musical training, starting with the piano, violin, guitar, and later to wind instruments like the clarinet and saxophone. I knew that I could pick it up quickly. So, I hired a private drum teacher, and by the time the film was ready to shoot, I was able to fake the songs like a pro.

That role could have been my big break because I would have had lots of lines and interaction with Robby and the other actors. Unfortunately, a writers' strike loomed just as shooting started, so the producer cut all the band members' lines to save time. As a result, I became one of the most highly paid extras in history. Without much interaction between Robby and his band members, the film didn't make much sense and ended up being one of his lowest-grossing films.

After that, I kept auditioning, but unfortunately all I got were stereotypical martial artist roles which required no acting. All you did was scream, make a few moves, and get killed by the star.

The last role I auditioned for could have made my acting career. I was cast, but when I learned that it was called *Charlie Chan and the Curse of the Dragon Queen* starring Peter Ustinov as the Chinese detective, I told my agent that I couldn't participate in a production where a white person played the Asian detective yet again! As it turned out, being in the movie would probably not have helped my acting career because the film critics Roger Ebert and Gene Siskel hated it, gave it "a two-thumbs down," and listed it as one of the worst movies of 1981. All the same, turning down that role was the nail in the coffin of my acting career. I never got called to audition again. For the third time in my life, standing up for what I believe in and refusing to participate in a production with denigrating stereotypes and yellowface put me at odds with the system.

The discrimination in the media industry substantiated my parents' fears and demonstrated the importance of Taoist principle of letting go—sometimes, accepting the facts, and letting life take its course can free you and help you overcome suffering. If I had adopted this thinking, I would have realized that the American audience was not ready for an Asian leading man, which is what I was aspiring to be, like every other actor. This awareness would have given me two clear choices: first, to continue working as an actor by adopting the persona and physical characteristics of someone like Dr. Fu Manchu, an archetype of the evil criminal genius and mad scientist; or, second, to save myself a lot of disappointment and time by not sending hundreds of letters to casting- directors asking them to consider me for non-stereotypical roles.

Remember that before computers enabled you to "copy and paste," each letter had to be individually typed by hand.

I tried to educate the system to no avail. I could never have imagined that it would take over thirty years for Hollywood to start to shift its thinking about Asians—a change not brought about by open-mindedness but by market conditions. Around 2012, when many movie theaters in the West closed due to the impact of home entertainment systems and China agreed to open its market to foreign movies, it made financial sense for American moviemakers to stop making Asians the villains; even casting a few in romantic leads. Unfortunately, by then, I was way past being cast in young leading roles.

Despite my silver screen dreams ending as a huge disappointment, I firmly believe that you need to be in the ring to win the fight, which continues to this day. Unfortunately, some fifty years later, established Asian American actors like Tzi Ma, Kelly Hu, and Peter Shinkoda face the same barriers, questions, and difficulties as I did. If you think the situation is better now, know that of the 1,300 popular films released between 2007 and 2019 only 44 (3.4%) had an AAPI lead or co-lead. One-third of those starred Dwayne Johnson who is of black and Samoan heritage. Factoring him out because most viewers don't think of him as Asian, only 2.3% of those films had an AAPI lead or co-lead.[26]

So, were all my efforts for naught? No. The silver lining was that my on-screen and on-stage experience—acting and teaching—had prepared me for a career as a professional speaker. It helped me develop my performance instincts and taught me to engage and retain the audience's attention. I discovered that presenting live to hundreds of people is among the finest forms of acting because if you don't grab their attention in the first two minutes, the next hour or so will be excruciating. Thank God for my acting training!

---

[26] N. Wang Yuen et al, "The Prevalence and Portrayal of Asian and Pacific Islanders Across 1,300 Popular Films," *USC Annenberg Inclusion Initiative,* (May 2021).

TZI MA ON TYPECASTING

In film, television, and theatre, stereotyping becomes typecasting in two ways: first, characters of certain ethnic groups are always portrayed in the same narrow and distorted ways; second, actors from those groups are always cast in the same types of roles. As a result, these actors are not able to get work playing a range of characters, not because they are not suited for those parts but because the industry cannot view them in a different light. Producers, directors, and screenwriters do not want to risk commercial success if audiences do not relate to ethnic characters, so they typically cast them in stereotypical and minor roles. Many Asian American actors are conflicted about accepting such roles; they want to work but do not want to propagate stereotypes that harm how their communities are portrayed. Also, they risk pigeonholing their own careers by being forever typecast as an Asian martial artist, nerd, gang leader, and so on.

In the following interview excerpt, Tzi Ma, who has had a long and varied career with roles such as the ambassador in the *Rush Hour* films with Jackie Chan and as the father in the live-action version of *Mulan,* speaks to the challenges he faces and highlights how little thought goes into portraying Asian characters in the industry.

Michael: Do you think that being Asian has helped or hurt your acting career?

Tzi Ma: I think it definitely hurt more than helped because they always see you as an ethnic first and as an actor second. Any actor worth their weight in salt will tell you, "I want to be seen as an actor, not as an ethnic." It makes no sense. You should be able to do any role that you're fit to do. It's not the color of your skin that determines the role you get.

Michael: When you go to a meeting with a director and casting agent, what questions do you have?

Tzi Ma: I try to go in there with a lot of questions, and it works very well for me. So, I might say, "This character's name is Vinh, right? V-i-n-h—that's a Vietnamese name, right?" The director responds, "Yeah, I think so."

They don't even know. They kinda-sorta know, but they don't really know. So, I say, "That's Vinh. Okay, that's cool. Then he leaves from Cambodia. So, is he Cambodian?" The director and casting director both respond with, "Uhhh," and then you see the confusion in their eyes.

So, I say, "Oh, so he's Vietnamese from Cambodia, comes to Seattle, and then chased by the Tongs, which is a criminal Chinese element."

Michael Lee: You're educating them about how little they know about Asians with your questions.

Tzi Ma: I have to, because if I feel that this role can be salvaged in some way, then I will make an effort. So, I say, "Here's what I think: I said Vinh is Vietnamese for sure, but he's ethnic Chinese Vietnamese and, by the way, that's very common. Most of the Boat People who got a chance to leave Vietnam during the fall of Saigon were ethnic Chinese. They got to Cambodia, which is a fairly short distance away. Then they finally become the Boat Persons who are being sent to the U.S. because the U.S. had certain obligations to the South Vietnamese people. So, since he's ethnic Chinese, he was hanging around in Chinatown because he speaks a little Chinese and he speaks Vietnamese. Then, because of the fact that he's living in Chinatown, he gets into a little trouble, and he's being pursued by the Chinese criminal element.

You should see the relief on their faces. They said, "Oh my God, that's the story!"

Michael: You're not just an actor; you're a screenwriter. I love it!

GET REAL!

After three years and tens of thousands of dollars in legal fees, the TV station paid me a settlement. In exchange, they were allowed legally to say that they had never discriminated against me. I used the money to purchase a second home in the Hollywood Hills in Los Angeles to use as the base for my movie production and acting career and, of course, as an investment.

Owning property is a Chinese cultural mindset because, in China, there are so many people and so little cultivatable land. Therefore, land is highly valued, thought of as something to pass on to the next generation, and as a sure sign of wealth. Of course, this outlook persists in Chinese immigrants. In my case, it had been ingrained very early in life. For as long as I can remember, I had wanted to own a home. At five or six years old, I recall my parents talking about how important it was to own your house so you wouldn't be subject to a landlord's whims and annual rent increases. They talked about being able to do what you want with the house, like adding a room and bath for me when I got to junior high school. When I started school, our home and backyard were the only places I felt safe from bullies. I spent most of my spare time playing in the backyard and in the garage where I learned woodworking from my father, building everything from a fort to a full-sized pool table.

In college, at age 22, I seriously started saving for a home, in addition to paying for my tuition at San Francisco State and sustaining myself. I refused to ask my parents for any financial help after I moved away from home and worked nights as a telephone salesperson for a home improvement company. To save money, I rented a one-bedroom apartment with two roommates for a total of $180 per month. I used my woodworking skills to turn the formal dining room and living room into two bedrooms, and we shared the bathroom and kitchen. It was challenging because the other guys not only used my pots and pans but also kept stealing my food, which was not plentiful.

Taking a tip from my mother, I used coupons to buy groceries and always waited for "double coupon day." I also ate a lot of cheap 10-cent ramen noodles, which I'm sure didn't help my arthritis with their salty broth. I didn't even buy tea but, instead, drank hot water at home and in restaurants on the rare occasions when I went out to eat. To save on commuting, I would pay 25 cents to ride the bus from school to downtown and get a free transfer pass as if I was going to ride another bus. Instead, I would use it to ride the bus back home after work at no cost by pretending I had just gotten off the cross-town bus. I'm not proud of cheating the system, but I felt it was a necessity to survive. I even bought a used bike and rode six miles each way to school if I couldn't get a ride from one of my roommates.

I saved every penny for the next five years until I had enough for a down payment for a home. It was not easy, but I love a challenge and felt that if my parents could buy a house in 1953, then I should be able to buy one too in more 'enlightened' times. As my parents often recounted, MacArthur Boulevard, Oakland's main street, separated the hills from the flatlands. It was the city's racial and social divide with the higher-income whites quite literally on high ground and the lower-income "others" below them. When my parents looked at homes to buy above MacArthur, they were told that they couldn't purchase a property there because of restrictive covenants in the owners' deeds that prohibited selling to non-Caucasians. These rules had been abolished two years earlier, but sellers and real estate agents were still acting as if they existed. Since lower-income people tend to be less educated and knowledgeable about the legal system, they are wronged far more easily.

I always felt angry that my parents had been discriminated against and that we had to live one house away from a very noisy freeway because the homes were cheaper there, and people were less likely to make a fuss about us being Asian. My parents had no choice but to buy below MacArthur where the homes did not appreciate much in value. Such discriminatory selling practices, along with lenders' systemic unwillingness to give home loans to minorities, have kept, and continue to keep non-whites from building wealth. Today, the average white family in America has approximately ten times the wealth of an average Black family largely because of their ability to buy homes in better areas.[27]

By 1977, when I was ready for home ownership, I was not impacted by most of these discriminatory practices thanks to the Fair Housing Act of 1968, which prohibited discrimination in the sale, rental, and financing of housing based on race, religion, national origin, and gender. My steady job as a producer enabled me to buy a small home in San Francisco; but still required sacrifices, like not taking vacations or owning a car, which meant I continued to take the bus everywhere. Even so, at the age of 27, I bought my first home for $50,000. I remember sitting in my living room for the first time in front of a crackling fire feeling so grown-up and secure. The house was mine, and no one could take it away from me.

When I invited my parents to see my house, I didn't tell them I had bought it. They asked how much the rent was, and I simply replied, "The mortgage is $450 a month." Immediately, they sat me down at my little card table, which was all the furniture I had, and asked when I was getting married. In their generation, and for Asians in particular, you only bought a home when you got married and needed a place to raise your kids. Historically, males in China were expected to own at least one property before embarking on their search for a wife. This social

---

[27] D. Irving, "What Would It Take to Close America's Black-White Wealth Gap?" *The Rand Corporation,* May 9, 2023, https://www.rand.org/blog/rand-review/2023/05/ what-would-it-take-to-close-americas-black-white-wealth-gap.

prerequisite continues today due to the "one-child policy."[28] implemented in China between 1980 and 2015—after which the fertility and birth rate decreased. Since sons were generally favored over daughters in China, there was a rise in the number of abortions of female fetuses along with an increase in the number of female babies killed or placed in orphanages. While this policy has since been rescinded, today there are an estimated 30 million more men in China than women. It's gotten to the point that owning a home is crucial for marriage in China, which is why young men, and their families will do all they can to buy property to make them more attractive in the marriage market, thus fueling the heavy demand for real estate. In 2021 the homeownership rate in China was over 90%[29] while in the U.S. it was about 65%.[30]

Asians in America seem to be similarly motivated. We had the second-highest percentage of home ownership at 63% in 2023 compared to whites at 73% in 2023. Unfortunately, due to discrimination, the rate for Native Americans was only 53%, Hispanic Americans was 51%, and for Blacks it was only 44%.[31] You can see that there is a significant racial homeownership gap in America that needs to be addressed. In fact, the nearly 30% difference between White and Black homeownership today is larger than the 27% gap that existed in 1960 when housing discrimination was legal, according to Urban Institute data.

Because of the way they were raised, my parents assumed that I was preparing to get married by buying a home. I said that I wasn't tying the knot anytime soon and that I had bought it for the tax benefits. My father had no idea what I was talking about because he owned his home free and clear by then. I explained, from my tax preparation experience, that since mortgage interest and property tax were deductible, my

[28] E. Feng, "China's Former 1-Child Policy Continues to Haunt Families," *NPR,* 21 June 2021.
[29] Y. Huang, S. He and L. Gan," Introduction to SI: Homeownership and Housing Divide in China," *National Library of Medicine,* (2020).
[30] More Americans Own Their Homes, but Black-White Homeownership Rate Gap is Biggest in a Decade," *National Association of Realtors,* (2023).
[31] Ibid.

mortgage installment was almost the same as my former rent payments after taxes, plus I planned to rent one bedroom for additional income. My father immediately responded, "When you go to jail for tax evasion don't expect us to come and visit you." It took my parents over a decade to trust that I knew what I was doing, but eventually, they invested in some rental properties with me.

While I was struggling financially after resigning from the TV station, I got my real estate license. Like most people, I thought that agents make 6% of the sale price or around $3,000 on a $50,000 home, the average home price in San Francisco at the time. I figured that if I sold ten houses a year that would exceed my annual salary as a television producer. It also seemed that they didn't work very hard, drove around in fancy cars, and always played golf on the weekends. Well, closing a sale was a lot more work than I could have ever imagined, and that is providing one finds clients in the first place! Thankfully, my small bladder and my sensitive stomach contributed to my success. Let me explain....

Shortly after getting my real estate license, I joined a Chinese American ski club, because I loved snow skiing. On my first ski trip, during the three-hour bus ride, I had to go to the bathroom located at the rear of the bus—this meant walking there from the front seat where I had sat to avoid getting car sick. When I turned around to head to the bathroom, I felt all fifty people looking at me as if I were going to make an announcement. Feeling awkward, I began stretching and talking to the first person I saw. All I could think of was to ask their name and how long they had been skiing. After a while, they would ask for my name and whether I had ever skied at the resort to which we were heading. Then I would ask what they did for a living, and they would naturally ask me the same. To this question, I learned to simply reply with "I'm a real estate agent who help people achieve the dream of home ownership." I discovered that no matter how interesting their career may have been as a doctor, lawyer, or other professional, we could only talk about that for a brief time. But everyone wanted to own real estate, and they all wanted to know how I was able to buy a home at such an early age and if I could help them do the same.

After a few ski trips, I got to know most of the members of the club, which was composed of around 200 young, successful Asians. As a result of these connections, I ended up being the second highest-producing agent in our real estate office, working part-time. This was the first time I experienced first-hand the benefits of the traditional Asian mindset about relying on one's community for support.

I still held out hope to get back into the media and stayed involved in projects, albeit part-time. In 1981, I hosted a television talk show on PBS in Southern California for a year. After this, I taught broadcasting at community colleges and really enjoyed working with students. I also started teaching management classes for the school where I earned my master's degree, Golden Gate University in San Francisco. It seems that I had a knack for taking complex material and making it simple to understand and fun to learn. I just taught the way I would want to learn. In other words, once you strip away the extraneous material, what did students need to know about the material and why was it important to them? The university liked my engaging teaching style so much that they asked me to teach their accelerated MBA degree program in Southern California and Arizona. This meant flying out of San Francisco on Friday mornings, teaching that evening and all day on Saturdays, and flying home that evening every other week for six weeks to complete one class. This schedule taught me how to think quickly on my feet, as I had to keep the class lively and interactive so I could maintain the attention of the students, especially when many classes were conducted in buildings during the summer with no air conditioning.

I also worked on two motion pictures—*Parts: The Clonus Horror* (1979) and produced *The Kill Squad* (1982) with Cameron Mitchell and Hope Holiday. Both were very low-budget, and I never saw a dime from them because the distributors kept all the profits without passing any on to the producers. Most people bought movie tickets with cash in those days, and there was no way to accurately track revenues. It was a difficult time for me financially, and the reality was that my silver screen dreams had already faded. All the roadblocks and discrimination I had faced in the media industry made me reluctant to keep beating the proverbial dead horse. So, I was compelled to "get real" about my life with real estate by focusing on it full-time. I saw it as a clear path not only to financial stability but also to upward mobility.

Despite my success as a Realtor® with Asian Americans, my not speaking Chinese was a problem with new immigrants. It's no surprise that they preferred to speak their language, especially when dealing with a complex topic like real estate. I would explain that I was a fifth-generation Chinese American, but they would never quite believe that I did not speak the language. Perhaps they saw me as a "banana," showing off how American I was or as a "jook-sing" airhead that I had lost my language and culture.

In any case, interacting with so many Asians on a daily basis, I became familiar with the tendencies, patterns, idiosyncrasies, and preferences of this market segment, including how the different generations of immigrants' view homeownership and real estate purchases. For example, since first-generation immigrants don't speak much English and are least familiar with the American culture, they tend to want to live in areas where other people speak their language and have excellent schools. Their American-born children, the second generation, typically serve as interpreters in their parents' business dealings. The third generation and beyond are usually very Americanized and may not speak the language of their ancestors. Yet, they are still influenced by their ancestors' culture. For example, my friend Lillian, a real estate agent, called me one day: "Michael, remind me again which is the unlucky direction for a home to face for Asians." I said, "Lillian, you're fourth generation. Why the heck do you care?" She said, "I don't, but when my parents come to visit, they won't stay in a home that faces the wrong direction." I reminded her, "The Chinese believe the devil lives in the north and, if he sees the front door of your house, he will be reminded to send bad luck your way. North is the unlucky direction for Chinese people."

On another occasion, I served as an expert witness in a court case where a Hispanic family had sold a Chinese family a home. The seller's son had committed suicide in the home, and this was not revealed to the buyers who believed this to be extremely bad luck and wanted to cancel the purchase. The court ruled that the death should have been disclosed because it is a material fact for some cultures, and since then, sellers in California and most other states must disclose a death in the home in the past three years.

Little did I know that all the superstitions, traditions, and belief systems that I had never placed any credence in throughout my life would open new opportunities for me. They deepened my understanding of my ancestral culture, and Asians in general, while enabling me to help members of my community claim their small share of "the new world," just as our ancestors had done more than one century earlier during the California Gold Rush.

SELLING THE AMERICAN DREAM

One of the many books I read growing up was *The Epic of America,* in which James Truslow Adams dreamed of a social order in which each person would be able to attain the fullest of what they are innately capable, regardless of the circumstances of their birth or social position. In the 1931 book, he coined the phrase "the American dream," but the dream is as old as our country itself. Despite many rags-to-riches stories, life in America has often been a nightmare for some ethnic groups, like Blacks, Hispanics, and AAPIs, long after the Declaration of Independence made its promises in 1776: "We hold these truths to be self-evident, that all men are created equal, that they are endowed by their Creator with certain unalienable Rights, that among these are Life, Liberty and the pursuit of Happiness."

America's history of brutal and systemic oppression of certain groups is no secret. So, what does the American dream stand for today? Well, for most people, it's quality of life—freedom to make your own life decisions, access to affordable education and healthcare, and homeownership.

When the early aspiring Chinese miners arrived in California, they discovered fields strewn not with gold nuggets but with disappointed prospectors and hostile locals. Sometimes, they found it difficult to earn enough to eat. Essentially, they were stranded because they were often unable to gather the needed funds for their passage home. Their dreams of staking a claim and making their fortune had been shattered by California's Foreign Miners' Tax imposed in 1850. Certain non-U.S.

citizens were charged the exorbitant fee of $20 every month for the right to mine. Europeans were not forced to pay the tax, which was the equivalent of approximately $750 a month in today's money. It was only collected from Chinese and Latinos, keeping them from owning claims and forcing them to work for white miners at low wages.

And that was only the beginning. More "alien land laws" were enacted to discourage 'undesirables' from settling permanently in the U.S. by limiting their ability to own property. Because the Naturalization Act of 1870 had extended citizenship rights only to African Americans, these laws prohibited primarily Chinese and Japanese immigrants from becoming landowners without explicitly naming any racial group. In 1879, California limited landownership to aliens of "the white race or African descent." In 1913, it prohibited aliens "ineligible for citizenship" from owning property or entering into leases longer than three years. In 1920, further restrictions prohibited any lease agreement with an ineligible alien and barred companies owned by ineligible aliens from purchasing land. Legislation drove Japanese farmers out of California agriculture, forcing many to rent or buy land in the names of their American-born children. Together with other discriminatory measures (the redlining and restrictive covenants that kept my parents from buying a property with greater appreciation potential as late as 1955), many alien-land laws remained in effect even after being ruled unconstitutional by the Supreme Court in 1952.

By the 1980s, when I made real estate my primary business, the American promises of freedom and prosperity were enticing Hong Kong Chinese into the San Francisco Bay, Los Angeles, New York City, and other areas. These immigrants were afraid that their homes and businesses would become worthless when the territory returned to Communist Chinese rule once the British 99-year lease on Hong Kong, Kowloon, and the "New Territories" ended. The agreement was that, for 50 years after the end of the lease in 1997, Hong Kong could continue to practice capitalism and political freedoms forbidden on the mainland. But after the violent putdown of the Tiananmen Square protest

(Beijing, China, June 3–4, 1989) when an undetermined number of protesting students were massacred, China honoring the agreement was doubtful.

With the influx of well-heeled Chinese from one of the most significant financial centers and trade ports in the world, I thought it would be wise to look into opening my own real estate company and start recruiting agents that spoke Cantonese and Mandarin. While the early immigrants, like my ancestors, had come from Canton and spoke Cantonese, more recent immigrants were coming from other parts of China and primarily spoke Mandarin. This was the most widely spoken native language in the world with nearly one billion within China alone.

It has taken two and a half centuries since the Declaration of Independence for U.S. legislation to reflect land ownership equality, but how easy is staking the ground for Asian Americans today? Between 1980 and 2019, Asians had the largest homeownership rate increase of any racial or ethnic group, from 52% in 1980 to 60% in 2019, with percentages varying for each ethnic group's economic and citizenship status, history in the U.S., and other factors. Unsurprisingly, higher citizenship rates and longer residency increase the likelihood of homeownership. However, factors like discrimination still play a significant role.

Swallowing the bitter pill that I was not going to make it big in the movies or TV, I stopped pursuing producing. I felt defeated at that time, as if it were the end of the world. However, I clung to a famous quote by Confucius, "Our greatest glory is not in never falling, but in rising every time we fall." It reminded me that, sure, you will fail at different times in life, but you can only truly fail by giving up. It also helped me see that after each failure is an end, then there is a new beginning and potential success. I guess I thought that I might be able to get back into the media at some point in the future.

Seeing full-time real estate as my new beginning, I decided to buy a real estate office, thinking that they make a lot of money. After looking for six months, I found one that was well located on a busy corner on the busiest street in San Bruno, California. The only thing I knew about the business was that it had 25 agents and offered tax preparation services. The combination was ideal for me because I had worked for H&R Block part-time as a tax preparer, and even obtained an Enrolled Agents license, which enabled me to represent clients who were being audited by the IRS. This combination of businesses also made sense for me because real estate slows down after the winter holidays until spring. The tax preparation business is busy from January through April 15th.

When I took over the business, reality set in, and it wasn't what I had imagined. Running a real estate brokerage is a 24/7 job with agents calling you with problems all day and night, including weekends, because there are always deals falling apart and threats of lawsuits. It also hadn't dawned on me that real estate agents are independent contractors who can leave your company at any time, so there was a constant need to recruit and train new agents. The amount of drama in this business was incredible! Even worse, when I saw that the company was only netting about $20,000 a year, I realized that I was making a lot more as an agent working fewer hours. Fortunately, the tax business was turning a good profit because there were almost no expenses and many of these clients wanted to buy or sell homes, so it was a free form of advertising for my real estate business. The silver lining was that I learned a lot about running a business and began to identify new opportunities. I was, after all, operating in the right location not only in terms of my physical office but also of geography.

With its ties to the Pacific Rim and Mexico, as well as its Gold Rush history, the San Francisco Bay Area has long been a destination for immigrants from abroad. As a result, it boasts one of the most diverse populations in the country, if not the world. Because of the open atmosphere during the 1960s and 1970s, it attracted many minorities who wanted and needed homes. In addition to catering to the Asian American market, I decided to hire African American, Hispanic, and more women agents until we had one of the largest real estate brokerages in the area. I credit our success to our inclusiveness and to serving market segments that benefited from working with agents they could relate to culturally.

Even with the growing minority population in the area, intolerance persisted. One evening, a young white couple parked in our lot because they wanted to go to the barbecue restaurant around the corner. I asked them to move their car as we were expecting several clients. The guy got very belligerent and said that they were only going to be about 30 minutes. We exchanged words, and they drove off in a huff. About two weeks later, I received an anonymous, hand-written letter calling me a "gook," telling me to "go home," and threatening me. It was obviously from the young man, who never had the courage to face me. It wasn't the first time I had been called a "gook," but it still really hurt.

Showing how deeply xenophobia runs in some people, astonishingly, for the next three years, I got his threatening and insulting letters every month like clockwork! I wasn't intimidated, but it was a constant reminder that not everyone thought that people like me were part of this country, and it was certainly discouraging. I often thought about Bruce Lee—not even he was able to break through the barriers despite his international superstardom. His quote, "Everyone under the sun is a member of a universal family" would come to my mind. After centuries of struggles in America, "the land of promised opportunity, freedom, and equality," people were still discriminated against based on their color, religion, and caste. Bruce felt that racism is an unfortunate tradition passed down from generation to generation, an outdated concept born out of fear and lack of knowledge. If anyone believes in racial differences, they have narrow thinking and perhaps do not understand what true love is. I tried to ignore both the blatant and subtle racism I commonly encountered, by remembering another one of Bruce's sayings: "Never waste energy on worries or negative thoughts, all problems are brought into existence, drop them."

Ironically, the ongoing painful reminder of the young man's persistent racism illustrated what my real estate business stood for—helping new immigrants and minorities claim their stake in the American dream, no matter how tattered it may be.

My father's father, Wong Choy Tin's membership to
Native Sons of the Golden State, 1920.

My mother's family: Dr. Rita Chow, Ruth Wong, Ronald Chow,
Mother May Chow, 1935, San Francisco, CA.

My father, John Wong (left),
with two US Army Air Forces buddies in 1942.

My parents' wedding in
San Francisco, 1948.

My parents' 60th Wedding Anniversary,
2008.

Me at age 3, with my parents, John and
Ruth Wong, 1953.

With my parents and brother, Daniel,
at Fisherman's Wharf, 1954.

My father's family. My father at top right, my mother below him,
holding newborn Daniel, and me below her, 1953.

My father's mother, Ow Shee Wong's Certificate of Naturalization, 1955/

My brother Dan and me in the backyard, 1957.

My family camping, Pine Crest, CA, circa 1960.

My cousins Joanne, Suzanne, and Henrianne, circa 1970.

I was acting in a play, "Year of the Dragon," with Frank Chin, San Francisco, 1976.

My "formal" actor's headshot, 1978/

My Martial Arts acting headshot, 1978.

On the set of "Perspectives," a TV show I produced, 1975-1977.

On the set of the Easter Seals Telethon I produced, hosted
by George Takei (left center), 1978.

My brother, Rev. Daniel Wong, and his wife, Flora,
at their wedding, Taiwan, 1979.

On the set of the movie, "Kill Squad," which I produced, 1981.

Christopher W. Strattan, Director of Photography, and me in front
of the poster for "Kill Squad," 1981/

My son, Christopher, age 2, and me at the Japanese Tea Garden,
San Francisco, 1987.

Christopher, age 3, and me with
my parents, 1988.

Christopher with my parents and me at his high
school graduation, Union City, CA., 2003.

My niece, Tiffany, my father, my brother,
Rev. Daniel Wong, and his wife Flora, at
our parents' 50th Anniversary, 1998.

Me and my brother Daniel with our
parents at their 50th Anniversary, 1998.

Giving a seminar on Public Speaking and Media Training for the
National Speakers Association, Tempe, AZ., circa 2010.

As part of my speaking and lecture seminars,
I break bricks on fire with my hands. 2010.

My aunt, Dr. Rita K. Chow, epitomizes the Art of Life- Long Learning. 2023.

Speaking on a cruise ship about Malaysian, Philippine, and Japanese cultures, 2023.

My wife, Miriam, and I are intrepid travelers. 2023.

DO, TEACH, SPEAK, WRITE

"Those who can't do, teach" is the saying, but I started teaching because I had real-world experience in broadcasting, real estate, and cultural issues. I found building bridges between cultures fulfilling and enjoyed being in front of inquisitive students. Since acting, interviewing, presenting, teaching, and public speaking were hardwired into me, over time these skills became interwoven into a professional path of teaching, speaking, and writing.

After I bought the real estate office in 1985, I met Jeff Tung, a second-generation Chinese American. We were about the same age, had similar interests, and he was very ambitious, like me. We hit it off immediately, and in 1987, I offered him half of the business. Over the next three years, we grew it into a large real estate office with over 50 agents.

Despite focusing on real estate and becoming involved in my local Board of Realtors, even being elected president, I decided to continue teaching. As educators, Asians are generally considered very knowledgeable but boring. I broke this mold by also being funny and engaging. One time, I taught an 8-hour class on IRS 1031 tax-deferred exchanges to a large group of real estate agents and got a standing ovation at the end because it was fun and practical.

In 1985, the California Association of Realtors (CAR) asked me to develop a class for agents on how to sell homes to Chinese clients. As already mentioned, Hong Kong Chinese were immigrating due to the impending return of the territory to Communist Chinese rule in 1997. They were coming to California in droves and driving agents crazy with their beliefs in things like feng shui. Also called Chinese geomancy, feng shui is an ancient practice that claims to maximize good energy and reduce the negative energy of places and structures like homes. Correctly directing the flow of Qi, or cosmic energy, through a building supposedly improves wealth, health, and happiness, while the wrong flow brings the opposite results. As illogical as all this seemed to me, I recognized how ingrained these beliefs were in Chinese clients. According to *The Guardian* article "Hong Kong: the city still shaped by feng shui": "Feng shui masters are still regularly consulted to help make the city's buildings harmonious and prosperous. In the past, emperors in China designed entire cities according to feng shui principles. Today, official adherence in cities such as Hong Kong is less explicit, but the practice still influences urban design and architecture through the choices of individual developers, architects, and the local population."[32]

In addition, the education staff at CAR said that agents needed to learn how to deal with Chinese buyers' constant negotiating. In America, we only bargained over the most expensive items like cars and houses, but the Chinese were masters of haggling looking for discounts on the home price, mortgage rate, escrow fees, and every other aspect of the transaction.

I explained to CAR that, as a fifth-generation Chinese American, I knew very little about new immigrants from Hong Kong and feng shui, but the association insisted because I was one of only a handful of Chinese agents with teaching experience at the time. So, I started compiling what I had learned over the years from my parents and others, like the belief that you should not buy a home at a "T" intersection because they believed that bad luck travels in straight lines and would come down the street directly into the home at the top of the "T" and that stairs that lead directly to the front door allow good luck to leave. I also did a lot of

---

[32] M. Keegan, Hong Kong: the city still shaped by feng-shui, https://www.theguardian.com/cities/2018/jul/19/hong-kong-the-city-still-shaped-by-feng-shui.

research by interviewing Chinese agents and their clients, learning more fascinating facts like they consider the number eight as lucky because the word for "eight" sounds similar to "fortune" in Chinese. Since they prefer addresses with eights, like 8888 Main Street, agents also started pricing homes with eights, like $138,888 —a practice that still exists today in the San Francisco Bay Area.

I realized very early on that most white people in general and agents in particular didn't care about culture because it didn't affect them on a daily basis, so I had to find a way to get them interested in attending my class. Since nothing is more convincing to any salesperson than the almighty dollar, I always subtly mentioned in my promotional materials that they would sell more homes if they learned how to be sensitive to their client's culture, and it seemed to work. Not only was I invited to speak on this topic throughout California, but also in many other parts of the country where Chinese were immigrating, which—over time— was almost every major metropolitan area of the United States.

To engage a rather tough audience like Realtors®, I would start every program with the question, "What things do Asian clients do that drive you crazy?" Agents would always say that they were frustrated that Chinese people would negotiate every part of the transaction from the price to the terms and even ask for a part of their commission. I would explain that, in the West, we don't haggle because we are relatively affluent whereas, in China, Latin America, and many other parts of the world, money is (or was) relatively scarce. That's why they will take the time to haggle over every little item from clothing to food in the market, while we will only bother to negotiate the most expensive items. Eventually, this led me to write another book about how to become a better bargainer called *Black Belt Negotiating*, with my Tae Kwon Do instructor, Sensei Grant Tabuchi. This book not only provided a system for negotiating real estate but just about anything people buy—from sandwiches to surfboards—using ancient martial arts principles.

I also kept hearing the following comment: "It frustrates me when immigrant clients who speak perfect English start talking in their own language in front of me!" The agents assumed that the clients did not like the house. After some thought-provoking questions from me, they realized that the clients were talking about whether they could afford the house or how much to offer. They knew that buyers don't stand around talking about how much they hate a house—they leave as fast as they can! I would then say to the agents, "So this is good for you. In fact, it might be the only buying sign you'll ever get!" I would tell them that it also means they are comfortable with you because my mother always told me never to speak Chinese in public because people would think that we're talking about them. At that point, the audience would realize that this was not a diversity training class but information that really would help them close more sales.

I would highlight not only the differences but also the similarities between cultures and how they impacted agents. For instance, the number four is not used in high-rise buildings in Asia because it sounds like the word for death in Chinese and Japanese. In America, we generally don't have office buildings, hotels, or hospitals with a 13th floor. This approach helped them relate to their clients by showing that we are not so different after all. Then I would compare and contrast Chinese people with other Asian cultures so the audience would understand the vast differences between specific cultures like Japanese, Korean, Vietnamese, and Filipino. During one class, it dawned on me that my whole purpose in life was to help people get past the differences they see on the outside; to recognize how similar we all are on the inside. If they did this, they couldn't discriminate against or harm anyone, including people like me.

To go along with the class, I put together a handout cleverly titled, "Selling Real Estate to Asian Clients." Despite the title that sucked, the program was extremely popular because it was practical and fun. When I was asked by Hispanic and African American real estate groups to present classes for their markets, it dawned on me that there were many similarities between how we were viewed and treated by whites. So, I combined them all into one course, "Secrets of Selling to Multicultural Real Estate Clients." Eventually, I was presenting at conferences all over the United States and decided to self-publish my first book, *Opening Doors: Selling Real Estate to Multicultural Clients*. No publisher thought it was a viable topic, so I paid $25,000 for 5,000 copies, a sizable investment at the time, but it was worth it because I eventually recouped my money and it led to speaking about cross-cultural selling at many National Association of Realtor® conventions, the Home Builders Association convention, car dealerships, and to companies like Coca-Cola.

What I was teaching was more than basic diversity training. For example, when I finished, salespeople knew that talking about culture helps develop a stronger relationship with prospective customers. In the same way, managers can develop better relationships with their employees from diverse cultures by getting to know them better. One way to do this is to ask people about their culture. However, I cautioned my audiences that they must ask everyone about their background, not just the people who look like minorities or new immigrants. Otherwise, it could feel discriminatory. The only exception is if they are talking to a Black person whose native language is English. I would suggest not asking an African American where their ancestors are from as it could bring up unpleasant issues around slavery. But if a Black person has a noticeable accent, it is usually safe to have that discussion with them.

However, before asking a client or coworker about their culture, I recommend they find out a little about their own background by doing some research or going to a website like Ancestry.com. I suggest opening the conversation with something like, "My grandfather came here from Italy, where are your ancestors from?" I stress that the wording of the question is important because if you simply ask, "Where are you from?" the answer could easily be "Toledo" instead of something like Thailand.

One event inspired me to improve my skills as a speaker. In 1986, I attended a real estate seminar in Hawaii attended by around 300 people and the speaker was captivating. I thought, "I could do that and get to travel to exotic locations as well!" When I approached her after the presentation, she told me she was what was called a "professional speaker."

I asked how I could become one, too, because I was a teacher. I'm sure she had heard that many times, but she suggested I join the National Speakers Association (NSA) and learn the profession. I did so with the sole purpose of earning the Certified Speaking Professional (CSP) designation, which would set me apart from other free public speakers. Well, the bar was high indeed! To qualify, at that time, you had to give 250 paid presentations to at least 100 different clients over five years and earn a minimum of $50,000 a year every year for five years or the equivalent total of about $700,000 today. This involved finding out when companies and organizations needed speakers, reaching the person who chose the presenters, proposing eye-catching topics, and then convincing them to hire me ahead of the hundreds of other qualified and better-known people. It was daunting, but I was determined.

I attended every NSA convention and workshop and learned how to perfect the craft as well as the business of speaking. I quickly discovered that I had a lot to learn. From voice projection to stage movement and content development, it was a very long learning experience. Public speakers are generally subject matter experts, who share their knowledge with the public or their peers for free. On the other hand, professional speakers know their topic but narrow down the information to meet the specific needs of the audience and then present it in a way that is captivating and memorable. Learning how to do this took much longer than I had ever imagined, but I did and along the way, I became president of our local NSA chapter.

In 1990, I was asked to teach broadcasting classes at Diablo Valley College in Pleasant Hill, California. Teaching college classes would not count towards earning my Certified Speaking Professional designation, but the president of the college wanted to build a complete broadcasting program and I was looking for a new challenge. So, I decided to move to the East Bay to help them grow the department, while still speaking professionally and selling real estate in my spare time to supplement my income. I sold my interest in the real estate company to my partner Jeff and moved to Lafayette, California.

So, I didn't start working towards my Certified Speaking Professional (CSP) designation in earnest until 1994, but on August 8, 1999, I became the first Asian American in the history of the National Speakers Association to earn this certification. I accomplished this goal by developing training for companies like Chevron, Boeing, State Farm Insurance, and many others, not only in the United States but also around the world. Since only 17% of all members of the NSA worldwide have earned the CSP designation, it was one of my proudest achievements. I'm still one of the very few Asian professional speakers in the world. Even so, I know that every time I get on the platform, I must be great, otherwise people will say that Asians are not good speakers. This is the challenge faced by anyone who is one of the few in their field.

I learned to start every program by walking out on stage, pausing for a long time as the anticipation built while the audience wondered what was going to happen. Then I announced, "I have a confession to make. I am Asian." This incredibly obvious statement always gets the audience laughing and breaks the ice, especially in diversity training classes where people naturally feel uneasy. There is a lot of resistance and fear because the earliest forms of this kind of education had a reputation for painting white people as villains and minorities as victims. To make my information easy to remember, I made sure that the content was fun and practical.

I would follow my "'confession" with, "I'm probably not like most of the new immigrants you meet because I'm a fifth-generation Chinese American. My great, great-grandfather, Quock Yow Choy, came to the United States in 1868, so I'm as American as apple pie. In fact, I'm so American that I don't even speak Chinese. Thanks to the California public school system... I speak Spanish!" This always gets even more laughter, and the audience is now relaxed and ready to learn from me.

Why do I start my programs this way? Well, I learned a long time ago that the first attribute about a person that people notice is gender and the second is ethnicity. Early in my speaking career, I realized that if I didn't say something about my background, the audience would be distracted by questions in their minds such as, "What nationality is he? Is he Chinese, Japanese, or Filipino?" Whenever I walk out on stage to speak in front of an audience that is not Asian (which is most of the time), I tell my joke about being a fifth-generation Chinese American, otherwise they won't listen to anything I say for at least five minutes. Whenever I forgot to start with this story, I could immediately see the puzzlement on the audience's faces while those inevitable questions about my background flashed through their heads.

Such thoughts and questions create a form of what I call "cultural static" that keeps people from clearly hearing others who are different. It clouds communication, so I teach people that it's okay to ask minorities about their culture. We know we look different from white Americans and expect them to wonder about us. It is perfectly natural to do so. We are all curious about each other's differences whether it's age, physical ability, or another factor outside of our own experience. This interest is healthy because it leads to learning new things and personal growth.

For instance, I have several friends who require wheelchairs to get around. Wanting to make sure that I was being considerate, I asked my friend, Bill, if I should stand up or kneel when talking with him. He thanked me profusely for my question and said, "If you're just coming up to say hello feel free to stand up, but if you plan to have an extended conversation, I would appreciate it if you would kneel, so I don't have to strain my neck looking up at you for a long period of time." I think my concern is a natural result of following the Confucian concept of "Li," a Chinese word that means respect, righteousness, and decency. It teaches behaving well with everyone and always doing good.

"Li" is innate in many people, but also learned through personal experience and empathy, which can be developed by imagining what it's like to walk a mile in another person's shoes. If I had to point to the seminal moment that led me to help people develop sensitivity for minorities, it would be my first day of school when I was ridiculed for being different; "a chink." Dying my hair blond, speaking English without an accent, or whitewashing my surname would never change that, but it seems to have motivated me to defy how Asians are perceived in America. It seems that I have been a contradiction to Asian stereotypes my whole life. I've always enjoyed the challenge of choosing traditionally non-Asian careers like a movie actor, television producer, professional speaker, and more. I have made a point of trying to break down barriers, escape from limiting boxes, and show others what is possible. I want people to know that Asians can do more than accounting and engineering. We are complex individuals with abilities, skills, and talents that are not predestined by race and culture. We also have dreams and aspirations like everyone else.

To this day, when I speak to someone on the phone in my perfect English, known only to them as Michael Lee, and then I meet them in person, they are often surprised. Some have even said, "I didn't know you were Oriental," with some apprehension because they had no idea how to treat me. My answer to that is simple, "Treat me just like anyone else!"

Yes, I am still seen as different in white America, but our differences are our strengths, giving us unique perspectives that we can offer the world. I added "Soon" to my name in 2000, when after my first book came out. I looked on Amazon.com and saw over 5,000 authors with some version of the name "Michael Lee." So, I added my nickname as my middle name to differentiate myself and reclaim my Asian identity. It would let people know instantly that I was Asian, but also added a touch of mystery because "Soon" is a common Korean name, not Chinese. Now, when you google "Michael Soon Lee," only I come up!

YELLOW PRIVILEGE

While I was studying culture and its historical impact in the United States, the phrase that kept coming up was "white privilege." A charged term and still real today, it refers to the advantages that whites have over non-whites in the same social, political, and economic circumstances. These advantages take many forms, like not being racially profiled and stereotyped, and being represented by the media generally in a positive way. The privileged group is also the measuring stick for everyone's success whether others have the same opportunities or not. Its characteristics become the social norm, including appearance, like the blue-eyed blonde being considered as the highest standard of beauty.

In America, whites take learning their history in school for granted. African American and Hispanic American history is starting to be more widely taught, but Asian American history is still virtually nonexistent in K-12 curricula. Now, white privilege is expanding into valuing comfort over honesty by banning Critical Race Theory (CRT), which states that race is a major factor in the U.S., without attributing racism to white people. The alleged reason for this ban is to prevent students from feeling bad or embarrassed about the involvement of whites in slavery and lynching, historical events that are deemed "divisive." Aren't we doomed to repeat past mistakes if we don't learn from them, or even learn about them?

Acknowledging the existence of systemic racism, as CRT does, is not racist. In fact, it sheds light on discrimination, which is based on what sociologists' call "racialization," meaning the notion that people of certain races are either less than human, or fundamentally different and should be treated accordingly. Colonialism, slavery, and Jim Crow laws were all justified by racialization. Yet, most scientists agree that race is a social construct since all humans share approximately 99.9% of the same genetic code.

While not all white people participated directly in the mistreatment of "other" races, their learned biases and silent consent allowed it to continue because it did not affect them directly—yet another aspect of being privileged. White privilege, being the status quo, is almost impossible to recognize if you're white. There is no denying that many Caucasians struggle in life, but white privilege still provides them with greater access to resources than people of color in the same situation. For instance, poor whites in the South in the 1800s were certainly a lot better off than slaves. When white business owners today don't hire people of color, they give whites more economic opportunities. Pew Research found that only 5% of whites say their race or ethnicity has made it harder for them to succeed, 62% say their race hasn't made much difference in their ability to succeed, and 31% say their race has made things easier for them. Minorities in America certainly cannot say the same thing.

Today, most Americans believe Asian Americans enjoy "yellow privilege" and that we are immune from the prejudice that impacts African and Hispanic Americans. When I look back on my life, I realize that I've had two emotions very close to the surface at all times, anger because I haven't been able to achieve my full potential due to discrimination, and guilt for having more privileges than Blacks, Hispanics, LGBTQ+ people, and sometimes white women. But as a professional diversity trainer, I am arguably more aware of racial privilege than most.

Yellow privilege is invisible in our lives as Asians but impactful, and like whites, we take it for granted. I experienced first-hand how different races are treated when I was pulled over for speeding while driving a Black friend to a party. I had never had a police officer approach with his hand on his gun, nor had I ever been ordered out of my car along with my passenger. The officer made us put our hands on the trunk while he checked our IDs. He then took me aside and asked me a lot of questions, like who my friend was, and if I was being held against my will. Finally, he let us go with a warning. My friend said he had never gotten off with a warning before, but it wasn't unusual for him to be stopped for absolutely no reason, frisked, and handcuffed while they checked his ID. He said his parents taught him to always keep his hands in sight so he wouldn't be shot. I could tell that he had been brought up with a fear of the police while I was taught that they were our friends.

One key benefit of both white and yellow privilege is a generally positive relationship with law enforcement and the judicial system. Asian Americans are six times less likely to be killed by police than Blacks, even less than whites. We are the least likely group to be affected by police violence[33] because we are less likely to be racially profiled. This results in lower arrest and incarceration rates, increasing the impression that Asians tend to be law-abiding. Despite that second-generation Asian Americans and southeast Asian immigrants are often involved with gang activity, we account for only 1.5% of federal prisoners, far lower than the 35% of African Americans, 21% of Hispanics, and 32% of whites.[34]

The view that we are law-abiding, non-threatening, and honest also has other advantages, like little resistance to us living in white neighborhoods, unless there are too many of us. We also face less overt discrimination despite that everywhere in America, except Hawaii, we are viewed as perpetual foreigners. So, in the U.S., some aspects of yellow privilege are geographically dependent.

When I lived in Hawaii, I didn't get funny looks when I walked into businesses. I saw food, hair, and skin products for Asians in the

---

[33] F. Edwards, H. Lee and M. Esposito, "Risk of being killed by police use of force in the United States by age, race–ethnicity, and sex." *Proceedings of the National Association of Sciences* 116 (34), (2019).

[34] A. Carson and E. Anderson, "Prisoners in 2015," *Bureau of Justice Statistics* (2015).

main aisles of stores, not in the "ethnic sections." I felt what it was like to be in the majority, and it felt good! In Hawaii, Asians have most of the privileges that white people are granted on the mainland. They live in every community without exception. They are not made fun of or feel ashamed when speaking their native languages in public. They have a positive relationship with the police and tend to be favored by school authorities. Asian and Hawaiian history is widely taught in schools and there are countless children's books that represent these races. When they speak with someone in charge, it is likely to be someone of their own race. They can take jobs with companies that promote affirmative action without having co-workers suspect that they were hired to meet a quota. The media features Asian reporters and stories about Hawaiians without the tendency to stereotype. In politics, in 2022, the majority of the legislators in Hawaii were Hawaiians/Pacific Islanders and Asian/Pacific Americans (65.79%) with about 22% Caucasian.[35]

On the U.S. mainland, yellow privilege does not include all the advantages of white privilege but confers Asian Americans with some exclusive benefits. In school, teachers automatically assume that we are intelligent and hardworking; if there's a commotion, we will be the last ones suspected of causing it as opposed to Blacks who are likely to be the first. We are seen as an asset to this country because of the services we provide; medical, technical, and so on. All these assumptions give us an initial advantage when applying for jobs. In addition, yellow privilege positively impacts other areas, including life expectancy. According to a 2019 Kaiser Family Foundation study, the average age at death of Asian Americans is 86.5 vs. 78.9 for whites, lower for Blacks and Hispanics who are less likely to have health insurance and access to medical care. Compared to other minorities we are subjected to less stress caused by overt racism—stress is proven to increase the risk of heart attacks, diabetes, and so on. Of course, other factors contribute to Asian longevity,

---

[35] Center for youth Political Participation, "Hawaii State Legislature," https://cypp.rutgers.edu/hawaii/

factors like a low rate of obesity and a unique diet, characterized by a low consumption of red meat and a high consumption of fish and plant foods such as soybeans and tea.

Be that as it may, yellow privilege is a double-edged sword in many ways. Since Asian Americans have reached or exceeded parity with Caucasians in areas like income and education, the notion is that we have become "white," in terms of the advantages we enjoy. Despite often having the highest level of education, we hit the so-called "bamboo ceiling" and are the least likely to be promoted. Managers often don't consider us for promotions, thinking that other minorities should be given opportunities, also assuming that we don't need more money. In 2020, the median annual household income was $74,912 for whites vs. $94,903 for Asian Americans, $55,321 for Hispanics and $45,870 for Blacks, according to the Peter G. Peterson Foundation.

The notion that we don't need promotions, raises or affirmative action and assistance programs, like welfare and food stamps, makes those of us who need them too embarrassed to apply. The reality is that not all Asian Americans—a group that encompasses roughly 20 major ethnicities and a vast range of economic statuses, religions, regions, and cultures—have benefitted equally from yellow privilege. We may be the wealthiest minority group in the country, but we also have the widest income gap. According to the Economic Institute, in 2019, the poverty rate for African Americans was 18.7%, followed by Hispanics at 15.7%, Asians at 7.3% along with Whites also at 7.3%. However, a White House study showed the diversity between Asians in America: the poverty rates of Hmong was 37.8%; Cambodians was 29.3%; Laotians was 18.5%; and Vietnamese was 16.6%. A key reason for this disparity is that some Asian immigrants arrived on skill-based visas and some as refugees. Other factors, like the length of time in the U.S. and our country's relationship with the ancestral country (e.g., the Vietnam War), have impacted the success of certain groups. The groups that benefit most from yellow privilege are the Japanese, Chinese, and Koreans. South Asians and Pakistanis are certainly beneficiaries, but the

U.S. Census Bureau has variously categorized them as Asian, Black, and white over the years although, ethnically, they are Caucasian.

By propagating the false belief that all Asian American groups are equally successful, yellow privilege glosses over the social issues that we face, including discrimination and violence. Being omitted from the race discussion, we have no platform or voice. In fact, we are often seen as "having it too good" to demand improvement. On the other hand, we are not compelled to take a stand against discrimination because, like whites, these are not burning issues for us. However, we should be vocal, because we are distrusted and resented by many Hispanics and Blacks due to the inter-racial antagonism triggered by yellow privilege and the model minority myth. This leads to violence against us because we are also stereotyped as passive and non-threatening, implying that we will not fight back.

Regrettably, yellow privilege has been used to propagate negative stereotypes against other minorities and to discount the systemic racism that prevents them from making forward socioeconomic strides. The media continue to leverage the model minority myth against Blacks and Hispanics to victim-blame and shame. In 2017, *New York Magazine* asked, "Today, Asian Americans are among the most prosperous, well-educated, and successful ethnic groups in America. What gives? It couldn't possibly be that they maintained solid two-parent family structures, had social networks that looked after one another, placed enormous emphasis on education and hard work, and thereby turned false, negative stereotypes into true, positive ones, could it? It couldn't be that all whites are not racists or that the American dream still lives?"

Yellow privilege was created to advance certain sociopolitical agendas domestically and internationally. Buying into the media hype, many people, including Asians, believe that racism toward us has diminished because we "proved ourselves" to be good Americans. But that is only a sliver of the truth because—to support the model minority myth—stories of successful Asians were highly publicized and those of less successful Asians omitted. We went from being portrayed as threatening, exotic, and degenerate at the outset of the 20th century to the model minority in the 1950s. Because so little was known about us in the U.S., being thought of as "inscrutable," it was easy to give us a quick public relations makeover without much push-back or fact-checking. As a result, Pew Research revealed that between 1940 and 1970, we went from segregated neighborhoods and schools to surpassing African Americans in average household earnings and closed the wage gap with whites.

Throughout U.S. history, other minorities attempted to combat racism by also portraying themselves as upstanding citizens capable of assimilating into mainstream culture. African Americans made such appeals in the 1940s but, after WWII, it was convenient for political leaders to hear only Asian voices. Being a tiny portion of the population, we were a preferable alternative to Blacks. Recent studies have found that in areas of the country that had larger Black populations in the middle of the 20th century, present-day white people showed a stronger implicit preference for white over Black people.[36]

Naturally, we contributed to our PR makeover, publicizing stories about our obedient children and traditional family values or highlight-ing our wartime service as proof of our Americanness, as in the case of the Japanese. The model minority myth was quickly co-opted by white politicians who saw it as a tool to maintain China as our ally against Russia during the Cold War. Aiming to portray the U.S. a racial democracy, they turned the purported Asian American success into pro-paganda. Congress overturned the Chinese Exclusion Act in 1943 as a goodwill gesture to China, our allies during World War II.

By the 1960s, anxieties about the civil rights movement compelled politicians to praise Asian Americans and victim-blame Blacks by ped-dling the view that "If you worked hard and kept quiet like Asians, you

---

[36] H.A. Vuletich, N. Sommet and B.K. Payne, "The Great Migration and Implicit Bias in the Northern United States." *Social Psychological and Personality Science*, July 2023 https://doi.org/10.1177/19485506231181718 .

could be successful like them." My parents and many other Asian families totally bought into the political spin and told us kids to avoid Blacks and Hispanics because they were lazy criminals. The myth was used to stir tensions between minority groups and prevent the formation of a unified front against an inherently biased system.

Yellow privilege can also be partly attributed to the "middleman minority," a little-known academic theory which closely describes my experience of our role in America. Members of my audience at speaking engagements and diversity trainings have consistently said that they see me as a comfortable bridge between minorities and whites. I seem to represent a non-threatening, buffering "other" in the stark Black-White racial divide. Although, in my case, this buffering is psychological, the middleman role is very real in the socio-economic structure. According to Walter P. Zenner, Professor of Anthropology at the State University of New York at Albany, "'Middleman' or 'trading' minorities are ethnic groups, which are disproportionately represented in occupations related to commerce, especially in the small business sector," as well as other go-between occupations like agent, labor contractor, moneylender, and broker that act as intermediaries between producer and consumer; employer and employee; owner and renter; the ruling elite and the masses.

Middleman minorities are found in societies where a huge division and status gap exist between the haves and the have-nots. Many minorities around the world have historically occupied this social position, like the Jews in Europe, the Chinese in Southeast Asia, and the Asian Indians in Africa. While possibly suffering discrimination, the middlemen are not part of the underclass because the elites, the haves, use them to avoid dealing directly with the masses and to bear the brunt of the hostility against them.

When they first arrive in a country, middlemen minorities are typically subjected to hostility due to their cultural, religious, or racial distinctiveness. They are forced into marginal lines of work, like the Chinese who were prevented from becoming miners by the Foreign Miners' Tax, so they did cooking and laundry, while California's Alien

Land Law in 1920 forced Japanese immigrants to engage in farming for wealthy landowners. Being targets of xenophobia and seeing themselves as temporary residents, they have no desire for full participation in the life of the host land. They form highly organized enclaves, which only highlight their differences from the surrounding society. They use residential self-segregation for protection and language (e.g., Chinatowns, Japan towns), establish language and cultural schools; maintain distinctive cultural traits and religion; often resist marriage; and generally, avoid involvement in local politics unless these directly affect their group; (Asians and Pacific Islanders make up only 0.9% of elected officials in the United States.[37]) They tend to ignore or downplay the hostility they face, including efforts to impede their livelihood, riots and killings, exclusion movements (e.g., the Chinese Exclusion Act) and expulsion, internment in camps (e.g., the Japanese during WWII), and even "final solutions," like the European Jews.

In the United States, Asians and Hispanics are often accused of taking jobs because they fill the gap between the top and the bottom of the socioeconomic food chain, where the top 1% of earners took 20% of income and the bottom 50% of earners took 10% in 2022. They are allowed to achieve some financial success and status compared to the underclass. Asians in particular were chosen for the middleman role, which is underpinned by the divisive model minority narrative, because we are not a substantial enough population to tip the scales of power and influence. As a result of our perceived success, envy, and prejudice fester beneath the surface until something triggers an outburst.

After 1965, when the U.S. ended the quota-based system of immigration, Koreans were given preference because they had high socioeconomic and educational attainment. By 1990, 568,000 Koreans had immigrated, mostly to Los Angeles County.[38] Unable to get other

---

[37] E. Lee, "Asian Americans Emerge as Force in US Politics." *Voice of America,* August 3, 2021.
[38] C. Esterline and J. Batalova, "Korean Immigrants in the United States," *Migration Policy Institute* (2022)

work due to the difficulty they had in learning English, many pooled their money to open small businesses in Black communities like the Watts area in Los Angeles—that was all they could afford. This surge of Korean-owned businesses created resentment in the Black residents because racism in financing prevented them from starting their own businesses.

The Koreans' role as middlemen was established in these areas, where they were forced to interact with Black and Brown communities, often in highly charged situations. It should be said that Koreans, like many other people outside the United States, had a built-in mistrust of Blacks due to American media, which commonly portrays them as violent, uneducated, and poor. Similarly, Black Americans had a built-in bias against Koreans, who had been depicted as untrustworthy during the Korean War when North Koreans were shown on television invading South Korea and killing American soldiers. There was little mention of the South Koreans who stood shoulder-to-shoulder with Americans.

Tensions between the two groups in Watts came to a head in 1991, when Mrs. Soon Ja Du, a Korean store owner, killed 15-year-old African American Latasha Harlins. Du accused Harlins of trying to steal a bottle of orange juice, which she had put in her backpack but for which she had the money in her hand. In anger, the girl threw the juice on the counter and began walking away when Du shot her in the head. In a judicial display of yellow privilege, Du received a remarkably mild sentence compared to those given to African Americans for murder—400 hours of community service, a $500 fine plus funeral expenses, and five years of probation. Black community protests to the light sentence became a regular occurrence outside of Du's store.

Coincidentally, two weeks before Harlins' death, four white Los Angeles Police Department (LAPD) officers were captured on video beating black motorist Rodney King. Everyone watched the police brutality on television. I was angry about this senseless, racially motivated violence, and it was the first time I questioned if the police were really "our friends," as I had been taught. One year later, I was angry again that the officers weren't found guilty because it certainly didn't appear that King had resisted arrest. The next thing I knew, Korean businesses in Watts were on fire! More than 50 people were killed and 1,000 injured, as the Black residents targeted 2,200 Korean businesses shouting "Latasha Harlins," causing an estimated half a billion dollars in damage.

The "Black-Korean conflict" became an enduring media storyline that shifted focus away from white racism and the LAPD, which was glad to see headlines of racial conflict in which they were not blamed. The King video, the acquittal, the riots, and the ensuing destruction served as a rude awakening to so many people on so many levels. To the Koreans in Watts, it became painfully apparent that they were abandoned by the system. Chang Lee, whose parents owned a store there said, "Nothing in my life indicated I was a secondary citizen until the LA riots. The LAPD powers that be decided to protect the 'haves' and the Korean community did not have any political voice or power. They left us to burn."[39]

Like so many other people, I couldn't understand why one minority group would destroy the businesses of another minority. Nothing could underline the importance of diversity training more. Churches and community organizers worked to increase understanding of cultural differences and educate the two communities about their shared histories of oppression. Many immigrant Koreans were unaware of the violence and discrimination black people have faced in America. After decades of community organizing, education, and empathy, many Korean Americans' racial attitudes about discrimination, civil rights, and restorative justice have changed. Today, more than nine in ten Korean Americans believe that there is some discrimination against black people and 70% agree that the government should do more to protect the civil rights of African Americans.[40] New research shows that half of Asian Americans

---

[39] K. Lah, "The LA riots were a rude awakening for Korean Americans," *CNN*, April 29, 2017. https://www.cnn.com/2017/04/28/us/la-riots-korean-americans/index.html

[40] J. Demsas and R. Ramirez, "The history of tensions—and solidarity—between Black and Asian American communities, explained," *Vox*, March 16, 2021.

across ten national-origin groups feel they have "something" or "a lot" in common with Blacks when it comes to government, political power, and representation.

Any society where some citizens enjoy certain advantages that others do not, is by definition, unequal, unfair, and discriminatory. These privileges, white or yellow, are shrewdly used to drive wedges between some communities to preserve the status quo for others. Responsibility comes even with partial privilege. Along with whites, Asians must fight to give everyone the rights that America promises but doesn't always deliver. Only when we work together can we truly attain liberty and justice for all.

BLACK VS. ASIAN—
A CONVENIENT NARRATIVE

Since Asians started entering the United States in large numbers in the 1850s, we have been used as a wedge against other minorities. Various ethnic groups have perpetrated hate crimes against us, but historical data—including FBI records—overwhelmingly shows that most perpetrators have been white. Yet, the media has tended to feature attacks on Asians by people of color, including African Americans. During the COVID-19 outbreak, hate incident reports surged to over 11,000 from March 2020 through March of 2023 according to the website StopAAPI hate.org. According to a recent study, white Christian nationalism, more than any other ideology, has shaped xenophobic views around the pandemic.[41] Many of the recent hate crimes that gained widespread media attention have, yet again, featured black assailants, increasing tensions between the African American and Asian American communities.

While there is no evidence that Blacks are responsible for this surge, or that they are particularly hostile to Asian Americans, the longstanding Black-Asian hostility narrative continues to be advanced. It is rooted in immigration and economic policies that have historically pitted these communities against each other. But white supremacy is what

---

[41] S.L. Perry, A.L. Whitehead, and J.B. Grubbs, "Prejudice and pandemic in the promised land: how white Christian nationalism shapes Americans' racist and xenophobic views of COVID-19. Ethnic and Racial Studies," 44(5), 759-772. (2021)

created these tensions through segregation and policing in low-income neighborhoods where minority groups are forced to compete for ever-shrinking resources.

That said, like all native-born people, Black Americans may be susceptible to xenophobic and nationalistic sentiments that blame others—in this case, Asian Americans, who can be seen as "forever foreigners"; even if they, too, are native-born. Some research indicates that African Americans may feel economic competition with new immigrants because of the racial hierarchy that has placed them at the bottom. Also, the yellow privileges given to the middleman minority in low-income areas where Asians and Blacks live side by side, have been used to create discord between the two communities. And intentionally so; for as long as they are divided, they cannot unite against systemic racism—the age-old "divide and conquer" strategy was particularly valuable during the civil rights movement.

In the 1960s, in terms of their sociopolitical standing, "Asian Americans became acutely aware that they had more in common with African Americans than with European Americans," writes activist-turned-author William Wei.[42] Of course, not all Asian Americans shared this sentiment; many bought into the model minority media spin, which was created when policymakers were agonizing about how to solve what they called the "Negro problem." The media popularized the idea that the protesting black and brown Americans were "problem minorities," in contrast to the passive, hardworking yellow Americans who were the "role model." Some Asian Americans espoused this idea, like Howard Imazeki, who stirred up controversy with a 1963 editorial calling on Black Americans to "better themselves" before asking for equal rights.

Growing up, my parents totally bought into the media stories that Blacks were mostly criminals and lazy ne'er-do-wells. I don't think they had any ill intent towards Blacks or any other ethnic

---

[42] H. Imazaki, "A Nisei Speaks to Negroes," *Colbert County Recorder,* August 22, 1963. https:// civilrightsshoals.com/object/editorial-grist-a-nisei-speaks-to-negroes/

minorities, but as the time approached for me to go to school, they sat me down and specifically told me to avoid Black kids. This wasn't hard at Fruitvale Grammar School because, in the 1950s, I don't recall seeing any dark-skinned kids at all. When I got to Oakland High, there were a lot of Black students, including the ones that my parents had warned me about. Of course, there were African American students who got good grades, but I never noticed them. Maybe it was just "confirmation bias," which is when you only see evidence that confirms a previously held belief. On the news, most crimes were shown being committed by Blacks, and many bad guys in movies and shows were Black. One time, when I was riding my bike three miles from home, there was a group of Black kids standing in the middle of the street. I assumed they wanted to take my bike, so I literally ran them over to get away.

At the same time, I was quite conflicted because many of the African Americans that I met were nice, friendly people. Against my parent's wishes, I began to make friends with some of them, and that's when I learned about the systemic racism that affected them. They told me about how bad the schools were in their neighborhoods and about being constantly harassed by the police. I thought I was poor until I found out how little they had to eat because their parents had jobs like housekeepers and shoeshines. I could see that it would be very difficult, even if they got good grades, for them to go to a university. The best most could aspire to was attending the local community college and then getting a job.

Getting to know Blacks as human beings, rather than media stereotypes of criminals, made me much more sympathetic to the civil rights movement and Dr. King's work. I began to see similarities between the struggles and discrimination that both Asians and African Americans faced. Many of my friends and my parents were against the civil rights movement, not because they didn't want Blacks to get equal rights; they were afraid that if we spoke up or protested, we would be put into internment camps. They felt that the way for us to get equal rights was to prove that we could be good citizens.

At that time, I also realized that my Black friends considered Asians to be foreigners and very hard to understand. They avoided Chinatown because they didn't understand the language or the food. It was so much fun taking Black friends to dim sum where they could pick dishes from the shiny metal carts that Chinese women would push between the tables. One time, the first thing I heard hollered out by the workers when we walked in was "*hot mo gui*," which means "black devil" in Chinese. I guess it was rare to see a Black person in a Chinese restaurant in those days. Introducing my friends to Chinese culture, language, and food was, I suppose, how I unofficially started my diversity training career. But it's always a two-way street, my black friends helped me understand many truths about their culture. My close friend Charles was always reading, like me. He spent hours in the library studying the history of African Americans because he wanted to understand the reason his people were still being treated as badly as they were. He explained to me that Blacks were not the only ones enslaved. In 1730, nearly 25% of the slaves in the Carolinas were Cherokee, Creek, or other Native Americans.

I became interested to know more, so I challenged Charles to explain why African Americans were stereotyped as lazy as my father said. After quite a bit of research, Charles found that one of the ways that slave owners coerced enslaved people into working hard was through the Puritanical teaching that work improves moral character. Otherwise, they had no incentive to do more than the minimum amount of work to avoid a beating. In other words, slaves would be rewarded in heaven for being docile, agreeable, and diligent; masters calling slaves "lazy" was the highest insult, which found its way into the media. It reminded me of my mother sending me off to school every morning with, "Work hard and don't be lazy."

I remember how shocked Charles was to learn that, during the Civil War, negotiations over prisoner exchanges failed because the Union wanted Black soldiers treated humanely and returned whereas the Confederacy wanted to send them back into slavery. He was even more surprised to discover that lawmakers in the South devised "unique forms of policing, sentencing, and confinement" to "capitalize on a loophole in the 13th Amendment that states' citizens cannot be enslaved unless convicted of a crime." The resulting Black Codes and Vagrancy Laws ensured that law enforcement could aggressively target newly freed Blacks. The Northern States were more subtle about it; they used the "disparate enforcement of various laws against "suspicious characters," disorderly conduct, keeping and visiting disorderly houses, drunkenness, and violations of city ordinances" to create "new forms of everyday surveillance and punishment of Black people in the Northeast, Midwest, and West." After these policies were implemented, the artificially inflated arrests and incarceration rates of Blacks were used as proof of their "inherent criminal tendencies"—a theme found at the heart of current stereotypes and biases.[43]

In 1964, aiming to reinforce the "black criminal" stereotype and discredit the civil rights movement, people like Goldwater, Nixon, and Johnson, began linking street crime to civil rights activism. Four years later, changes in federal criminal justice policy resulted in more arrests, incarcerations, probations, harsher sentencing laws, and more criminal justice subsidies for prison guards, probation officers, prison food, and other suppliers. In 1968, there were about 182,000 people in prison, but since these changes there are more than 2.1 million people behind bars in 2022, almost 4.5 million on probation and parole, and 70 million with criminal convictions. Since Charles discovered this information in our senior year of high school, Washington has been spending billions of dollars each year to keep people imprisoned for as long as possible. Mass incarceration is big business with devastating social consequences, especially for the most targeted group: Black men make up 13% of U.S.

---

[43] E. Hinton, L. Henderson and C. Reed, "An Unjust Burden: The Disparate Treatment of Black Americans in the Criminal Justice System," *The Vera Institute of Justice*, (2018).

population but 35% of the incarcerated in the country. According to a 2021 report by The Sentencing Project, Black Americans are incarcerated at nearly five times the rate of whites.[44]

The two-parent family was a hot topic across the country in 1965 when a government report by Daniel Patrick Moynihan called Black families a "tangle of pathology "that led to a 24% Black "illegitimacy" rate while the white rate was 4%.[45] I asked Charles about another of my father's claims that Blacks were not successful because they had so many families with single mothers. He reminded me that, because of segregation, Black men are more likely to attend inferior schools and are not prepared to compete for jobs with better-educated people. He explained that this is why he studied so hard. The heroin epidemic at the time was also sending disproportionate numbers of Black men to prison, eliminating job opportunities for those who had served their time. Charles explained that Black women don't want to marry men who can't provide for their families and that welfare laws created a financial incentive for poor mothers to stay single. I understood that the issue was a lot more complex than Black men not wanting or marry or stay with the woman they got pregnant. Almost fifty years later, about 64% of Black children are still born to single mothers.[46] Even after a post-welfare-reform decline in child poverty, those mothers are far more likely to be poor and to pass that poverty onto their children. The cycle continues.

My interactions with Black friends in high school began expanding my understanding of the social issues I saw around me. I realized that there are two sides to every story and that we should not always believe what the media (or our parents) tell us. I started to learn to think for myself and to question more of the facts that I formerly

---

[44] A. Nellis, "The Color of Justice: Racial and Ethnic Disparity in State Prisons," *The Sentencing Project*, (2021).
[45] D. Moynihan, "The Moynihan Report: The Negro Family, the Case for National Action," *Office of Policy Planning and Research. U.S. Department of Labor*, (1965).
[46] Ed. "Child Well-Being in Single-Parent Families," *The Anna E. Casey Foundation*, (2023).

took for granted, just as the Black vs. Asian narrative began gaining momentum.

The current media focus on stories of Black against Asian violence intends to undo these gains, drive the wedge deeper, and obscure the history of Black-Asian solidarity against structural racism. For example: In 1869, African American abolitionist, Frederick Douglass, advocated for Chinese and Japanese immigration. During the Philippine-American War (1899-1902), prominent African Americans Henry M. Turner and Ida B. Wells spoke out on behalf of the Filipino freedom fighters. From 1965 to 1975, African Americans protested the Vietnam War along with many young Asian Americans and others. Malcolm X and Martin Luther King Jr. spoke out, while Muhammad Ali was convicted for refusing induction into the U.S. armed forces. He saw the war as genocide and said, "Why should they ask me to put on a uniform and go 10,000 miles from home and drop bombs and bullets on Brown people in Vietnam while so-called Negro people in Louisville are treated like dogs?" Black people were getting drafted at vastly higher rates compared to whites and mistreatment of black soldiers on the battleground was widespread.

In the late 1960s, rumors circulated that the government planned to incarcerate African American radicals to end the protests against the Vietnam War. When African American activists failed in their attempts to repeal the law that would enable authorities to repeat the Japanese incarceration during WWII, the Japanese American Citizen League (JACL) and Asian American student activists joined forces with them. The legislation to repeal the law, sponsored by Senator Daniel K. Inouye, Congressmen Spark M. Matsunaga, and Chet Holifield, was passed in 1971.

In 1968, the Third World Liberation Front was formed by Black and Asian activists and other student groups at San Francisco State University to demand the establishment of race and ethnic studies in college and university curricula in California. As a result of their joint efforts, Asian Americans like me were able to learn about our history in this country and recognize how, like Blacks, we had faced discrimination.

In 1982 Chrysler plant supervisor Ronald Ebens and his stepson, laid-off autoworker Michael Nitz, mistook Chinese American Vincent Chin for being Japanese whom they blamed for hurting the American car industry. The two white men beat Chin to death, and when convicted they only received three years' probation and a $3,000 fine with no jail time for murder. In 1984, with the support of Rev. Jesse Jackson and NAACP leaders, Asian Americans pursued a federal civil rights case against the men after which one defendant was sentenced to 25 years in prison while the other was found not guilty. This demonstrated to the Asian community the power of using the legal system and working with Black leaders who had more experience in such matters. The multicultural alliance that came together helped to form the basis of the "Rainbow Coalition," which was central to Jackson's 1984 presidential campaign.

After George Floyd's death at the hands of a Minneapolis police officer in 2020, Asian Americans supported the Black Lives Matter (BLM) movement in protests and behind the scenes within their own communities. For instance, more than a dozen AAPI organizations came together to produce a toolkit that includes ways to support the movement for Black Lives. In May of 2021, BLM and Stop Asian Hate activists rallied in San Francisco to dismantle white supremacy, which has harmed Black Americans in a very different way than it has harmed Asian Americans. Social media videos showed Blacks chanting things like, "We are on these streets fighting for Asian lives," but the narrative around Black and Asian tensions is still used by mainstream media to discount the white supremacy that creates and drives their rhetoric.

What we need to realize is that, historically, darker skin has been deemed undesirable and equated with being poor under Western and Eurocentric views. Therefore, anyone who is not white falls to the bottom of this hierarchy. Today, Asian Americans are perceived as "honorary whites," primarily because we're currently the preferred alternative to Blacks. For Asian American and African American communities to move forward in harmony, it is important to remember that the Black vs. Asian hostility narrative is politically convenient for those in power. Of course, it's not only up to minorities to build solidarity; it's the responsibility of all Americans to understand the role that white supremacy has played in creating these rifts, which are exploited again and again.

The U.S. Census bureau predicts that around the year 2044, minorities in America will become the majority and in many states like Hawaii, New Mexico, California, Texas, Nevada, and Maryland this is already a reality.[47] This prospect seems to frighten many people who are afraid they will lose power and control. What many don't realize is that the growth of the minority population in the U.S. is due to births, not immigration. Minorities are younger and have larger families than whites. Building a wall will not affect these factors.

They also don't realize that diversity is good for business. Companies with high levels of diversity, equity, and inclusion report higher employee engagement and retention. In addition, businesses with a diverse workforce are 35% more likely to experience greater financial returns and 70% more likely to capture more markets.[48]

Today, because of the increasing numbers of minorities, there is a tremendous sense of fear and panic that has pervaded our country. Like many, I saw the election of Barak Obama as a sign that Americans were willing to elect anyone President of the United States regardless of their race. Unfortunately, his election was also a sign to some people that white people might be losing power in America. Now equality seems like such a distant dream again as racists get bolder every day openly spreading hate and violence across the country.

---

[47] D.L. Poston and R. Sáenz, "U.S. whites will soon be the minority in number, but not power," *Wayback Machine*, (2017).
[48] A. Stahl, "3 Benefits of Diversity in the Workplace," *Forbes*, 17 December 2021.

To you who are afraid, all I can do is offer an ancient Chinese proverb that says, "The Eight Immortals crossing the sea all have their own particular skills." In other words, we all have our own special skills to contribute to the success of the country. If you deny anyone the right to use their unique skills, we will all not be as successful. Let's work together rather than against each other and we'll all be much happier.

ENDING ANTI-ASIAN HATE

The pandemic brought a sharp rise in anti-Asian hate incidents that included being coughed and spat on, refused service, vandalism, verbal harassment, and physical assault. Verbal harassment/name-calling has the highest percentage of occurrences at 63.7%. Despite the recent anti-Asian hate movements and legislation aimed at tackling Anti-Asian incidents, incidences are still occurring.

The largest federal response to this surge since the start of the pandemic has been Congress's COVID-19 Hate Crimes Act. This legislation aims to improve hate crime data collection, bolstering hate crime tracking by designating a Justice Department official to specifically review potential hate crime incidents, providing grants for regional law enforcement agencies to set up reporting hotlines, and offering training to police on how to handle hate crime responses.

While these many attempts at addressing this surge in anti-Asian hate crimes have aimed at helping the reporting and aftermath of these incidents, this report shows that these legislations are overlooking prevention. Hate crime laws have important symbolic meanings. They send a message to two groups: they send it to the perpetrator, informing him that our community will not tolerate his intolerance. And then at the same time, they send a message to potential victims that they are welcome in our community.

In order to make communities safer, Stop AAPI Hate says that resources should go towards long-term community-center solutions education, culturally competent victim services, and prevention programs that get at the underlying causes of racial bias; encourage restorative justice, rather than punitive justice; break the cycle of violence because it holds perpetrators accountable by educating them; and support victims by giving them a voice and a choice. Stop

AAPI Hate has also called for investment in education, outreach, and "more holistic solutions to combating hate in schools and places of business."

Unfortunately, hate crimes against Asians have the media focusing on members of other minority groups as the perpetrators. A hate crime is defined by the FBI as a criminal offense motivated by bias against the victim's race, religion, disability, sexual orientation, ethnicity, gender, or gender identity. While historically whites have been responsible for most hate crimes reported to the FBI, the media has featured attacks on Asians being carried out by people of color.

Ultimately, the pandemic has exposed the cracks in America's society, bringing forth the layers of systemic racism and legacies of injustice that many Americans have chosen not to pay attention to until now. We must recognize the role that white supremacy has played in deliberately pitting one group against another.

In my interview with Kelly Hu which took place during the peak of the pandemic, we talked about the incidents of anti-Asian hate. I wanted her perspective and thoughts on this issue. Inevitably, the Black vs. Asian narrative came up since it was being pushed by mainstream media at the time.

Michael: Is there anything you would like to say that might help reduce some of the violence against Asians at this time?

Kelly: I think that highlighting people and situations that happened on social media really helps. I remember in the beginning of the pandemic when Asian people were getting attacked, I was posting things and get comments like, "That's not really happening," "An isolated incident," or "I'm married to an Asian woman, and I have a half-Asian daughter and I don't see any of that." Now, with video, they cannot deny it. They cannot pretend that it's not happening. By us putting that out there, showing that it is happening, that people are specifically targeting the Asian-American community, then they have to address it. I think forming organizations because they have been {able} to help people fight back, or people police the Chinatowns or Asian communities. I feel like we can't really rely on the police as much as we used to. We really have to start looking out for ourselves, and one another, in order to make a dent.

I wish I knew exactly how to stop it because I would absolutely form a whole campaign around it, but I don't know. I don't have the answers except that we need to build more solidarity and really get together and help the Black community as well, even though people are saying a lot of the crimes against the Asian community are coming from Black people. I think that we need to support their community as well if we expect them to support us. We have to be out there and be very bold and visual about it so that people see that we are in solidarity in order for us to also get understanding and solidarity from the Black and Hispanic, or any other minority communities. Or even the white community because we really do need that. We need everyone to come together and see what is going on with the Asian community and address it.

MICHAEL'S ADDENDUM

I firmly believe that the most effective way to reduce anti-Asian hate is to increase people's understanding of who we are as people. Again, that is why I have written this book. Most importantly, we need to engage the white community. An August 2020 poll by NPR/Ipsos found that white Americans have been the least engaged in trying to understand racial injustice issues in this country. The challenge is that Caucasians generally couldn't care less about social justice because it doesn't affect them.

So how do you reach people, who aren't interested in supporting movements like Black Lives Matter and who may even take offense at what these groups are protesting? You've got to show them what's in it for them. I learned this a long time ago when I started training real estate agents how to sell to Hispanics, African Americans, and Asians. The only way I was able to get them to attend and pay attention was to tell them that by learning how to be sensitive to other people's cultures they would increase their sales and make more money.

If you look at all the contributions of minorities to this country in medicine, commerce, and more, just imagine if more of us had a chance to flourish without the fetters of discrimination and violence. Let's start by educating everyone about the history of all groups in the country without leaving out the parts of which we might be ashamed.

Most Americans acknowledge institutional racism exists in the country. More than half, 58%, agree that there is systemic racism built into the American economy, government, and educational systems.

So, what actions can white people take to promote racial justice?

- Get to know More Asians. It's easier to fall victim to bigoted thinking and stereotypes when you don't personally know people from that community and are completely ignorant of their culture. While white people in America like to say that they support "diversity in the workplace," our society continues to be remarkably segregated.

- Try going to a Japanese, Chinese, Korean, Thai, Burmese, or other Asian restaurant and get to know the owner. Learn about them and their food, and you'll be surprised that what you thought was wrong. For instance, many popular dishes in Chinese, Japanese, Korean, and Indian restaurants are not found in restaurants in each of those countries.

- You can intentionally get to know more Asians. If you carpool, look for one to share the ride with. You'll be surprised by what you can learn and how you can bond during a commute to work. If your workplace has communal seating, deliberately join a group of Asians for lunch—first listen, then share. At meetings, get into the habit of sitting next to someone you don't know well, especially an Asian. They're often quiet and reluctant to open up, so break the ice by asking them where they went to school. You'll be surprised how just a small bit of initiative can make a big difference.

- Try asking an Asian friend or colleague about the hot topics of the day, including their feelings about anti-Asian hate. Share your feelings about it and Black Lives Matter as well.

- Join the Asian diversity committee at work. If there isn't one, help to start one. You'll likely be remembered because you'll probably be the only non-Asian in the group.

- Talk to your kids about race and Asians. Try discussing some of the little-known facts in Asian American history in this book. It's crucial that kids begin to learn about issues of race and equity early (in an age-appropriate manner) so they can begin to develop their own awareness of injustice.

- If you're in a leadership position in your organization mentor an Asian. There doesn't need to be a formal mentoring program. Find a young Asian in your organization *who* shows promise and takes them under your wing. Also, encourage your peers in senior ranks to do the same. Many Asians believe that, if they just work hard, leaders will automatically select them for mentoring rather than being proactive and asking for your help.

- Work with your Human Resources department to encourage them to develop objective selection processes. Subjectivity in hiring often weeds out people of color before they get a fair chance. Too often when selection processes or other decisions are made without clear-cut objective criteria, people of color end up getting the short end of the stick. Indeed, unconscious bias often encourages decision-makers to prefer a candidate who is more like them. Asians are often less effusive about their levels of experience than other groups so often don't make the first round of interviews.

- Don't work for a company that isn't diverse. Many companies talk about their commitment to diversity, but their hiring numbers betray their reality. If you find yourself in an environment that isn't consistent with your values of racial justice and human rights, leave.

- Insist on diversity in leadership teams. Asians in America are the least likely of any ethnic group to be promoted to senior management positions. Despite representing almost 7% of the population and 12% of the professional workforce, when it comes to promotions to the top executive level, only 1.5% of Asians will make it, according to the Ascend Foundation which provides training and education for Asian professionals. Today, there's no excuse for leadership teams to have few or no Asians and other people of color. Once there is increased diversity, make sure there's real inclusion as well.

- Challenge your own stereotypical beliefs. Changing your behaviors and actions starts with changing your thoughts. When you first see an Asian do you automatically think they're smart, good at math, and technologically savvy? Think about the Asians you know and ask yourself if they all fit this stereotype.

- Speak up publicly. Microaggressions and inequities are pervasive in the workplace, and Asians are no exception. The sad fact is that most corporations do have a bit of a corporate caste system, and when those in positions of power stay silent, little changes. So, when you see something, say something.

- If you're a parent, arrange for cultural exchanges with schools in Asia. Go out of your way to make sure your kids include Asian children in their parties and sleepovers.

- Make sure that you have a diverse group of friends. Practice real friendship and intimacy by listening when people of color share their experiences and perspectives. Encourage Asians to share if they seem a bit shy. It's difficult because it can be extremely painful.

- Educate your children about how Asians in America have been treated and discriminated against since the 1800s. This will help them to understand that we are not all new immigrants and have been contributing to this country for over 150 years. They will know that we are made up of many different and varied cultures. They will understand that we are not so different.

White supremacy exists in every institution. We are each responsible for addressing it wherever we work, play, and worship. Be aware of it and ask people of color if they experience it. If not, why not? In addition to showing how discrimination and unequal opportunity harm people of color, it's important to explain how systemic biases affect all of us and prevent us from achieving our full potential as a country. We can never truly become a land of opportunity while we allow racial inequity to persist. Ensuring equal opportunity for all is in our shared economic and societal interest. In fact, eight in ten Americans believe that society functions better when all groups have an equal chance in life. While educating our youth is the most important step to ending anti-Asian hate, we need the support of white people.

TOUGH LOVE & SELF-SACRIFICE

In the whirlwind of doing, teaching, writing, and speaking that had been my life for fourteen years, I returned to broadcasting in 1999 to produce and host a national radio show called *Minding Your Business* about running a small business. I also started finishing my doctorate degree in business which I had started in 1993 because I thought that becoming the Dean of a university might have a greater impact on more students than just teaching. In 2000, I became the Chairman of the MBA program at John F. Kennedy University, and in 2001, Dean of their Business School. In my office, I had two large black-and-white framed photos of JFK and Martin Luther King, Jr. They reminded me every day that, no matter how tough the job got, I probably would not be in that position without the sacrifices those two great men had made.

It's true what they say that you never forget where you were when… It was a Friday, 10a.m., after my first class at Brett Harte Junior High School on November 22, 1963. I stepped out into the hallway, which was eerily silent. Kids were looking down, some in disbelief, and many girls were crying. "President Kennedy was shot in Dallas," my friend Earl told me. No one knew how badly he had been injured but just being shot was a shock to all of us. To us, he was invincible, and it made us all feel very vulnerable. An hour later, the word was being passed around that he had died. How could such a young, handsome, and charismatic person die? I wondered what would happen to his commitment to putting a man on the moon, and more importantly, to the civil rights movement that he supported? He had even interceded on Dr.

Martin Luther King's behalf when the civil rights leader was sentenced to hard labor for violating his probation by participating in a sit-in demonstration in Atlanta in 1960.

On Saturday, I watched on television as his coffin was carried on a horse-drawn caisson to the United States Capitol to lie in state. Lines of people in tears passed slowly by his coffin. The route was the reverse of his inaugural parade in 1961. I had watched him come triumphantly into the office and now he was leaving office and this life to the sound of muffled drums. On Monday, which had been declared a National Day of Mourning, my family and I watched the funeral on television without a word. What was there to say? We knew our world would never be the same. I was disconsolate that he was cut down along with my hopes for a better future. His agenda included limiting U.S. involvement in Vietnam. In 1963, he introduced the Civil Rights Act, and I resonated deeply with his description of the issue not just as a constitutional matter, but as a "moral issue." Not long ago, I visited his gravesite at Arlington National Cemetery in Virginia, where an eternal flame still burns. It was incredibly moving.

In 1968, I was in my senior year at Oakland High and trying to get good enough grades to graduate because I was so disinterested in what I was being taught. However, I was coming out of my shell and trying to get noticed. I would do things like come into the middle of class after faking an illness, so the girls would notice me, but in reality, everyone probably thought I was just sickly. On Thursday, April 4th, I took the bus home, turned on the TV, and saw reports that Dr. Martin Luther King, Jr., had been shot in Memphis, Tennessee. I was totally devastated and so angry. How could someone shoot another one of my heroes? Why would you kill a man who preached peace and non-violence? I went to my room, closed the door, and cried for over an hour. I felt such emptiness because that proud, gentle man whom I admired so much was gone; even though I knew that he was in constant danger. He had hinted that he might be killed in his "I've Been to the Mountaintop" speech, less than 24 hours before his assassination. On TV, I saw him say, "I've seen the Promised Land. I may not get there with you. But I want you to know tonight, that we, as a people, will get to the Promised Land." I thought he was just being melodramatic, but did he really know he would be killed? Nevertheless, after his assassination, my Black friends and I wondered if the civil rights movement would be able to continue.

By that point, I was firmly against the war in Vietnam. Earlier that year, I had watched Dr. King deliver his "Beyond Vietnam" speech on television, saying that the war effort was "taking the Black young men who had been crippled by our society and sending them eight thousand miles away to guarantee liberties in Southeast Asia which they had not found in southwest Georgia and East Harlem." The same was true for Asians in America. I very much wanted to meet Dr. King because I sensed he would understand my anger and frustration about the injustice we all experienced in this country. Many years later, when I was speaking in Atlanta, Georgia, I attended Sunday morning service at Ebenezer Baptist Church where Dr. King was baptized and ordained as a minister. I was warmly welcomed by the parishioners, many of whom had heard him preach there. I could still feel his loving presence in the room.

Then, on Wednesday, June 5th of 1968, we were decorating the school for senior graduation…Senator Robert F. Kennedy was running for president. I liked him, not only because he looked and sounded like his brother, but because he was also a staunch supporter of civil rights. As U.S. Attorney General, he prosecuted corrupt Southern electoral officials and answered late-night calls from Coretta Scott King about her husband's imprisonment for demonstrations in Alabama. He undertook the most energetic and persistent desegregation of the administration that Capitol Hill had ever experienced. He demanded that every area of government begin recruiting realistic levels of Black and nonwhite workers; even criticizing Vice President Johnson for his failure to desegregate his own office staff. On that morning, I arrived at school to learn that Senator Kennedy had been killed the night before. I was still numb from Dr. King's assassination just two months earlier, and now it seemed like the path to peaceful change was impossible. In less than five years, the three men I admired most were shot and killed. Were any of us safe?

A sense of desperation pervaded the country. I was filled with a sense of fear and foreboding. I thought about how the world might have changed had they lived. To my surprise, President Johnson got the Civil Rights Act and the Voting Rights Act passed, but minorities supported Kennedy because of his concern for poverty and equal employment opportunities. RFK's killing led to the election of Richard Nixon who, while opening diplomatic relations with China, also ordered secret B–52 bombings of North Vietnamese base camps in Cambodia to show them that he was willing to escalate the war. It was a difficult time for me to be optimistic about the future.

Those painful experiences taught me so much about commitment and self-sacrifice. Due to the fearless efforts of those three men, and countless others, I sat in the Dean's chair. The coincidence that my deanship was at John F. Kennedy University was never lost on me; almost every time I stepped into my office until 2004 when I left. There was so much more I wanted to accomplish.

Did I find fulfillment in this relentless drive to achieve? Was this compulsion to achieve more innate, or instilled in me? Probably both since we are products of nature and nurture. Since childhood, I have been driven by the desire to earn my parents' praise, especially my father's—this, coupled with my desire to be seen as an equal to white Americans, has fueled my ambition throughout my life. Every time I reach a benchmark, I set for myself, I raise the next one much higher, seeing every achievement as a part of my American dream.

Like most Chinese Americans of my generation, I am a product of "tough love." But that wasn't just how my parents raised my brother and me. When I was growing up, I never heard them say, "I love you" to each other. My Asian friends had the same experience. Of course, I intuitively knew that my parents loved me and that each culture has a different way of expressing affection.

Anthropologist and cross-cultural researcher, Edward T. Hall, who created the field of intercultural communications in 1959, spoke about "high-context" cultures and "low-context" cultures.[49] Context refers to the unspoken information around what is said, or not said, in words, for example, the setting and the relationship between the parties. According to Hall, in high-context cultures like China, Japan, France, Spain, and Brazil, actions speak louder than words, and more is implied than overtly stated. You are expected to understand that you are loved by the care and support you receive from your parents. Nothing needs to be said. However, in low-context cultures such as the United States, Australia, and the United Kingdom, the setting and relationships are not as important, so thoughts and feelings need to be explicitly expressed. In the West, we say, "I love you," so much in cards and songs that it almost loses its meaning.

While one type of culture is not better than the other, they are certainly very different. Their differences are emphasized in multicultural environments, where they are observed side by side. I was surrounded by white friends, whose low-context-culture parents said, "I love you," all the time, even when they said "goodbye." It made me wonder why my folks didn't say it to me. I didn't understand that one of the most obvious ways my high-context-culture parents expressed their love was by working hard every day to provide for us. Years later, I realized that food was one way that Asian parents communicate love to their children. After I moved out of their house, my parents would always prepare my favorite meal, steamed fish, and rice, whenever I went to visit. I regret not realizing earlier in life how many times they had communicated that they cared about me without uttering the "three magic words."

As for how they expressed their love for each other, their relationship dynamics changed during the year when I was in Hawaii and my brother was enrolled at the Moody Bible Institute in Chicago. As empty nesters, they were alone with each other for the first time in decades. When

---

[49] E. Hall, *The Silent Language*. Doubleday, 1959.

I returned from Hawaii, I stayed on their couch for a couple of weeks until I got resettled in the San Francisco Bay Area. Well, I thought my parents had been abducted by aliens and replaced by two white people who looked like them! They were no longer the serious, sullen couple who had raised me; they were much more light-hearted creatures that laughed a lot and made silly jokes with each other. That was the first time that my father hugged me and that I saw him being affectionate with my mother.

It was as if a huge weight had been lifted off their shoulders and, looking back, it had. No longer burdened with the duty of raising children, they could finally enjoy each other's company, which they seemed to be doing to the fullest. I began to see that meeting expectations, as an Asian in America, is not just tough on children; it also takes its toll on parents. However, I didn't fully appreciate that until I had to make an extremely "tough love" decision in my own life.

I didn't have a real girlfriend, or even gotten past "first base" with a girl until I got to San Francisco State University in 1972 at the age of 22. With time, my confidence grew because I had become a successful television producer, who was able to convince famous and difficult-to-reach personalities to be on our show. I felt much more attractive to women because of my status and increased communication skills. I discovered that all they wanted was to be understood, so I honed my listening skills to a very fine edge. Realizing that the key to building any relationship was listening to the other person and discovering their needs also gave me insight to successful selling.

Despite my listening skills and attentiveness, unlike meeting my clients' needs, unfortunately, the only way I knew how to relate to women was physically. This resulted in many short-term and unsatisfying relationships. For me, sex became synonymous with emotional intimacy, which it obviously is not.

In 1977, I met a woman named Rhoda, and we began dating on and off. She had a wonderful family, and we enjoyed each other's company. However, in 1979, I met the love of my life, Lorraine. She was a gorgeous, intelligent woman who worked in the advertising department of the newspaper where we promoted our real estate open houses. For one year, I was in absolute heaven, and we made plans to wed. One day over dinner, Lorraine handed me back the engagement ring I had given her and told me she couldn't marry me because she had been diagnosed with leukemia. She explained that it is a cancer of the blood cells and that the survival rate, at that time, was less than 30%. I insisted that I wanted to spend whatever time she had with her, but she said she didn't have the energy to fight the disease and have a relationship with me at the same time.

Out of desperation and grief, I restarted my relationship with Rhoda but, in 1985, it became clear that we couldn't live together. We had very different outlooks on life. As I was about to break it off for good, she told me that she was pregnant and wanted to keep the baby. I admit that I had mixed feelings because I was in the middle of a very promising career and had already decided that the relationship was not right for me. To make matters worse, not two weeks after Rhoda's news, Lorraine called and said, "Guess what? I'm cured!" Apparently, if you survive leukemia for five years the doctors say you can live a normal life.

What a dilemma! Do I abandon my child to be with the woman that I loved with all my heart, or do my duty and raise my child? I explained the situation to Lorraine, and she said that she wanted an answer in two weeks because, after five years, she wanted to resume her life. Those were the longest two weeks of my life, during which I agonized every day about what to do. Eventually, I decided to stay with Rhoda and the baby because I was brought up with Confucian values, meaning that family always comes first, and my happiness was second-ary. Whether an Asian is born in the U.S. or outside does not seem to have a significant impact on the priority placed on parenthood. Asian immigrants and U.S.-born Asians are equally likely to say that being a good parent is one of the most important things in their lives.

I certainly felt this pressure when my son Christopher was born in 1985. Even though I was trying to cobble together a decent living after being blacklisted from television, teaching part-time and doing real estate, I devoted as much time as I could to him. Rhoda and I stayed together for five years. After we went our separate ways, I spent every weekend with our son until he went off to college.

My biggest mistake as a parent was thinking that spending time with Christopher was the same thing as being present with him. Every weekend, we did things like going to a ballgame, but I would read the newspaper at the same time. Or we would watch TV together, while I worked on my computer, multitasking to make the most of the time that I felt I had before I became debilitated. I am always in pain of some sort, despite the no-red-meat diet, exercise, and SAM-e supplements. Since I was diagnosed with spinal arthritis in 1973, physical discomfort is a constant reminder that I could become crippled at any time. I'm dictating this manuscript because my fingers are stiff. I have had to give up Bikram Yoga after twenty years because my back hurts afterward for days; I'm afraid the pain won't stop. I used to lift weights three days a week, but now my elbows and shoulders hurt. I also have arthritis in my knees, so I don't do much hiking that I used to love. However, I still find time to walk and do whatever exercise my body will allow these days.

Instead of hindering me, pain seems to drive me to be productive and creative. While I multitasked during my time with my son, I didn't realize how much he felt ignored until he started lashing out as a teenager and, by then the damage to our relationship had already been done. While I felt that spending time with him demonstrated my love, I think he saw our time together as me doing my Asian duty as a parent and little more. I learned that "time together" is not the same as "quality time." In hindsight, the moments I treasure most were sitting on his bed on Sunday mornings, taking turns reading comics to each other. I tried to be the opposite of my parents, and like a typical low-context-culture American parent, I always told him I loved him and hugged him every time I saw him, but I didn't understand that he saw my actions as a contradiction to that.

Today, Christopher is a very fine and smart young man. Our relationship is one of mutual respect and love, but we're still working on it.

If there is one thing I regret in life, it would be how I squandered my time with him. Yes, I was worried about how little time I might have to make my mark on the world, but I've learned that the true legacy we leave is our children, not our careers. Unfortunately, now I find myself constantly calling him to see when we can get together; the tables have turned. It reminds me of the 1974 song "Cat's in the Cradle" by Harry Chapin about the young boy who's always pleading for his father's attention, but he's too busy. Later in life the boy gets even by being too busy for his father.

If I were to give advice to parents, I would urge them to focus all their love and attention on their children because they grow so fast. Careers come and go, but your time with your kids is fleetingly short. I like to say, "When your kids are young, they think you're a god who knows everything. When they become teenagers, suddenly, they think you're an idiot who knows nothing. If you're lucky, in their twenties, they start to realize that you actually know something about life that can benefit them."

As for the love of my life, Lorraine eventually married. She had twin girls, and we'd seen each other a few times over the years, but it was never the same. There is an ancient Chinese proverb that says, "If you are at peace, you are living in the present." It always reminds me that, while memories are precious, there is no future in the past. I decided not to waste my time thinking about what could have been and focus, instead, on living my life to the fullest.

THE REBELLIOUS ONE

One day in 1976, my brother Daniel suddenly announced that he was going to become a missionary to Taiwan. My parents were so excited to have a man of God in the family! I wasn't so enthusiastic and told my parents that I believed he was just going there to look for a wife. They were horrified that I was so blasphemous because he said, "God called him." I wanted to ask if God had called collect but resisted the temptation! However, it seemed to me that he didn't care for Asian American girls who were very independent, as he tended to prefer more traditional women.

I also debated God's plan with my parents because my brother didn't speak Taiwanese. I told them, "It seems rather inefficient of the Almighty. Why wouldn't He just call on a missionary in Taiwan who already spoke the language and save the airfare?" Yes, I have always been a bit (or a lot) of a smart-ass. I even bet them that he would meet a girl on his first three-month mission. To his credit, Daniel mastered Fukienese, the main dialect of Taiwan, but as I predicted, he met a lovely girl named Flora. The next year, he returned to Taiwan for another three months, and afterward, they decided to get engaged.

Dan invited us to Taiwan for the wedding in January of 1979, but I declined, saying, "He'll be back soon enough." My parents were furious with me for missing such a momentous event and went without me. One of the highlights of the event was when my father had to give a speech welcoming my brother's wife into our family. Because he didn't speak the Fukienese dialect, he had to have a translator. As soon as he started his speech, the whole room broke out in uproarious laughter.

What he didn't realize is that while he, an Asian American, was speaking English, his red-haired Caucasian interpreter was speaking Fukienese! I understand that it was quite a sight.

A week after the marriage, they moved to Texas so Dan could continue his theological studies and, eventually Flora's whole family emigrated to the U.S. I didn't get any points for correctly predicting this outcome, however. In fact, I hadn't been scoring many points for many years, pursuing careers that my parents did not understand dating women of all ethnicities, hanging out with hippies, and participating in the civil rights movement in college, and more. I did ask my parents what happened to God's plan for Dan to become a missionary to Taiwan, and they said, "God changed His mind." I didn't dare respond, "If God knows the future how He can change His mind?" For a brief time in my youth, I attended seminary school, and it was questions like that which caused the school to ask me to leave and never return after one semester.

Perhaps the contrast between Daniel's more traditional Chinese mindset and my approach was pushing me to succeed and prove myself to my parents even more. Would my path have been easier had I conformed to my parents' expectations? Perhaps, but "I did it my way," as the famous Frank Sinatra song says, racing from achievement to achievement to make the most of my life and hoping to change how my parents saw me.

Now, as empty nesters, my parents shifted their own relationship dynamics, clearly enjoying being with each other. It was wonderful to see! Over the years, they also slowly began trusting me and treating me as an equal. They started to see me as more educated than they were, so they increasingly began to rely on my financial advice. I got them to invest in some stocks and buy a small rental property with me. It provided them with a good tax shelter and helped to increase the income that they had for retirement.

After fifty years at the Alameda Naval Air Station making custom parts for military airplanes, my father retired. He was extremely good with his hands so he became interested in origami and started selling his work at Chinese events like New Year's festivals just so he could buy more of the special paper he needed. He certainly wasn't doing it for the money, but—at some point—I realized that he didn't have a head for business, not even at the most basic level. One time, I watched his sales in San Francisco's Chinatown moving very briskly. When I looked closer, he was selling a cool Chinese origami warrior made of two, one-dollar bills for one dollar, so he was losing a dollar on each one. I watched in dismay as kids bought them and immediately unfolded them to pocket their profit. After I pointed out his mistake, he changed his price to two dollars, but that still didn't value his time.

Dad also actively attended local reunions of the Fourteenth Air Service Group (14th ASG), which consisted of nine units made up of Chinese American enlisted men with a combination of white and Chinese American commanding officers. These units had the largest concentration of Chinese American personnel in the American armed forces (about 10% of all the Chinese Americans in the military). The 14th ASG took shape in Venice, Florida, in 1944, but the move to create all-Chinese-American units had begun earlier. In November 1942, Lieutenant Sing Y. Yee of the 859th Signal Service Company in Springfield, Illinois, received permission to recruit other Chinese Americans to serve in China in support of General Claire Chennault's "Flying Tigers" in the China-Burma-India Theater (CBI). They came to fame by using their P-40 Warhawks painted with sharks' teeth to beat the Japanese, against superior odds, and kept the Burma Road open to the Allies who used it to transport material to China. My father volunteered for this group after he got bored sitting around at a base on the West Coast. This is where he learned to repair aircraft, which is what he continued to do after the war for the Alameda Naval Air Station.

My mother was a wonderful party planner who loved organizing family reunions. She enjoyed studying her family history, putting together our family tree, and tracing her lineage back to her great-grandmother, Jenny Kwok, who came with her husband from China in 1868. They landed in Monterey, California, where they worked in the fishing and canning industries. When we attended celebrations of the Chinese in Monterey, I learned about the area's first Chinese inhabitants, who set up camp in 1851 at Point Lobos. Upon discovering the rich bounty of

Monterey Bay, these experienced fishermen established additional settlements at Pescadero and Point Alones, near what is today Cannery Row's bustling tourism center. According to the Monterey County Historical Society, "By 1853, there were some 500 to 600 Chinese fishermen working the deep waters off Monterey. The Chinese community had become well enough established that Cabrillo Point—the site of today's Hopkins Marine Station north of Cannery Row—became known as 'China Point.' These skilled Chinese seamen launched the first commercial fishing industry in Monterey, taking first abalone and later other varieties of fish, including cod, halibut, flounder, yellowtail, sardines, squid, and shark, as well as oysters and mussels from the bay waters."[50]

By 1900, 200-800 pounds of fresh catch were sent daily to the fishmongers on Clay Street in San Francisco. The Chinese also produced dried fish, abalone meats, and shark fins. Some of this dried product found its way to the mines of the Sierra Nevada Mountains, but much of it was destined for shipment to the immigrants' home province of Canton, China. The Chinese fishermen were so successful that serious conflict developed with Italian American fishermen, who began to work the waters of Monterey Bay in the later 1800s, contributing to the tension and prejudice against Monterey's Chinese fishing community.

An impressive sight in those early days of Cannery Row was the arrival of large, ocean-going Chinese junks with their massive triangular sails. They would anchor off China Point to unload Oriental goods for the local Chinese, and then load dried squid —a sought-after food staple and fertilizer in China. A visitor to the area in 1879, Robert Louis Stevenson wrote, "The boats that ride in the haven are of strange and outlandish design; and, if you walk into the hamlet, you will behold costumes and faces that are unfamiliar to the memory. The joss stick (incense) burns, the opium pipe is smoked; the floors are strewn with strips of colored paper—prayers, you would say that somehow missed their destination—and a man guiding his

---

[50] J. Kemp, "Chinese Start Monterey Fishing Industry," *Cannery Row Historic Newspaper*, 1995 Winter/Spring.

upright pencil from right to left across the sheet, writes home the news of Monterey to the Celestial Empire."[51] Stevenson's fascination with the Chinese was similar to many Americans' inexperience with all things Asian. Some 150 years later, when I read his vivid description, I could imagine my great-great grandparents going about their daily lives in Monterey.

My parents flew regularly from Oakland to Toronto, Canada, to visit my brother, who had become the Assistant Pastor of a Chinese Church there. I was very happy to see them traveling and being out of the house. Unfortunately, after returning from one of these trips, my father had his first heart attack. He had severely blocked arteries and was given a triple bypass. Despite the fact that he was now healthier than ever, he never wanted to travel again, perhaps out of fear that he might suffer another heart attack away from home. My philosophy is to travel as long as I can and if I die during some foreign adventure who cares. My mother did fly up to see my brother once or twice, but she didn't want to leave my father alone. She wanted to see the world, at least on cruise ships, where the rigors of travel are minimized. But she always had an excuse like not being able to find a compatible roommate or the high cost, so she never realized her dream.

Towards the end of their lives, I would visit them at least once a week and always take them to one of their favorite Chinese restaurants. I think my paying for the meals every time was a sign that I was now a responsible adult. We would reminisce about what we were like growing up and the challenges my brother and I gave them. I was always the "rebellious one" and my brother was the "good one." We would laugh about how at twelve years old; I told my parents that I was not going on any more family vacations because it was just too stressful for us kids. My parents had to get up early and pack all the camping gear and then unpack it whenever we got to whatever god-forsaken place we were headed which made them tired and irritable. I told them to go on vacation by themselves, and I would look after my 9-year-old brother, which I did. I think they really enjoyed driving to places like Las Vegas and staying in cheap hotels without us. In

---

[51] R.L. Stevenson, *Across the Plains* (1892). Digitized by the Gutenberg Project.

the meantime, I would invite all the neighborhood kids to play hide and seek in our house. My brother and I would clean up the place before they came home, sometimes just in the nick of time.

In 2009, my mother was robbed at knifepoint by a young Black kid who wanted her purse. She refused to let go (probably because it contained her priceless coupon collection) until he finally knocked her down. She called the cops, and they caught the kid trying to use her credit cards. It turned out that he was the son of a Black Oakland police officer, and his father did everything he could to get him off. However, because she was one of the few people to show up in court to testify, he was convicted and hopefully learned his lesson. No one intimidated my mom!

At the end of 2009, she fractured her leg tripping over an uneven spot in the sidewalk and spent three months in skilled nursing. After that, she went to an assisted living facility because she had to use a wheelchair. My father went to live with her to keep her company. On June 10th of 2010, they found my father, John Git Wong, dead of a heart attack at age 87. My mother was always a very stoic person, and even then, I never saw her shed a tear, but I know she missed him. She just kept herself busy as usual with the funeral arrangements.

My mom stayed at the assisted living facility for two more years but always talked about going home. The staff and I kept insisting that it wasn't safe for her there because there were steps going into the house and the doorways were too narrow for a wheelchair. Finally, in 2012, she got her way and returned to her house in Oakland, using a walker to get around. A month later, she was found on the floor, having fallen, and broken her hip again. After another stint in skilled nursing, she was back in assisted living.

During the last five years of my mother's life, I took over all her finances. She would save all the bills in a pile, and I would write out the checks and have her sign them. While she was away, I maintained the home to let her have the hope of returning. Unfortunately, she was never able to go home again.

In June of 2013 she went into hospice care when all her organs began to fail at age 89. Yet, she hung on for three weeks, saying goodbye to friends and family. I slept on the floor and administered morphine nightly as needed, telling her that it was okay to let life go, but she was a very tough old bird and wouldn't go until she felt it was time. Unfortunately, I was at work when she passed away. The caretaker present said that when my mom, Ruth Marian Wong, took her last breath on July 16th of 2013, she felt a presence swirl around the room several times. Then suddenly, zoom, it went out the door, which slammed closed with a bang. I guess that was my mother's way of making one last big exit!

Looking back, I am certain my parents were proud of me but would always talk about my brother first because they clearly understood what he did for a living and regarded being a minister as a sacred calling. They didn't really understand what I did as a real estate broker, television and film producer, and professional speaker even though they had seen me address many Asian groups. I had invited them to the opening of the two films I had worked on, and I don't think they comprehended the role I had played in getting them produced. I always gave them copies of my books, but they had no idea of how much work went into writing one. After they died, and I went to clean up their house, my books looked like they hadn't been opened. It was very frustrating for me, because you always want the respect of your parents, particularly if you are Asian. Fortunately, at some point, I think they just stopped worrying about me and focused all their concern on my brother. They saw me as more independent than him and worried more about his financial future as a minister than about mine. While he was doing quite well as a teacher and pastor at a Christian university in Toronto, I guess you never stop thinking of your kids as children.

I still miss my parents every day and often catch myself about to call their phone number to see how they're doing. Thanks, Mom, and Dad, for the strength and pride in our culture that you've given me. I trust you're happy with the legacy I'm leaving, but I know it will never be enough…

THE BIG SPINOFF

"We have a job for you to speak at a major oil company," said the owner of one of the speakers' bureaus that often hired me. I was really excited because it was not often that I got to speak at a Fortune 100 company with its huge training budget. And then he added, "Well, it's for the Asian Employee Network within the corporation, so they have a budget that's only 10% of your normal fee."

At the time, in 2001, I was getting paid $15,000 for a keynote, so this was quite a disappointment. But the bureau owner was very persuasive, "We'd like you to do this as a favor to us because we'd like to develop a relationship with this company, and we're sure you'd like to develop a relationship with them as well. Besides, their world headquarters is just up the road from you. You could drive there and be back within two hours." I reluctantly agreed, saying, "I'll do it but there better be spinoff" —this is when you speak for one group at a large company, and later other divisions book you for talks. Some speakers I knew had made entire careers working for just one big organization.

So, I called the president of the employee network, whose name was Miriam, for the details of the program. It was to be a 90-minute keynote about the challenges and opportunities for Asians in the workplace. On the day of the presentation, I met Miriam, a very attractive Filipino woman, who escorted me through security to a huge room for about 300 people. "Do you think it will fill up?" I asked. I had spoken before to minority networks where they planned for 50 people and only 20 showed up. She replied that it would probably be standing room only, explaining that the president of the company would be giving the opening address. To say that I was taken by surprise would be an understatement.

I have never felt such pressure in my life! I had spoken over 1,000 times to audiences large and small around the world, but it took every bit of that experience to calm my nerves. When it was time for me to take the stage, I decided to focus my attention on a friendly face, Miriam's. I began and they laughed hysterically when I said that I was a fifth-generation Chinese American who spoke Spanish, not Chinese. Then I related the challenges I had faced in my life, as an Asian, and how I had overcome them. I explained how I had learned to speak up in meetings by asking good questions and to take credit for my work despite that my mother always told me, "Never pat yourself on the back." Then I advised them that if they didn't claim credit for their work, others would be happy to take it. Some even shed a few tears when I mentioned my challenges in only being able to date Chinese girls in high school and nodded in agreement when I said that people assume that all Asians are alike.

For a professional speaker, that presentation was one of those extraordinary moments, when it feels like you have the audience in the palm of your hand. Although it was certainly not the first or last time, I received such a terrific response from the crowd, over the years, I realized that I love speaking to Asian audiences, because they can relate to my experiences so easily. In particular, I enjoy connecting with Asian Americans who, like me, feel caught between two worlds, never quite fitting into either.

I received a very long, standing ovation and was invited to lunch by the event organizers. I ended up being seated next to Miriam, and we got to talking. It turned out that we were both divorced, so I asked her out on a date. It took a few months because her father was ill, but eventually, we had dinner in San Francisco—a magical three hours that absolutely flew by.

I had never felt so comfortable with anyone in a long time. Despite how we met, I didn't feel like I had to act the part of the successful professional speaker and could be myself with all my flaws and weaknesses.

I had no idea how much pressure I was feeling, trying to find acceptance in the American world as well as in the Asian world, until I didn't have to worry about it for a few hours.

In the coming weeks, as I reflected on how I felt spending time with Miriam, certain things about my past romantic relationships began to come more clearly into focus. For example, I recalled how—after seven years in a relationship with a white woman whom I considered my ideal mate—I was unhappier than I had ever been in my life. Of course, the reason was not solely because she was white and I was Chinese. There were challenges in the relationship that were beyond our control. But I began to ask myself some uncomfortable questions: Why did I stay in that relationship for so long? Did I see that relationship as some sort of social validation as an American?

As I continued my soul-searching, I realized that any success I achieved placated my insecurities only temporarily. I saw how the constant conflict between the external images we project, and how we really feel inside, inevitably takes its toll. What also became crystallized in my mind was that the only thing that matters is not how a partner makes you "look" to other people, but how they make you feel. And Miriam made me feel comfortable being myself for the first time in my life. Her son, Ryan, was only five years old but he was very active, and I was determined to spend more quality time with him than I did with my son Chris.

I guess that marrying a woman who wasn't Chinese had always been a very real possibility for me. My parents certainly were not in favor of that and, much to their chagrin, my first serious girlfriend was Japanese. Even though I was only in high school, my mother's warning to me as a teenager "never bring a Japanese girl into this house" still rang in my ears. Except I wasn't in their house anymore, so I was able to make choices without their approval. Unlike my brother Daniel, who genuinely wanted a more traditional life, I felt free to explore outside the cultural norms. Chinese men tend not to intermarry much because they feel more comfortable being able to share their language, foods, and beliefs. I've noticed that minorities, in general, tend to gravitate toward people who understand and have experienced similar kinds of discrimination. I never had any intention of settling down with the culturally appropriate person just to meet family expectations. Yes, I did envision myself getting married, especially when I met my first real love, Lorraine. While I still believe we would have had a great life together, that was not in the script. Was the fact that she was a second-generation Chinese American a factor in how well we got along? I am not sure, but the cultural commonalities certainly made things easier.

At any point in my life, had you asked me whom I might end up with as a life partner, the last ethnicity I would have said was Filipino. Growing up, my parents always told me to avoid them, saying that they were "lazy and wasted their time singing and dancing all day." When I met Miriam, I didn't know much about Filipinos, except that Chinese and Filipinos are different in many ways. Filipinos tend to be Catholics while many Chinese are Buddhists or Presbyterians. Some Filipino foods like *pancit, Karkare*, and lumpia are similar to Chinese *chow mein*, ox tail soup, and egg rolls respectively, but on the whole, the cuisines are quite different. In Chinese families, the parents are the heads of the household, but in Filipino families, the children provide for their parents the moment they start working. They become the financial heads of their family and even support relatives in need. However, both cultures are similar in the importance they place on family and maintaining traditions.

In terms of personality, Filipinos tend to be vivacious and outgoing. They do love singing and dancing but obviously not all the time! All this is the polar opposite of reserved Chinese people. For that reason, Filipinos used to make me feel a bit uncomfortable, but Miriam seemed to be the perfect counterbalance for me. In time, through our relationship, I learned more about Filipino culture and history. While I knew that Filipinos are heavily influenced by Spanish culture, I didn't know that the Philippines were named after King Philip II of Spain. The Philipines were occupied by Spain for over 300 years, and locals often intermarried with Spaniards, which is why many have Spanish surnames like Cruz and Lopez, while others have Filipino surnames like Balindong and Manalo.

Many people don't know that the Philippines are an archipelago of some 7,000 islands, which were probably connected to mainland Asia at one time. Believed to be of Asian descent, from the 10th century AD onward, Filipinos began trading with Chinese and Arab merchants. A major cultural and trade crossroads, the archipelago was comprised of hundreds of territories and tribal groups with no single national identity. After Ferdinand Magellan claimed it for Spain in 1521, the Spanish conquistadors created a feudal system of government where Spaniards owned vast estates worked by the Filipinos. Friars converted the Filipinos to Catholicism. Today, the Philippines have the third-largest Catholic population in the world.

After escaping forced labor and enslavement during the Spanish galleon trade, Filipinos established their first recorded North American settlement in St. Malo, Louisiana, in 1763. Later, mariners, adventurers, and domestics migrated to the West Coast, Hawaii, and Alaska to work in the fishing and whaling industries.

During the Spanish-American War (1898), the United States paid Spain $20 million to annex the archipelago. Filipinos fought back and declared the Philippines independent on June 12, 1889. But, on August 13, Spanish Gov. Fermín Jáudenes secretly arranged surrender to the USA. This resulted in the Philippine-American War (1899-1906) during which 20,000 Filipino revolutionaries and 4,200 American troops died in combat, while upward of 200,000 Filipino civilians starved to death, died of disease, or were killed. By 1902, the Roosevelt administration had declared victory.[52]

U.S. Philippine Commissioner William H. Taft deemed Filipinos as "ignorant, superstitious, and credulous in remarkable degree," so the U.S. aimed to Americanize every aspect of life on the islands but never

---

[52] *Encyclopaedia Britannica*, 15th ed. (2018), s.v. "Philippine-American War."

quite succeeded. Over time, they began treating the Philippines more as a trading partner than a colony.

Mass Filipino migration to the U.S. began during the colonial period. Demand for labor in Hawaii and California attracted thousands of immigrants, known as Sakadas (plantation workers), who replaced the Japanese. Sakadas came as American Nationals but were not given full citizenship rights and were the first Filipino Americans to experience discrimination. Later, Filipino immigrants (known as Pinoys) suffered extensive racial discrimination resulting from immigration policies, oppressive farm management, and anti-miscegenation laws that banned interracial marriage and, in some cases, sex between members of different racial groups. Another group, the Pensionados were privileged young men who came to the U.S. in the early 1900s as government-sponsored scholars. They were meant to return to the Philippines to administer the colonial government, but some remained.

During the Great Depression, in 1932, Congress voted to phase in Philippine independence over 10 years to free the U.S. from the financial liability of the islands. In 1934, the Tydings-McDuffie Act was passed to limit Filipino migration to 50 persons per year but was later offset by the U.S. Navy's recruitment of Filipino Americans during WWII. After the Japanese invasion and occupation of the Philippines in 1941, 1,000,000 civilians and military personnel died. After Japan's surrender, the U.S. recognized the Republic of the Philippines in 1946. Between 1935-1965, more Filipinos immigrated to the U.S.—war brides, veterans, students, and professionals, mostly in the healthcare field.

The 1965 Immigration and Nationality Act liberalized immigration laws, so in the mid-1970s, economic and political refugees from the authoritarian Marcos regime and short-stay visitors were added to the Filipino American community. In 1986, the People Power movement ousted Pres. Ferdinand Marcos, who had come into power in 1965, and restored democracy to the Philippines. A few years later, the 1990 amendment to the Immigration and Naturalization Act brought an influx of Filipino-born WWII, Vietnam War, and Korean War veterans.

From 2000 to 2019, Filipino Americans grew from 2.4 million to 4.2 million people, making them the third-largest Asian American group in the U.S.

One of those immigrants who arrived in San Francisco was Miriam, at age 18. She immediately started looking for work as a secretary for which she had trained in the Philippines. She failed her first typing test miserably because she was used to manual typewriters, and everyone here was using the high-tech IBM Selectric. Determined to master the new technology, she went on any job interview she could find that required a typing test just to practice! Before long, she was much faster than average and felt confident enough to apply at a major oil company, as suggested by her sister who worked in their research department. She was accepted into the typing pool in their San Francisco office. Wanting to accomplish more, she obtained her bachelor's degree while working full-time. She then attended one of Arizona State University's first online hybrid MBA programs and earned her master's degree. Over the years, Miriam worked in procurement, environmental, legal, and human resources; eventually becoming a manager of the global diversity department where she stayed until her retirement.

After three years of dating, we got married in 2004. I sold her condo and my small house, and we bought a large home in San Ramon, CA, where we raised her son, Ryan. At the time, my son, Chris, was just graduating from my old alma mater, San Francisco State University, with a degree in finance and moved into a rented home in the Bay Area.

I was always a bit jealous of Ryan because, unlike me, he was very outgoing and made friends easily. Today, he has grown into a very caring and supportive young man who works for a social media company.

Like me, Miriam is very Americanized, so we used that commonality to bridge our different cultures. For me, it was a great help that her mother was so welcoming, as were the rest of her family, all eight brothers and sisters. Chinese parents tend to be much more aloof, but Miriam got used to it. My parents were initially against the marriage because traditional Chinese culture dictates that you only marry another Chinese.

However, I had already softened them up by dating all kinds of races, including a Black woman. Eventually, they fully accepted Miriam and treated her like the daughter they never had. She was fully involved in their lives and care, even at the end.

It turns out that Filipinos can be the perfect complement for some workaholic Chinese people like me. While also driven to succeed at everything she does, Miriam makes sure that we always take time off to enjoy life, and she makes me laugh every single day. What a great example of the power of diversity even within the Asian culture!

As for my hopes for a big spinoff at the big oil company, it turned out that if you're romantically involved with a corporation employee you cannot be hired in any capacity, as that would be considered a conflict of interest. Dating and eventually marrying Miriam precluded me from getting other paid speaking gigs there, but she was the best possible spinoff I could have ever asked for!

MISCEGENATION AND MARRIAGEABILITY

The earliest interracial marriages between Chinese and foreigners were between Chinese diplomatic envoys and students studying abroad. One of the first to do this was Arcadio Huang. Born in Fujian province in 1679, Huang traveled to France, where he worked on a Chinese French dictionary and helped European scholars make huge advancements in the understanding of the Chinese language and culture. In 1713, he married a Parisian woman named Marie-Claude Regnier despite that many considered such relationships unthinkable.

When Asians began arriving in significant numbers in the U.S., plays like George Ade's *The Sultan of Sulu* (1902), Joseph Jarrow's *The Queen of Chinatown* (1899), and David Belasco's *Madame Butterfly* (1900) expressed American anxiety about interracial interactions and racial contamination, especially with Asians. "Miscegenation," a term coined in 1863, refers to the interbreeding of different races. Anti-miscegenation laws were introduced in North America in the late 17th century and remained in many states until 1967, until a case, quite literally, of loving. The Lovings' marriage was deemed illegal because Mildred was Black and Native American and Richard was white. The ACLU took their case to the Supreme Court and won on June 12, 1967. Chief Justice Earl Warren wrote in the decision, "The freedom to marry, or not marry, a person of another race resides with the individual, and cannot be infringed by the State." Since then, the number of such marriages has increased from 3% to 19% in 2019. Most importantly, public approval of interracial marriage rose from around 5% in the 1950s to 94% in 2021.

Marriageability, like attractiveness, is "socially constructed" according to social scientists, meaning that its definition is historically specific and changes with context. We, Asian Americans, are the perfect example of this: we went from being considered filthy and unassimilable in this country to be America's most marriageable minority group. This underlines the point that whom one chooses to date and marry is the result of social perceptions, opportunities, and constraints.

At present, Asians are at the lead in the U.S. when it comes to interracial marriages, with just over one-third (36%) of newlywed Asian American women who had a spouse of a different race or ethnicity, compared with 21% of newlywed Asian men in 2015.[53] High rates of intermarriage, especially Asian women with white men, have been viewed as an indicator that Asian Americans are successfully "assimilating," signaling acceptance by the white majority, and their own desire to become part of the white mainstream.

Marriageability is also socially constructed by gender. Asian women intermarry at twice the rate of Asian men, and studies of on-line dating reveal that while Asian women are highly preferred among males across racial groups, Asian men are the least preferred of all men among women. In my adolescence, when I desperately wanted a girlfriend and there were not enough Asian girls in my school, I used to resent Asian women who dated or married white men, because I felt they were giving up their culture and giving into the white man's "Asian fetish."

As we have seen in previous chapters, in recent times, movies and television seem to be making an effort to portray Asian males as desirable romantic partners. Is this mandated in some way or a reflection of a shift in perspective? Whatever the case may be, it can only help.

---

[53] "Intermarriage in the U.S. 50 Years After Loving v. Virginia," *Pew Research Center* (2017).

THE BAMBOO CEILING

n the talk I gave to the Asian Employee Network that led to meeting Miriam, I shared some of my own experiences with the "bamboo ceiling." This term was popularized by Jane Hyun's in her 2006 book, *Breaking the Bamboo Ceiling: Career Strategies for Asians.* As defined by Hyun, it is a combination of individual, cultural, and organizational factors that impede Asian Americans' career progress; subjective reasons like "lack of leadership potential" and "lack of communication skills" that cannot be explained by job performance or qualifications.

Asians are the most highly educated group in the U.S. They were behind 19% of high-impact patents and have won one-out-of-ten Nobel Prizes in physics and chemistry since 1980. Yet, according to the Equal Employment Opportunity Commission, they are the least likely group to be promoted to management and executive positions. Among the nation's top companies, one in every forty-five white men and one in every sixty white women are executives. For Asian managers and professionals, only one in every ninety-six men, and one in every one hundred and twenty-four women hold a top job. Many statistics and studies substantiate the existence of the bamboo ceiling, but a distinction must be made between East Asians and South Asians. Of the sixteen Asian CEOs in the S&P 500 in 2017, only three were East Asian, whereas thirteen were South Asian. This pattern was consistent over the years and across companies in the S&P 1500. The discrepancy is even more striking considering that the United States East Asian population is about 1.6 x larger than the South Asian population. Since surveys indicate that motivation, education, and ambition are high and comparable in the two groups, the only plausible explanation for East Asians not being able to move to top-level positions is level of assertiveness.

Researchers found that East Asians were consistently less assertive than South Asians and whites.[54] This—combined with the prevalent belief that Chinese, Japanese, Koreans, and other East Asians don't possess typically American leadership skills like outspokenness, persuasion, and charisma—hold us back. We are generally thought of as quiet, submissive, and efficient worker bees. Our traditional values like deference to authority figures, respect for elders, self-effacement, and restraint create the false perception that we either have no interest in leadership or won't be good at it. Another reason for the dearth of Asians in leadership roles is the myth that we are the successful minority who don't need to be considered for promotions whereas others should be.

The bamboo ceiling extends to many fields other than business. In the U.S., people of East and South Asian descent are stereotyped as athletically inferior to other races. This has led to much discrimination in the recruitment of Asians for professional sports, with the exception of sports that require little to no physical contact like figure skating, skiing, or ping-pong. In politics, in 2022, twenty-one members of the 117th Congress (3.9% of the total membership) are of Asian, South Asian, or Pacific Islander ancestry. Nineteen of them (16 Democrats, 3 Republicans) serve in the House, and 2 (both Democrats) serve in the Senate.[55] In the legal profession, Asian Americans comprise 13% of associates at major law firms, but just 4% of equity partners which is the lowest ratio among minority groups.[56] Asian Americans are also underrepresented in university leadership positions. Asian Americans make up only 3.4 percent of executives and administrators in higher

[54] M. Somers, "A cultural clue to why East Asians are kept from US C-suites," *MIT Management Sloan School* (2021).
[55] "Membership of the 117th Congress: A Profile," *The Congressional Research Service*, (2022).
[56] K. Sloan, "More Asian Americans on the federal bench; progress lacking at Big Law," *Reuters*, December 25, 2022.

education, according to Education Department statistics, and just 1.5 percent of college presidents.[57]

I have bumped up against the bamboo ceiling many times, starting with my first career-track job in television. I thought that if I worked fourteen hours a day for seven days a week, I would be automatically recognized, but I kept getting passed over for promotions that went to white people with far fewer qualifications. Of course, one can argue that was in the 1970s, and being Asian in a white industry was extremely difficult, but the same thing kept happening two decades later in other fields.

In 1995, I was teaching television production at Diablo Valley College (DVC) and chairing the Broadcast Communications Arts Program. After building a class of thirty into a state-certificated program with three hundred students, I felt that I could have greater influence over more students as a Dean. To this end, I took a job as the Evening Supervisor at DVC that made me (under the direct supervision of the Dean of Students) responsible for 14,000 students and instructors. So, in addition to my other university duties, selling real estate, and speaking to real estate groups, I worked in this capacity from 6 p.m. to 10 p.m. every weekday evening. If nothing else, I can certainly brag that I was an incredible time manager!

In 1999, the Dean of Students became ill and was looking for a temporary replacement. Having met with her five nights a week for four years, I was the logical choice. We got along splendidly, and she trusted my judgment but gave the position to a white instructor. Since no one else was as qualified as I was, it became obvious that I was not considered because I was Asian. I went to Human Resources to start a discrimination complaint. My argument was that I was currently the acting Dean in the evening, and to prevent me from getting the full title, they brought in a white male instructor who had not done the job in years and had never expressed any interest in it until the Dean became sick, whereas I had always let her know of my aspirations. The

---

[57] J. Ono, "Why So Few Asians Are College Presidents," *Chronicle of Higher Education* (2013).

president of the college asked me to drop the complaint as a personal favor so I let it go. Realizing that my career at the college was over, I accepted a position as a part-time Chair of the bachelor's program at nearby John F. Kennedy University (JFKU). A year later, I was also given the chairmanship of the master's program.

In 2003, the Dean at JFKU was promoted, and I was named Acting Dean and demonstrated that I could create programs, increase enrollment, cut costs, and build good working relationships with the other deans, departments, and the president. To my surprise, the university opened the position to a national search, but I applied since I was, again, the logical choice. For the next six months, the hiring committee considered everyone from inside and outside the school except me. Finally, almost as an afterthought, I was given an interview. The last question they asked was how I felt the university was doing in accomplishing its diversity goals. I used their search process as an example of how minorities were often overlooked, even when the right candidate was under their noses. I explained that, according to the American Council on Education, only 1.5% of all college and university deans were Asian, a number substantially less than our percentage of the population. Having nothing to lose, I also explained how it felt to be treated as an "other," or outsider despite having been part of the university family for three years. While there were no minorities on the interview panel, there were several gay women who understood how unfair and insulting it was to me not to be seriously considered for the job I had been doing successfully for nearly a year. Eventually, I was officially named the Dean of the School of Management. I continued building the program and adding new specializations, including an international degree in management. I also oversaw the move of the campus to a new location, which was quite a task, but we got it done on time.

"The superior man is modest in his speech but exceeds in his actions." This quote of Confucius is key to understanding the Chinese perspective on hard work and self-promotion. It emphasizes proving oneself with actions, and not blowing one's own horn. Overt displays of individualism and boastfulness are repelling to the Chinese sensibility; but, in America if you don't claim what is yours, you will be overlooked. That's how it is for everyone in the workplace, but Asians also have to contend with the bamboo ceiling. The truth is that some of our noblest values as Asians do not 'translate' well in the American career landscape.

The bamboo ceiling is a nexus of factors like stereotypes, discrimination, and inaccurate perceptions, but the differences between the Asian and American cultural and value systems also play a part. Our modesty renders us invisible. Our reserved nature, which sometimes prevents us from speaking up and overtly taking charge, is seen as a lack of leadership. Our quiet reserve is misunderstood as the absence of an opinion or ideas. From an early age, Americans are taught to question teachers and challenge authority while Asians are taught the opposite. Our deference to superiors is often interpreted as a sign of weakness rather than respect. Many times, our hard work and diligence make us too valuable to promote or be moved laterally within the company. Remember that in my first TV job I became so fast at threading film projectors that I kept being assigned to the projection room instead of running the camera or audio during the news, which I would've preferred.

In my talks to Asian groups over the years, I have often touched on these issues. Some of the best advice I have given is, "Don't be like me!" In 2000, I had the opportunity to develop a six-week workshop on the bamboo ceiling when the Asian Business League of California asked me to put together a program called "The CEO of YOU" about how Asians can develop stronger leadership skills. Keenly aware that gender-specific stereotypes negatively impact Asian men and women differently, I decided to split the group along gender lines for half of every class, and then bring everyone back together to work on leadership. To facilitate the women's session, I brought on Kimi, a female Japanese American co-leader.

While all women can be stereotyped either as passive and docile or called out as "abrasive" or "bossy" in the workplace, gender, and race place Asian women in a unique predicament. If they assert themselves, men think of the evil Dragon Lady. Due to the tiger mom stereotype, not only are they seen as overly preoccupied with parenting rather than work, but also no one wants someone that harsh to be their boss. According to Margaret Chin, author of *Stuck: Why Asian Americans Don't Reach the Top of the Corporate Ladder*.[58] Asian women are also often hypersexualized and typecast as hyperfeminine. Being both people of color and women, they contend with both bamboo and glass ceilings. Yet, the 'Asian effect' is 3.7 times greater than the 'gender effect.' Asian American women can find themselves saddled with extra work, not being credited but held to higher standards, and plateaued despite many having high educational and career achievements. The women in the program shed light on additional deterrents, like not pursuing higher-level positions because they didn't want to earn more than their spouses. We asked them to talk to their significant other about how they would feel if they earned more money. It turned out that not one had a problem, even encouraging it, saying they would be glad to stay home with the kids. For South Asian Indian women, their responsibility for their in-laws also conflicts with their desire to advance professionally.

In the workplace, Asian men are often viewed as too data-driven, rigid, cold, calculating, and inscrutable. They are stereotyped as quiet, timid, and passive employees who won't stand up for themselves—ironic, since it is assumed that we are all born knowing karate and being tech-savvy, which makes us nerds, not team leaders! We are generally thought to be socially awkward, which implies we can't raise money or build working relationships. Last, but not least, we are stereotyped as being insensitive and disrespectful towards women thanks to popular movies like *The Joy Luck Club*. That's obviously not a good image for a leader in the world of #MeToo. All this in addition to other negative

---

[58] M. Chin, *Stuck: Why Asian Americans Don't Reach the Top of the Corporate Ladder,* (New York: NYU Press, 2020).

stereotypes; for example, that South Asian Indians and Pakistanis will work for free or low pay.

In the workshop, we explored how to break free from stereotypes and educate others without chastising them. We showed participants how to take credit for their achievements without bragging. We showed how sharing kudos with the team could be very effective, as group harmony is a very Asian trait. East Asians are strongly influenced by Confucianism, which is characterized by humility, conformity, and interpersonal harmony. Consider Western proverbs like "the squeaky wheel gets the grease," in contrast to Asian ones like "the nail that sticks out gets hammered down." This style works in East Asia where most company leaders and employees are Asian. South Asian cultures, on the contrary, encourage assertiveness in communication, as exemplified by the Indian tradition of debate. In India and Pakistan, it's not unusual to observe loud and animated conversations ending in a handshake or respectful bows.

I based the "CEO of YOU" program on the premise that it's much easier for Asians to become more assertive than to get the whole of corporate America to change; in other words, adapting to the work world as it is and slowly shifting the system from within. When I tried to convince casting directors to consider me for typically non-Asian roles, I got nowhere. It would have been easier for me to accept the typecasting with some modifications. So, in the workshop, we devoted a great deal of time to strengthening leadership skills, relationship building, agility, motivation, decision-making, conflict management, negotiations, and critical thinking. We also addressed how CEOs interact with their boards of directors, how employees can develop positive working relationships with the board, and some of the politics involved when working with a board. We brought guest Asian American managers and CEOs to talk about their experiences. The students were quite amazed to hear about all the challenges they had to overcome as minorities in the workplace.

A big part of the class was presentation skills training. One of the easiest ways to gain visibility in any company is to give confident and compelling presentations. Unfortunately, public speaking is difficult for most people, and even harder for Asians because we were taught to avoid the spotlight. However, once we provided our students with the basic structure of how to give a talk, it became much easier for them. We got them practicing from the first day and worked on it until they became comfortable with getting in front of groups and speaking extemporaneously.

We also provided a basic five-step formula for assertiveness to make sure the participants got what they wanted at work without being confrontational: 1) Judging a situation and being assertive only when it's appropriate; 2) The importance of standing up for yourself; 3) How to say "no" without feeling guilty; 4) Clearly expressing your wants, needs, and opinions; and 5) Maintaining self-control while being assertive.

Another major component of the program was strengthening networking skills. Since childhood, Asians are taught to be self-sufficient and not ask for help from anyone outside their family because that would be a sign of weakness. In Asia, even in their careers, people rely more on family than business contacts. Nepotism is common, and it's typical for several members of one family to work in the same organization. To succeed in American business, however, you need to network with colleagues as well as those in higher positions. We also explained the importance of getting a mentor, who will not only guide but also facilitate upward mobility within the company, and demonstrated how this can be done.

We addressed issues like diversity and inclusion. Most Americans believe that Asians are all the same, so we taught the group how to gently teach others the difference between Asian cultures. Of all demographic groups in the workplace, only 16% of Asian men and 20% of Asian women said they felt fully included at work. These percentages were significantly below the next lowest group, Black women, at 22%.[59] We made suggestions about how they can feel more included and explained that inclusion means feeling free to speak up, ask questions, and present

---

[59] "New research shows a critical need for greater workplace inclusivity among Asian American workers," *Bain & Company* (2022).

ideas without fear of retribution or concern that their comments might damage their relationships or reputation.

We made it clear to our students that when the culture we live in is white male, it's our responsibility to adapt. The frank and practical nature of the program made "The CEO of YOU" extremely popular. It ran for years and led to several of the participants being elevated to the "C-suite" at their companies. Eventually, I was presented with the highest award for service from the Asian Business League.

WHEN OPPORTUNITY KNOCKS...

In 2005, while I continued to grow the School of Management at John F. Kennedy University, I also served on the hiring committee for a new president. It was my job to make sure that we had diversity both in the committee and with candidates. However, my speaking career was really taking off, so I decided to leave the university after the new president was hired.

During that period, I was giving between sixty and eighty talks a year all over the country to major corporations and real estate groups. Being in the public eye so often, I had a built-in audience and the opportunity to reach even more people through my publications. Not everyone could attend my talks, but I could certainly help expand their knowledge through my books. So, I approached literary agents with several book proposals. I wanted to get my first self-published book *Opening Doors: Selling to Multicultural Real Estate Clients* released by a major publisher by making it more general, as well as my self-published book for real estate agents called *Defending Your Commission*. I also had an idea for a book on negotiating based on ancient martial arts principles.

Well, there can be too much of a good thing! In 2006, I was given advances by three major publishers to write all three books: John Wiley and Sons asked me to write *Cross-Cultural Selling for Dummies* based on my first book, AMACOM Books asked me to write *Black Belt Negotiating* with my martial arts instructor, and Kaplan Books paid me to write *111 Ways to Defend Your Commission*. Any writer will tell you that writing one book is a huge challenge, but three books in a year is insane! However, when opportunity knocks, you open the door because it rarely knocks twice. With that said, I'll never do that again.

My 12-hour days consisted of writing a chapter for one book followed by reviewing the edits of another and then making final edits for the third. I was working non-stop and everywhere—in airports, airplanes, and hotels, going from one public speaking engagement to the next. It was a crazy year, but I survived…barely. The hardest thing was that I hardly saw Miriam or our sons.

All three books came out in 2006, and my speaking increased as a result. Unfortunately, in 2008, the recession hit when the housing market crashed because lenders had been giving homebuyers "stated income" mortgages since 2005. Basically, as a buyer, you could declare any income on your loan application without having to prove it. Thinking that opportunity to grab a piece of the U.S. real estate market and the American dream had finally come knocking, people jumped into the market. Some bought a home for themselves, but others went "all in." My hairdresser bought three homes and my manicurist bought five to rent out thinking that they would be able to refinance their loans when the interest rates rose. These variable interest rate loans started out at low "teaser" rates, but in three years, they jumped up with unaffordable balloon payments. Borrowers defaulted and home values collapsed due to a glut of foreclosed homes on the market.

While most people understand how much devastation was caused by the U.S. housing crash, it's a little-known fact that it disproportionately affected minorities. Many people, particularly Black and Hispanic borrowers, were given higher-rate subprime mortgages, even when they could have qualified for regular loans. These non-prime mortgages had been designed for borrowers with lower credit scores, usually below 600, who could not be approved for conventional loans. Even for upper-income Black households, subprime financing was more common than it was among low-income white households. As a result, between 2007 and 2010, nearly 8% of black and Latino families lost their homes to foreclosure, compared to 4.5% of white families. Between 2005 and

2009, the median net worth of black households dropped by 53%, while white household net worth dropped by 17%.[60]

The flood of foreclosures from 2008 onward affected the rest of the U.S. economy. Many lost their jobs, companies stopped hiring speakers like me, and there were few buyers for real estate—a "double whammy" for my two primary income streams and 2010 was difficult for almost everyone, including me. For the next few years, I took jobs like Director of Education for a for-profit school, taught real estate classes, managed real estate offices, and sold real estate. Since 2015, I have been a Broker-Associate for RE/MAX Realty and have been speaking to real estate groups across the country, including at fourteen National Association of Realtors® conventions.

When COVID-19 hit in February of 2021, I figured that I was going to get a vacation from real estate. For a short period of time, we were not allowed to show homes, but —in about a month—we were designated as an essential business. My sales skyrocketed because, by default, I found myself dealing with homebuyers who were earnestly interested. During the normal course of business, buyers often call for information about a property, and then you never hear from them again. During the pandemic, they had to complete a contact-tracing form providing us with their names and numbers, so they were much less likely to be just "looky-loos."

So, in a completely unexpected way, opportunity came knocking again. I was closing two to three, million-dollar homes a month, which put me into the top 5% earning real estate agents in the country. I had clients from South America, the Middle East, and many other parts of the globe. In the San Francisco Bay Area, most of my clients were South Asian Indians. My training in multicultural selling certainly didn't hurt!

During COVID, I also presented dozens of online classes for the National Association of Realtors' *At Home with Diversity* program,

---

[60] D. Gruenstein, W. Bocian, W. & K. Ernst, "Foreclosures by Race and Ethnicity: The Demographics of a Crisis," *CRL Research Report* (2010).

which teaches agents how to treat homebuyers and sellers fairly. One of the big lessons of the program is that most agents don't intentionally discriminate against people whose culture is different from their own, but the bias can be very subtle. For example, they may assume that minorities want to live in the same area as others from that group. I explain that this is not always true, urging them to ask their clients to state their preferences. I also tell the agents that I wouldn't want to live in Chinatown, or in a heavily Asian neighborhood because I know that homes have the most stable values in well-integrated areas. The prices won't crash if one group moves out for some reason.

In 2021, Miriam retired and urged me to retire as well, so we could travel. I told her that I could donate my time to working in a soup kitchen or use my nearly 50-years' experience in real estate to help clients with difficult transactions part-time and donate the money I made to help feed the homeless. This would keep my mind active and occupy my time but still allow for travel. Miriam and I have been speaking on cruise ships around the world two to three times a year. Our programs provide information on food, language, music, and more. We love helping people understand different cultures and being comfortable in various countries. It just makes their experiences richer and more memorable.

One truly memorable trip for us was at the end of 2021, on the first sailing of the Azamara Club Cruises since the lockdown. The crew was so happy to be back at work that they lined up and gave all the passengers an ovation as we boarded. We sailed through the Greek Isles, and it was incredibly empty. In Santorini, a tourist hotspot that is typically packed with people, the streets and shops were vacant. Shopkeepers were selling off their goods at a discount because it was already the end of the tourist season. We went to a restaurant overlooking the harbor and were immediately given a table with a perfect view. Looking back at that trip, we now realize that we had the opportunity to experience places that are typically shoulder-to-shoulder in such a beautiful and relaxed way.

Today, I have cut back to working with just one homebuyer and seller at a time rather than six or seven. I'm also only speaking a couple of times a month. With that said, I'm writing this on the plane from Frankfurt, Germany, to Israel for a month's tour of the Holy Land and the Middle East. Once a workaholic, always a workaholic...

NOT THE LAST CHAPTER

Under the constant threat of developing ankylosing spondylitis, I've lived my life as if each day would be my last. This disease is often called "Bamboo Spine" because it can cause widespread fusing of the bones in the spine resulting in one long bone resembling a long, grooved stick of bamboo.

When first diagnosed, I felt I had no control over my life and no way out. I became depressed to the point where I didn't want to get up in the mornings. I never knew how much pain I would have to endure that day, or when and if I was going to end up looking like the Hunchback of Notre Dame. All I could think about was how easy it would be to swallow a bottle of sleeping pills and end it all.

Fortunately, my research helped me find an approach that worked for me which included avoiding red meat, taking natural supplements, and exercising. I learned to live with the pain and embraced my situation. I took it one day at a time, determined to accomplish as much as I could for as long as I could. I felt that we must do the most with whatever we are given to achieve our fullest potential for the benefit of all mankind. Otherwise, what's the point of living?

Growing up I saw my parents living rather boring, ordinary lives and felt there was more out there for me. Even before the possibility of a "bamboo spine," I saw life as a gift that we should share with others by doing our best. I suppose that drive was innate and cultural, rooted in both the Asian work ethic and Protestant values that emphasize diligence, discipline, and productivity. I'm not a big believer in organized religion, because I don't think that going into a building makes you holy any more than going into a garage makes you a car! But I believe that there is a God because I don't think this beautiful, complex world happened by accident. I also believe that we are all here for a reason, but that life throws us curve balls, and it's how we deal with them that determines whether we are able to fulfill our purpose or not. Life isn't fair but, as in poker, any hand can be a winner depending on how we play the game. At the age of twenty-three, my soul's game plan had already become evident: could I make the most of my life despite my health challenge and being Asian in a white majority country?

I have always rooted for the underdog; those are the stories I like to see in movies and read, books like *Think and Grow Rich* by Napoleon Hill. Rags-to-riches, and against-all-odds stories renew my hope and faith because that's the position I have been in my entire life. I think fate had me born in America because of the tremendous opportunity this country offers. Had I been born to a farming family in China in 1950, I would have been among the 260 million Chinese living in poverty at that time. No matter how hard my family worked, there would have been no way to improve our circumstances since individual land owner-ship was not allowed. From 1958 to 1962, agricultural reforms caused one of the largest famines in human history, resulting in an estimated thirty million people dying from starvation. Even if I had survived, with my arthritis, I probably would have been deemed an "unproductive resource" and exterminated because it's unlikely I would have received much medical treatment. Even if I had been able to pursue my love for learning, I likely would have been among the half-million intellectuals and dissidents who were sent to remote labor camps for 'retraining' dur-ing that time.

Life as a minority in America is certainly not a "bed of roses." Roses have thorns, but I'm not angry about having to face discrimination. If anything, it makes me stronger and more confident every time I find a way past it. I wish I could have reached my fullest potential as many white people can, but I can honestly say that I'm proud of what I have achieved despite all the challenges I've had to overcome. I am thankful for the life I have had and for the life I have now. But if you forced me to answer the question, "What do you wish you could have done in your life but did not?" my answer would be, "More acting and producing major motion pictures." I was always tantalizingly close, just on the periphery, but never quite there.

I would have pursued acting full-time, but I just couldn't see how I would secure my financial future. It's a long shot even if you are not a minority. Also, the roles I would have been offered would have been stereotypes, so I would have had to compromise. God, I hate that word! The best compromises are those you make willingly after weighing the pros and cons like choosing to go into acting or real estate. The worst compromises are those you are forced to make, like paying the bills or portraying characters that perpetuate negative stereotypes. Could I have done more in acting by accepting such roles? Could I have gone farther in my television career by not protesting the elimination of social issues from our show? Should I have stayed in a marriage that didn't make me happy so I could be with my son every day?

It's so easy to play that stupid mind game, "could have...should have..." Ultimately, I played the cards I was dealt at the time in the best way I knew how and followed my own moral compass. It's easy to be led astray and lose your way if you don't have a solid set of personal values. Mine have always been to help others before I help myself because what you do always comes back around; to outwork everyone else because it's the only thing I can control; to replace negative thoughts with positive ones; to have a small circle of true friends; and to leave the world better than I found it. For me, mistakes of the past are just lessons for the future.

We all have regrets that can lead to feelings of disappointment, even remorse if you let it progress to that point. One regret I have is never having the courage to "pick a lane." I pursued real estate, acting, producing, teaching, writing, and public speaking; sometimes all at the same time, to diversify my risks and income, when I could have possibly been exceptional at any one of those professions. I was good at each, but my risk-averse Asian background wouldn't let me put all my eggs into one basket, which is what it takes to be uber-successful sometimes. Another regret is not having a better work-life balance, which resulted in my biggest regret—not spending more quality time with my son, Chris. I realize now that my career probably wouldn't have suffered had I done that. All the same, my greatest personal achievement was being willing and able to spend as much time as I did with him despite my workaholic mindset and worries over my physical condition. I learned to share with him my biggest accomplishments and failures, knowing that he will never judge me. Today, I trust his judgment more than my own. Through him I've grown as a person, as a father, and as a man.

My second greatest achievement was learning to ask for help despite my huge ego, which constantly told me that I could solve all my problems on my own. Others helped me to speak more professionally, write and publish books and so much more. Eventually, I understood that "no man is an island" and the importance of "knowing thyself." It took courage, even desperation, to be willing to examine every aspect of my life and question what had brought me to any given point, why I did what I did, and whether I wanted to change my path. My soul-searching helped me choose the things that truly made me happy. This inner growth opened me to dating Miriam, to spending quality time with Chris, and to realizing that I was put on this earth not to accumulate wealth but to be of service—to the students I have taught, the real estate clients I have helped, the salespeople who made more money while becoming more sensitive to cultural differences, and more. There's an old saying, "The best way to find yourself is to lose yourself in the service of others." I still find myself constantly looking for ways to give to others and to use the talents and experiences that I have. Why not try to be better every day and contribute to society rather than be a burden?

Part of why I have worked so hard is so that I wouldn't have to live off welfare or Social Security, especially if I was disabled. (That's so Asian!) I want to live life on my terms as much as, and as long as I can.

Facing disability at a young age totally changed the way I feel about life and death. At the time of the diagnosis, I evaluated my short journey to that point, and since then, I've repeated that process many times. I try to live consciously and with intention, navigating my course as best as I can, so as not to be blown around like tumbleweed. I see life as a constant state of expansion—experiencing more, learning more, achieving more, helping more, loving more, dreaming more, more of everything until there is no more.

When I bought my first house, which was the fulfillment of a life's dream at a young age, it led me to want to build a portfolio of rental houses as part of my retirement plan. I say this to illustrate that—while I am very happy with what I've accomplished—I'll never be completely satisfied. There's always another rung to climb. That's what gets me up in the morning but drives Miriam crazy. For me, being content is like being dead inside. Obviously, I still have more personal growth to do....

I've been blessed with a high IQ and belonged to groups like MENSA, where most people were intellectually superior but many of them could not even balance a checkbook! Intelligence certainly helps, but my biggest advantage in life has been my attitude. I've never viewed anything as impossible. To me, every problem is just a series of steps that lead to the solution. I don't think of anything I've faced as a disadvantage, whether it's being a minority or having arthritis of the spine. Life is full of seeming disadvantages, which are simply challenges to overcome. Even when you are discriminated against, you can either get mired in bitterness, or you can find a way to prevail. In my case, it fostered the empathy and compassion that have guided my life and driven my career because I know how it feels to be treated as less than or like you don't exist.

White privilege can give some people an advantage. It's like two people in a footrace, where one must start twenty-five feet behind the other at the starting line. The person in front doesn't feel like they have an advantage, but the one behind feels like it will take every ounce of effort and luck just to catch up. I've learned to never look at the person ahead of me but always measure my progress against myself. Understanding that I am the only standard that counts was part of my most important soul lesson in this life: self-love.

Yellow privilege gives some Asians an advantage that we can use to help others. We are starting behind the leader but not as far back in the pack as others. We should use our position to give them a hand as well.

It's been a long journey to self-acceptance, from hating being different to embracing my differences as a superpower. For instance, since I'm often the only Asian speaker at a conference, I'm easy to remember. Attendees may not remember my name, but they always remember that "funny Asian guy with the thought-provoking message".

Self-love has always been tough for me. I have always sacrificed my well-being to please others and probably settled for less than I deserved. Not long ago, I asked Chris what movie he wanted to see the next time we got together. He gently reminded me that it was my birthday that we were celebrating, so I should choose the film. It's still a constant struggle to put myself first in many instances. But I make a conscious effort to practice self-love through good nutrition, exercise, and healthy social interactions with clear boundaries. I realize that self-forgiveness is a big part of self-compassion and self-care. I reward myself with simple things, like buying myself an ice cream for no reason. It's hard to think negative thoughts when you're rewarding yourself or when you are busy moving forward in life. I am a textbook example of the power of positive thinking! Sure, I acknowledge unpleasant feelings when they come up, but I don't dwell on them because that's a total waste of time. I can't change the past, but I can take action to learn from my mistakes and make better choices next time.

I am grateful for what I have, especially for the people in my life. My happiest moment was when I married Miriam; I was never so satisfied or full of joy. I just knew it was right. Every day, I am thankful for having her, and I tell her so. A nice car, house, and job appease the ego, but meaningful relationships uplift the spirit. My family and friends have made my life worth living and a fun ride. I appreciate and celebrate them now, because—like the tide—people come and go from our lives. If I had a chance to do it over, I would have learned to live in the moment sooner, rather than always looking for the next mountain to climb.

I hate to leave anything incomplete, which is why I finished my doctorate after 20 years even though I didn't need it; I was already the dean of the School of Management. I suppose that not completing something feels like a failure to me. That kind of regret and sadness is natural in advanced age, but the clock has been ticking loudly in my head since my diagnosis with arthritis of the spine. Today, the pace at which I work is slower because I'm not worried about paying the mortgage or saving for retirement. I celebrate my successes but still have goals, no matter my age. Right now, I'm the Activity Chairman for a large senior men's group where I coordinate activities that help the guys connect, stay active, and improve the quality of their lives. I also take a few, select speaking engagements around the country and work with a couple of past real estate clients.

Okay, I admit that I'm scared to death of stopping because stopping would feel like death. And anyway, why should I stop? Aren't we meant to savor life to its last drop?

If I were to depart tomorrow, I would have no regrets because I have given it my all. At the moment of death, I would think about my family and friends, hoping that I have impacted their lives in a positive way and done as much as I could for them. I would like to be remembered as a caring, helpful, and positive person. I would like my legacy to be that I helped a few people get past differences and see the humanness in others. It may sound trite, but I can say that I have genuinely tried to contribute to the world every day. Despite all the progress our society has made, it seems that today we have been separated more than ever by political, religious, racial, and other differences. Unless we find a way to bridge those gaps, I'm afraid our country is destined to wither and die.

If I had the opportunity to say one thing to humanity, it would be: Our differences hold our greatest gifts; they are something to celebrate because they make the world more interesting. How boring would life be if we only had vanilla ice cream rather than over 1,000 choices? If I had to share one pearl of wisdom, it would be Dr. King's, "Let's not judge people by the color of their skin but by the content of their character."

A strong character is forged by challenges, which are just opportunities for growth; they don't happen *to* us but *for* us. Deciphering the message and meaning behind our trials and tribulations may be half the battle because then we can stop seeing ourselves as victims and start picturing ourselves as warriors! Maybe fate chose ankylosing spondylitis as part of my growth trajectory because the disease inflamed my determination, motivation, and ambition. I could have stooped to self-pity, inertia, and despair under the threat of the "bamboo spine," but instead I stood up stronger, straighter, and taller. Maybe my determination to live to the fullest, for as long as I could, kept the condition at bay. Mind over matter?

In any case, the metaphor of the "bamboo spine" is fitting! Bamboo is the strongest woody plant on earth with a tensile strength superior to steel—28,000 pounds per square inch versus 23,000. Also, bamboo is strongly associated with Asia, and it is a major theme in Chinese painting, calligraphy, and poetry. It stands for grace, moral integrity, modesty, and loyalty. But it also represents loneliness and the human condition. The people in our lives are but fellow travelers on the road, and life is a journey for one. We come into the world, live in the world, and leave the world alone. Each one of us is one bamboo stalk among many, but working together we are so much stronger.

Bamboo also symbolizes longevity. It survives in the harshest conditions, bending but not breaking, and staying green year-round. My "bamboo spine" has made me strong, resilient, and evergreen. Even today I'm determined that this is not my last chapter. While answering some questions posed by my editor, after philosophizing for several pages, my last words to her were: "How's that for a start?"

APPENDIX

ASIAN AMERICAN HISTORY TIMELINE

As with any historical accounting, not every detail can be included. However, the following are what I believe to be major milestones, which will help readers understand the history of Asians in America.

October 17, 1587: The first Asian-origin people known to arrive in North America—Manila Filipinos known as "Luzonians" or "Luzon Indians," who were part of the crew of the Spanish galleon Nuestra Señora de Buena Esperanza. The ship set sail from Manila and landed in Morro Bay in what is now the California Coast as part of the Galleon Trade between the Spanish East Indies, including the Philippines and the colonies in North America.

1600s: Chinese and Filipinos reach Mexico on ships of the Manila galleon trade.

1763: First recorded settlement of Filipinos in America. To escape mistreatment aboard Spanish galleons, they jump ship in New Orleans and flee into the bayous of Louisiana. These "Manila men" established a small settlement called St. Malo, along with seven other villages on the outskirts of New Orleans. Since there were no Filipino women with them, they married Cajun and Native American women.

1781: Antonio Miranda Rodriguez, of Filipino ancestry, is one of the founders of Pueblo de Nuestra Senora Reina de los Angeles, known today as the city of Los Angeles.

1785: Three Chinese seamen arrive in the continental United States aboard the ship Pallas in Baltimore, MD.

1790: First recorded arrival of Asian Indians in the U.S. They were known as East Indians in North America to differentiate them from Caribbean Americans (or West Indians).

- The Naturalization Act of 1790 restricts citizenship to "free white persons" of "good moral character." In effect, it divides the Nation between white and racial minority populations, each would be accorded different and unequal rights and treatment. Racial minorities would be limited in their citizenship, voting, residency, jury, property, and family rights. Asian Americans, including Chinese Americans, would be directly affected by this legislation until it was rescinded by the passage of the Walter-McCarran Act of 1952.

1812: Filipinos serve under General Andrew Jackson's American forces in the War of 1812 and as artillery gunners at the Battle of New Orleans.

1815: With the establishment of the Old China Trade in the late 18th century, a handful of Chinese merchants were recorded as residing in the United States.

- Filipinos work as shrimp fishermen and smugglers in Louisiana.

1830: The first U.S. Census notation of Chinese in America records three Chinese living in the United States.

1830s: East Asian groups begin immigrating to Hawaii, where American capitalists and missionaries had established plantations and settlements. Originating primarily from China, Japan, Korea, India, and the Philippines, these early migrants were predominantly contracted plantation workers.

1834: Afong Moy, the first Chinese woman known to have visited the U.S., is exhibited in a theater in New York as "The Chinese Lady."

1839: With the annexation of Hawaii by the United States, a large population of Asians lived in U.S. territory and more continued to immigrate. As Americans established sugar cane plantations in Hawaii in the 19th century, they turned, through organizations such as the Royal Hawaiian Agricultural Society, to the Chinese as a source of cheap labor as early as the 1830s.

1840s: Filipino migration to North America continued with reports of "Manila men" in early gold camps in Mariposa County, California, in the late 1840s.

1842: China is defeated by the British Empire in the first Opium War, resulting in the Treaty of Nanjing, whereby China is forced to cede the island of Hong Kong and open ports to foreign commerce.

May 7, 1843: Referred to as the United States' first ambassador to Japan, a 14-year-old fisherman by the name of Manjiro is considered America's first Japanese immigrant. He was shipwrecked on a Pacific atoll, rescued by a whaling ship, landed in the U.S. in 1843, and participated in the California gold rush.

July 3, 1844: U.S. and China sign a first treaty of "peace, amity, and commerce."

1846: A series of crop failures in southern China leads to poverty and a threat of famine among peasant farmers.

1847: Yung Wing and two other Chinese arrive in the U.S. for schooling. Yung Wing graduates from Yale in 1854 and becomes the first Chinese to graduate from a U.S. college.

1848: On January 24, gold is discovered by James W. Marshall at Sutter's Mill in Coloma, California. The news brought approximately 300,000 people to California from the rest of the United States and abroad, including China. The famine in China causes many to sail west to make their fortunes and hopefully return home as rich men. The first Chinese (two men, one woman) immigrate to the U.S. and land in San Francisco.

1849: There were 325 Chinese residents in California.

1850: Chinese American population in the U.S. is about 4,000 out of a population of 23.2 million.

- Chinese in California form associations for mutual protection against assaults.
- California imposes a high Foreign Miner's Tax mainly aimed at the Chinese, who were considered odd and competitors to white Americans. Most Chinese were unable to pay the tax, so they were forced to cook or do laundry for miners since there were few women out West at the time. Doing "women's work" was the beginning of the stereotype that Asian men were not masculine and would not fight back when attacked.

1851: A group of growers in Hawaii formed the Royal Hawaiian Agricultural Society to address a growing labor shortage in the sugar cane fields. The growers instituted a contract-labor system under which the first group of Chinese recruited came under five-year contracts at $3.00 a month plus passage, food, clothing, and a house. An advance of $6 was made in China to be refunded in small installments. During the five-year period, they were only paid subsistence wages after which they were free to leave.

- Before the end of the century, 46,000 Chinese workers had come to Hawaii.

1852: Lured by the Gold Rush, more than 20,000 Chinese arrive in California (it was a myth that all Chinese wished to get rich quickly and return—only 50% reportedly were able to go home).

- The first group of 195 Chinese contract laborers land in Hawaii.
- Chinese first appear in court in California.
- Missionary Willian Speer opens a Presbyterian mission for Chinese in San Francisco.

1853: Several hundred years of Japan's isolation end as U.S. Commodore Matthew Perry forces it to open its door to foreign commerce.

1854: People v. Hall, the California Supreme Court case that denied the rights of Chinese immigrants and Chinese Americans to testify against white citizens. In this case, George Hall shot and killed Ling Sing, a Chinese immigrant. The primary witness to the crime was also Chinese, rendering him unable to legally testify. This meant that any member of the race could be beaten and murdered with impunity creating fear among them and causing them to retreat to the safety of Chinese ghettos later dubbed "Chinatowns."

- Chinese in Hawaii establish a funeral society, their first community association in the islands.

1857: San Francisco opens a school for Chinese children (changed to an evening school two years later). Missionary Augustus Loomis arrives to serve the Chinese in San Francisco.

1858: California passes a law to bar entry of Chinese and "Mongolians."

1859: Chinese are excluded from San Francisco public schools.

1860: The Chinese American population in the U.S. is 34,933 out of a total population of 31.4 million.

- Japan sends its first diplomatic mission to U.S.
- A California law bars Chinese Americans, Indians, and African Americans from public schools.

1861: Some seventy Chinese and Filipinos enlist in the Union Army and Union Navy during the American Civil War. Smaller numbers serve in the armed forces of the Confederate States of America.

1862: The Pacific Railroad Act chartered the Central Pacific and the Union Pacific Railroad Companies, tasking them with building a transcontinental railroad that would link the United States from east to west. Over the next seven years, the two companies would race toward each other from Sacramento, California, on the one side to Omaha, Nebraska, on the other.

- The Central Pacific Railroad Co. needed thousands of laborers, so a job ad was placed but only a few hundred white laborers responded. It was suggested that Chinese be used but averaging just 5 feet in height and weighing only 120 pounds, the Chinese were not considered fit for the job. They were thought to be too small and weak for the dangerous, strenuous job of building the railroad.

- "An Act to Protect Free White Labor Against Competition with Chinese Coolie Labor, and to Discourage the Immigration of the Chinese into the State of California" established a monthly "police tax" for all adults "of the Mongolian race." As mining opportunities declined, more Chinese turned to the railroads to earn a living.

- The United States prohibits the importation of Chinese "coolies" on American vessels.

- Six Chinese district associations in San Francisco form a loose federation.

1863: Chinese laborers generally arrived in California with the help of brokers in Hong Kong and other ports under the credit-ticket system, where they would pay back money loaned from brokers with their wages upon arrival. In addition to laborers, merchants also migrated from China, opening businesses and stores, including those that would form the beginnings of Chinatowns.

1864, January: Out of desperation, the railroad started an experiment using a crew of twenty-one Chinese workers. In head-to-head competitions, they beat experienced white railroaders by a wide margin. Two years later, about 90% of the workers were Chinese, totaling 12,000 men who hoped to be accepted as equals.

1864-1869: Chinese railroad workers received 30-50% less pay than whites for the same job and had to provide their own food. This led to the belief that Asians were coming to America to steal "white jobs," yet whites were not willing to do the work. They also had the most difficult and dangerous work, including tunneling and the use of unstable explosives, which ended up killing over 1,200 of them. Because they were considered less than human, their bodies were often buried on the side of the tracks while the work continued. This attitude about the lack of worth of Asian lives still exists today.

1867: Two thousand Chinese railroad workers strike for a week. The railroad refuses to feed them and the strike collapses.

1868: The United States and China ratify the Burlingame-Seward Treaty, which sanctions mutual emigration between the two countries.

- The Meiji Restoration in Japan brought about great social disruption and agricultural decline. Farmers were forced to leave their land, workers were left jobless by foreign competition, and stories of a booming U.S. economy spread. Many Japanese men left Japan for the United States to seek their fortune. In the same year, the Hawaiian consul general secretly hired and transported 148 contract laborers to Hawaii starting a flood of immigration from Japan.

- Known as the "Gannenmono," 153 Japanese—including six women and a child—are the first immigrants to Hawaii from Japan to serve as temporary migrant workers on sugar plantations.

1869: The Fourteenth Amendment gives full citizenship to every person born in the United States, regardless of race.

- Japanese immigrants arrive in California and form the Wakamatsu Colony on Gold Hill.

- J.H. Schnell takes a select group of Japanese along with 50,000 mulberry trees for the cultivation of silkworms to California to establish the Wakamatsu Tea and Silk Colony.
- Chinese Christian evangelist S.P. Aheong starts preaching in Hawaii.

May 10, 1869: The Central Pacific and the Union Pacific Railroad Companies struggled against great risks before they met at Promontory Point, Utah. While the Central Pacific Railroad hired thousands of Chinese laborers, after the line was finished, they were hounded out of many railroad towns in states such as Wyoming and Nevada. Most wound up in the Chinatown areas of large cities where they were mostly ignored by the police.

1870: The Chinese American population in US is 63,199 out of a total population of 38.5 million.

- About half the Chinese in the United States are working in mining, making up more than a quarter of all miners.
- To get rid of these hard-working but strange foreigners, California passed a law banning the importation of "Mongolian" women—widely interpreted to include Chinese and Japanese women—so Asian men could not bring their wives to start families. This foreshadowed the federal Page Act of 1875.
- The U.S. economy took a turn for the worse. Looking for a scapegoat, the public cast blame on Chinese immigrants, who were less than one percent of the country's population.
- Chinese railroad workers in Texas sue the company for failing to pay wages.
- Congress grants naturalization rights to free whites and people of African descent, omitting mention of Asian (or "Oriental") races.
- Congress approves the Naturalization Act, barring Chinese from obtaining U.S. citizenship. The Act also prevents immigration of

Chinese women, who have marital partners in the United States. Chinese and Japanese men must show evidence in support of a woman's moral character in the case of prospective and actual wives of Chinese and Japanese descent.

- The Benevolent Society of Hispanic Filipinos is founded in Saint Malo, New Orleans. It is the first Filipino association in the U.S.

October 24, 1871: Approximately 500 white and Hispanic Americans attacked, harassed, robbed, and murdered the Chinese residents of the old Chinatown neighborhood of the city of Los Angeles. A total of nineteen Chinese immigrants were killed, fifteen were hanged by the mob during the riot, but most had already been shot to death before being hanged.

1872: California's Civil Procedure Code drops law barring court testimony by Chinese.

1875: The first American drug law was passed in San Francisco, banning the smoking of opium in opium dens. The reason given for this law was that "many women and young girls, as well as young men of a respectable family, were being induced to visit the Chinese opium-smoking dens, where they were ruined morally and otherwise." This was followed by other laws throughout the country, including federal laws that barred Chinese people from trafficking in opium.

March 3, 1875: The Page Act of 1875 is enacted, prohibiting the recruitment of laborers from "China, Japan or any Oriental country" who were not brought to the United States of their own will or who were brought for "lewd and immoral purposes." The law explicitly bars "the importation of women for the purposes of prostitution." Based on stereotypes and scapegoating, the act is enforced by invasive and humiliating interrogations at the Angel Island Immigration Station outside San Francisco. It effectively blocks Chinese women from entering the country and stifles the ability of Chinese American men to start families in America. This caused some to return home but many, who could not afford the passage on their menial wages, lived, and died alone in America.

1876: U.S. and Hawaii sign the Reciprocity Treaty, allowing Hawaiian sugar to enter U.S. duty free.

1877: Denis Kearney organizes an anti-Chinese movement in San Francisco and forms the Workingmen's Party of California, alleging that Chinese workers took lower wages, poorer conditions, and longer hours than white workers were willing to tolerate.

- There is anti-Chinese violence in California and around the country where many are killed by lynching or shooting. The fear of attack by whites is palpable.
- Anti-Chinese violence in Chico, California.
- Japanese Christians set up Gospel Society in San Francisco, the first immigrant association formed by the Japanese.

1878: California rules that Chinese are ineligible for naturalized citizenship because they are not considered white or Black. Chinese were deemed not citizen material and many face hostile, and often violent, treatment from locals.

1879: California's second constitution prevents municipalities and corporations from employing Chinese.

- California state legislature passes law requiring all incorporated towns and cities to remove Chinese outside of city limits, but the U.S. circuit court declares the law unconstitutional.

1880: The Census counted 105,465 Chinese and 145 Japanese, indicating that Asian immigration to the continent by this point consisted primarily of Chinese immigrants, the majority of whom were in California.

- U.S. and China sign a treaty giving the U.S. the right to limit but "not absolutely prohibit" Chinese immigration.
- Section 69 of California's Civil Code prohibits issuing of licenses for marriages between whites and "Mongolians, Negroes, mulattoes and persons of mixed blood."

1881: King Kalakaua of Hawaii visits Japan during his world tour.

- Removal of Queen Liliuokalani from the throne in Hawaii.
- Sit Moon becomes pastor of the first Chinese Christian church in Hawaii.

1882: U.S. and Korea sign first treaty.

- On May 6, the Chinese Exclusion Act is signed into law by President Chester Arthur, prohibiting virtually all immigration from China for ten years. It is the first immigration law to do so based on race or national origin. The law also prevented Chinese immigrants from becoming naturalized U.S. citizens. It became the first significant law restricting immigration into the United States in order to maintain white "racial purity." It increases demand for Japanese immigrants on the West Coast. Congress extends its provision every ten years until 1943, when World War II labor shortage pressure and increased anti-Japanese sentiment leads to its demise and Chinese immigrants are allowed to become naturalized citizens.
- The 1882 Chinese Exclusion Law is amended to require a certificate as the only permissible evidence for reentry.
- Chinese community leaders form Chinese Consolidated Benevolent Association (CCBA or Chinese Six Companies) in San Francisco.

1883: Chinese in New York establish CCBA.

1884: Joseph and Mary Tape sue San Francisco school board to enroll their Chinese daughter Mamie in a public school.

- Chinese Six Companies sets up Chinese language school in San Francisco.
- United Chinese Society established in Honolulu.
- CCBA established in Vancouver, Canada.

1885: In Hawaii, resistance from plantation laborers protesting low wages and tensions between various native and immigrant groups encouraged plantation owners to import more labor from different Asian countries to keep wages low. Between 1885 and 1924, about 30,000 Japanese went to Hawaii as government-sponsored contract laborers.

- Following the Chinese Exclusion Act, large numbers of young Japanese laborers, along with smaller numbers of Koreans and Indians, began arriving on the West Coast of the United States where they replaced the Chinese as cheap labor in building railroads, farming, and fishing. Growing anti-Japanese legislation and violence soon followed.
- San Francisco builds new segregated "Oriental School" in response to the Mamie Tape case.
- First group of Japanese contract laborers arrives in Hawaii under the Irwin Convention.

September 2, 1885: Angered that they're taking away "white" jobs, white coal miners attack Chinese laborers in the Wyoming territory during what comes to be known as the Rock Springs Massacre. Twenty-eight Chinese are killed, with fifteen more injured by the mob, which also looted and set fire to all homes in the area's Chinatown. Federal troops are brought in to return Chinese miners, who had fled, to Rock Springs, and Congress eventually agrees to compensate the workers for their losses.

1886: Forcible expulsion of Chinese begins in many areas of the western U.S.

- Residents of Tacoma, Seattle, and many places in the American West forcibly expel the Chinese.
- End of Chinese immigration to Hawaii.
- The Japanese government lifts its ban on emigration, allowing its citizens for the first time to make permanent moves to other countries.
- Chinese laundrymen win in the Yick Wo v. Hopkins case, declaring that a law that is enforced with racial discrimination is discriminatory.

1886-1911: More than 400,000 men and women left Japan for the U.S. The two most popular destinations were the archipelago of Hawaii and America's Pacific coast.

1886-1925: The sugar planters in Hawaii brought in 180,000 Japanese workers. Taking refuge from Japanese imperialism, from growing poverty and famine in Korea, and encouraged by Christian missionaries, thousands of Koreans migrated to Hawaii in the early 1900s.

1887: The "Chinese Must Go"" movement was so strong that Chinese immigration to the U.S. declined from 39,500 in 1882 to only 10 in 1887.

May 27-28, 1887: Seven white horse thieves ambush a group of Chinese miners who had set up camp along the Snake River in Oregon, murdering all thirty-four men and mutilating their bodies before dumping them in the river. Three members of the gang stand trial in the Hells Canyon Massacre, with one testifying for the state, and all are found not guilty by an all-white jury.

1888: The Scott Act declares 20,000 Chinese reentry certificates null and void.

1889: The U.S. Supreme Court decision in Chae Chan Ping v. U.S. upholds the constitutionality of Chinese exclusion laws.

- The first Nishi Hongwanji priest from Japan arrives in Hawaii.
- The first two Korean women, wives of Korean diplomats, enter the U.S.
- "The San Francisco Bulletin" initiates its "yellow peril" campaign against Japanese immigration.

1890: The Chinese American population in U.S. is 107,488 out of a total population of 62.9 million.

1890s: Japanese, Korean, and South Asian immigrants arrive in the continental United States to fill demands for labor. Japanese immigrants were primarily farmers, facing economic upheaval during the Meiji Restoration; they began to migrate in large numbers to the continental United States after the Chinese exclusion.

1892: The Geary Act further "required Chinese to register and secure a certificate as proof of their right to be in the United States" if they sought to leave and reenter the country, with imprisonment or deportation as potential penalties. It also renews the exclusion of Chinese laborers for another ten years and institutes mandatory registration by all Chinese.

1893: Japanese in San Francisco form first trade association, the Japanese Shoemakers' League.

- Attempts are made to expel Chinese from towns in southern California.
- In Fong Yue Ting v. United States, the U.S. Supreme Court rules that Congress has the power to expel the Chinese.

1894: Saito, a Japanese man, applies for U.S. citizenship, but U.S. circuit courts refuse because he is neither white nor black.

- Japanese immigration to Hawaii under the Irwin Convention ends and emigration companies take over.
- Sun Yat-sen founded the Xingzhonghui in Honolulu.

1895: Lem Moon Sing v. U.S. rules that district courts can no longer review Chinese habeas corpus petitions for landing in the U.S.

- The Hawaii Sugar Plantations' Association (HSPA) was formed.

1896: Shinsei Kaneko, a Japanese Californian, is naturalized.

- Bubonic plague scare in Honolulu; Chinatown burned.

1898: The Treaty of Paris ends the Spanish-American War and forces Spain to cede the Philippines, Guam, and Puerto Rico to the United States. In return, the United States paid Spain $20 million for the Philippines, which became a U.S. colony.

- The U.S. Supreme Court admits Wong Kim Ark, a Chinese American born and raised in the United States, back into the United States. Ark was initially denied entry due to the Chinese Exclusion Act. The case rules that U.S.-born Chinese cannot be divested of their citizenship.
- Hawaii joins the U.S. as a territory. Most residents are Asian and receive full U.S. citizenship.
- Japanese, Chinese and Filipinos make up the population in Hawaii.

1899: Chinese reformers Kang Youwei and Liang Qichao tour North America to recruit supporters for the return of the Chinese emperor to power.

- First Nishi Hongwanji priests arrive in California and set up North American Buddhist Mission.

1900: The Census counted 24,326 Japanese residents and 89,863 Chinese residents in the U.S. Initially, Japanese, and South Asian laborers filled the demand that could not be met by new Chinese immigrants.

- The bubonic plague makes a resurgence in San Francisco. Its origins were traced back to an Australian who came to America via ship, but the first person to contract the plague in the United States was an immigrant from China. Immediately, the public turned against the entire community with police swarming Chinatown, forbidding residents from leaving. However, white residents could come and go as they pleased. Chinese mistrust of law enforcement and government grew.

- April 2, 1900: The Hawaii Organic Act makes all U.S. laws applicable to Hawaii, ending contract labor in the islands because it was basically a form of legalized slavery.

- Japanese Hawaiian plantation workers begin migrating to the mainland.

1901: The first Korean immigrant arrives in Hawaii on a Japanese ship.

1902: The Philippine Organic Act made the Philippines into an American protectorate as an "unorganized" territory making Filipinos become quasi-Americans.

- Congress extends Chinese exclusion for another ten years.

- Immigration officials and the police raid Boston's Chinatown and, without search warrants, arrest almost 250 Chinese who allegedly had no registration certificates on their persons.

1903: A shipload of Korean immigrants arrives in Hawaii to work on pineapple and sugar plantations. By 1905, a total of 7,226 Koreans had gone to Hawaii (including 637 women and 465 children) to escape the famines and turbulent political climate of Korea. When their plantation labor contract expired after five years, around 50% of Korean workers moved to the mainland and established self-employed businesses such as laundry stores and nail salons and the other half returned to Korea.

- 1500 Japanese and Mexican sugar beet workers strike in Oxnard, California.

- The first group of 209 Filipino students (pensionados) arrive in the U.S. for higher education. Most return to the Philippines to teach and take government posts.

1904: Congress makes the Chinese Exclusion acts indefinite.

- South Asian Indians begin coming to North America, in particular, to British Columbia, Canada.

- Law enforcement officials arrest 250 allegedly illegal Chinese immigrants without search warrants.

- Japanese plantation workers engage in first organized strike in Hawaii. Shortly after, more Koreans are imported to work as strikebreakers against Japanese workers.

- Punjabi Sikhs begin to enter British Columbia.

1904-1917: South Asian Indian immigrants also entered the United States as laborers, following Chinese exclusion. Recruited initially by Canadian-Pacific railroad companies, a few thousand Sikh immigrants from the Punjabi region immigrated to Canada, which, like India, was part of the British Empire. Later, many migrated into the Pacific Northwest and California, and became farm laborers. Ironically decried as a "Hindu invasion" by exclusionists and white labor, the "tide of the Turbans" was outlawed in 1917 when Congress declared that India was part of the Pacific-Barred Zone of excluded Asian countries.

1904-1925: About 2,000 Korean women immigrate to Hawaii and California as "picture brides" of the bachelor immigrants who were already working as plantation laborers.

1905: Section 60 of California's Civil Code is amended to forbid marriage between whites and "Mongolians."

- Chinese in mainland U.S. and Hawaii support boycott of American products in China.
- Koreans establish Korean Episcopal Church in Hawaii and Korean Methodist Church in California.
- San Francisco School Board attempts to segregate Japanese schoolchildren.
- Koreans in San Francisco form Mutual Assistance Society.
- Asiatic Exclusion League formed in San Francisco.
- The Japanese government in Korea halts all emigration of Koreans.

1906: The U.S. government creates the Bureau of Immigration.

- Anti-Asian riot in Vancouver.
- Japanese scientists studying the aftermath of the San Francisco earthquake are stoned.
- Japanese nurserymen form the California Flower Growers' Association.
- Koreans establish Korean Presbyterian Church in Los Angeles.
- Fifteen Filipino laborers recruited by the Hawaiian Sugar Planters' Association arrive in Oahu, marking the beginning of a massive Filipino immigration to Hawaii and eventually to the U.S. mainland.
- San Francisco School Board places children of "Mongoloid" ancestry in segregated schools.
- April 18, 1906: A major earthquake and fire in San Francisco destroys all municipal records, including immigration records. "Paper sons" can claim they are U.S. citizens and have the right to bring wives and children to America.

1907: President Theodore Roosevelt signs Executive Order 589 prohibiting Japanese with passports for Hawaii, Mexico, or Canada to re-emigrate to the U.S.

- Japan and the U.S. reach "Gentlemen's Agreement" whereby Japan stops issuing passports to laborers desiring to emigrate to the U.S. As a result, labor contractors in Alaskan fisheries and on California and Hawaii farms and plantations begin recruiting Filipinos.
- Koreans form the United Korean Society in Hawaii.
- First group of Filipino laborers arrives in Hawaii.
- September 4, 1907: Spurred on by the inflammatory rhetoric of the nativist Asiatic Exclusion League, hundreds of white workers swept through the coastal town of Bellingham, WA, at night, looking for Indian immigrants. The Indians, who were laborers in Bellingham's lumber mills, were predominantly Sikh men from Punjab. The rioters pulled Indian workers out of their bunks, set their bunkhouses on fire, stole their possessions, and beat them. Some Sikh men were beaten so badly they had to be hospitalized.

1908: Japanese form Japanese Association of America.

- Canada curbs Asian Indian immigration by denying entry to those who have not come by "continuous journey" from their homelands (there is no direct shipping between Indian and Canadian ports).
- Asian Indians are driven out of Live Oak, California.
- Japanese picture brides begin arriving in the U.S.

1909: Koreans form Korean Nationalist Association.

- Seven thousand Japanese plantation workers strike major plantations on Oahu for four months.

1910: Chinese American population in the U.S. is 94,414 out of a total population of 92.2 million. The Census, the first to count South Asians, recorded that there were 2,545 "Hindus" in the United States.

- Administrative measures are used to restrict influx of Asian Indians into California.

- January 21, 1910: The immigration station Angel Island opens in California's San Francisco Bay, serving as the country's major port of entry for Asian immigrants, with some 100,000 Chinese and 70,000 Japanese being processed through the station over the next 30 years. Known as the "Ellis Island of the West" and located six miles off San Francisco's coast, the island was a military reserve during the Civil War. Immigrants are required to undergo humiliating medical examinations and detailed interrogations. Those without proper documentation were quarantined there for days to years in a "prison-like environment," according to the National Parks Service. Closed in 1940, it's now a California state park.

1911: Sun Yat-sen (1866—1925) was influential in overthrowing the Qing (Manchu) dynasty (1911/12), served as the first provisional president of the Republic of China (1911–12) and later as de facto ruler (1923–25). He was known as the father of modern China.

- Pablo Manlapit forms Filipino Higher Wages Association in Hawaii.

- Japanese form Japanese Association of Oregon in Portland.

1912: Sikhs build gurdwara in Stockton and establish Khalsa Diwan.

1913: California passes law prohibiting "aliens ineligible to citizenship" (i.e., Asian immigrant males) from buying land or leasing it for longer than three years. Various Western states, including Washington, Oregon, and Arizona, followed its lead. This law, specifically aimed at Japanese farmers, kept them from building wealth in the country and forced many of them to purchase land in the names of their American-born children. It was not until after World War II that the Supreme Court and California reversed their decisions.

- Sikhs in Washington and Oregon establish Hindustani Association.
- Asian Indians in California found the revolutionary Ghadar Party and start publishing a newspaper.
- Pablo Manlapit forms Filipino Unemployed Association in Hawaii.
- Japanese form Northwest Japanese Association of America in Seattle.
- Korean farmworkers are driven out of Hemet, California.

1914: World War I begins. Germany sought to break up the French-Russian alliance and was fully prepared to take the risk that this would bring about a major war.

- Aspiring Asian Indian immigrants, who had chartered a ship to come to Canada by continuous journey, are denied landing in Vancouver.

1915: Japanese form the Central Japanese Association of Southern California and the Japanese Chamber of Commerce.

- January 21, 1915: Telesforo de la Cruz Trinidad receives the Medal of Honor for actions on the USS San Diego, becoming the first and only Asian American and Filipino in the U.S. Navy to receive the Medal of Honor.

1916: More than 18,000 Filipino farm workers (sakadas) have immigrated to the Hawaiian Islands to work on sugar plantations.

1917: America enters World War I. Despite numerous instances of discrimination, many AAPI's joined the U.S. Army and served with distinction on the battlefields of France. Following the war, soldiers of

Asian ancestry were recognized for their contributions to the war effort and allowed to become naturalized citizens.

- Syngman Rhee founds the Korean Christian Church in Hawaii.

- February 5, 1917: Congress passes the Immigration Act of 1917, which includes an "Asiatic Barred Zone," banning Chinese, Asian Indians, Burmese, Thai, Maylays, and others. Japan is not on the list of those excluded, as prohibitions against immigrants from that country are already in place, nor is the Philippines, as it is a U.S. territory.

1918: World War I ends and veterans of Asian ancestry are granted U.S. citizenship. Great Britain, the U.S., and Japan fight for control of China, and communist influence begins to spread in Asia.

- Asian Indians form the Hindustani Welfare Reform Association in the Imperial and Coachella valleys in southern California.

- Arizona passes an alien land law.

1919: Japanese form Federation of Japanese Labor in Hawaii.

1920: There are 26,634 Filipinos in the U.S.

- Initiative on the California ballot is passed to eliminate loopholes in the 1913 alien land law.

- 10,000 Japanese and Filipino plantation workers go on strike.

- Japan stops issuing passports to picture brides due to rising anti-Japanese sentiments.

- Filipinos become the main labor force in Alaska canneries after U.S. immigration laws exclude Japanese and Chinese laborers from entering the country.

- Call for barring Filipinos intensify on the U.S. mainland.

1921: Washington and Louisiana pass alien land laws.

- Japanese farm workers driven out of Turlock, California.

- Filipinos establish a branch of the Caballeros Dimas Alang in San Francisco and a branch of the Legionarios del Trabajo in Honolulu.

1922: Takao Ozawa v. U.S. declares Japanese ineligible for naturalized citizenship.

- New Mexico passes an alien land law.
- Cable Act declares that any American female citizen who marries "an alien ineligible to citizenship" can lose her citizenship. (Repealed in 1936).

1923: Webb v. O'Brien rules that sharecropping is illegal because it is a ruse that allows Japanese to possess and use land.

- Frick v. Webb forbids aliens "ineligible to citizenship" from owning stocks in corporations formed for farming.
- U.S. v. Bhagat Singh Thind declares Asian Indians ineligible for naturalized citizenship.
- Idaho, Montana, and Oregon pass alien land laws.
- Terrace v. Thompson upholds the constitutionality of Washington's alien land law.
- Porterfield v. Webb upholds the constitutionality of California's alien land law.

1924: The Asian Exclusion Act, which is part of the Immigration Act of 1924, excludes all Asian laborer immigrants (particularly Japanese) from entering the United States except for Hawaiians and Filipinos. By this time 180,000 Japanese immigrants had arrived on the mainland.

- The U.S. Border Patrol is created, as an agency under the Department of Labor, to regulate Chinese immigration to the United States across the U.S.-Mexico border.
- 1,600 Filipino plantation workers strike for eight months in Hawaii.

1925: U.S. legislation requires that Filipinos must serve three years in the U.S. Navy in order to become eligible for U.S. citizenship.

- Warring gangs in North America's Chinatowns declare truce.
- Hilario Moncado founds Filipino Federation of America.
- Chinese wives of American citizens are denied entry.

1927: In the infamous case of Lum v. Rice, the Supreme Court found that states possess the right to define a Chinese student as non-white for the purpose of segregating them in public schools.

- Vigilantes force all Filipinos out of Wapato and Toppenish, Washington, to protect white women from interracial dating.

1928: Filipino farm workers are driven out of Yakima Valley, Washington and later there is an anti-Filipino riot in Watsonville, California. This was a clear message that they were also not welcome in America.

1929: Annual immigration quotas are declared permanent.

- An anti-Filipino riot erupts in Exeter, California, and a mob burns their camp to the ground.

1930: Chinese American population in U.S. is 102,159 out of a total population of 123.2 million. There are 30,00 Filipinos in California and 63,052 in Hawaii.

- Anti-Filipino riots in Watsonville, San Jose, and San Francisco, California. Filipinos are blamed for the decline of wages of fig, lettuce, and asparagus harvesters.
- The Los Angeles Superior Court rules that Filipino/white marriages performed since 1921 are not valid.

1931: Amendment to the Cable Act declares that no American-born woman who loses her citizenship (by marrying an alien ineligible to citizenship) can be denied the right of naturalization later.

- Filipinos in the U.S. armed forces become eligible for U.S. citizenship.

1932: Anna May Wong, at the height of her career, stars with Marlene Dietrich in *Shanghai Express*.

1933: Salvador Roldan vs. LA County tests the anti-miscegenation laws. The anti-Filipino forces, however, soon get legislation added onto existing laws to include Filipino-white in anti-miscegenation prohibitions.

1934: Filipino lettuce pickers in the Salinas Valley, California, go on strike.

- Morrison vs. California holds Filipinos ineligible for citizenship.
- March 24, 1934: Tydings-McDuffie Act gives "Commonwealth" status to the Philippines but places an annual quota of fifty on Filipino migration—effectively excluding their entry.

1935: The U.S. Congress passed the Filipino Repatriation Bill to encourage Filipinos to return to the Philippines voluntarily without officially deporting them while also satisfying the anti-Filipino sentiment without an international incident. It offers free transportation for Filipino residents of the continental United States who wished to return to the Philippines but could not afford to do so on the condition that they never return. Only 2,100 take the offer.

1936: American Federation of Labor grants charter to a Filipino-Mexican union of fieldworkers.

1937: Gobind Behari Lal becomes the first Asian American to win a Pulitzer Prize in Reporting.

- Last ethnic strike in Hawaii.

1938: One hundred and fifty Chinese female garment workers strike for three months against the National Dollar stores (owned by a Chinese).

1940: The American Federation of Labor charters the Filipino Federated Agricultural Laborers Association.

- Martial artist, Bruce Lee, is born in San Francisco Chinatown.

October 1941: The Munson Report, commissioned by President Roosevelt, concludes that Japanese Americans are loyal and would pose little threat to the U.S. in event of war.

- December 7, 1941: Japanese planes attack Pearl Harbor, Hawaii, bringing the United States into World War II. After the attack, racist propaganda depicted Japanese immigrants as potential spies and a threat to American freedom.

- December 8, 1941: The U.S. declares war on Japan. After declaring war on Japan, 2,000 Japanese community leaders along Pacific Coast states and Hawaii are rounded up and interned in Department of Justice camps.

- December 8, 1941: The Alien Enemies Act designated Japanese, German and Italian nationals as enemy aliens.

- December 8, 1941: Ten hours after the attack on Pearl Harbor, the Japanese Imperial Army invades the Philippines. Through 1945, the Filipino resistance movement works closely with the U.S. Army to fight the Japanese invaders.

- December 20, 1941: Congress passes Public Law 360, which allows Filipinos in the U.S. to serve in the Armed Forces. By 1945, hundreds join the segregated units of the First and Second Filipino Infantry Regiments in the U.S. Army to fight the Japanese in the Philippines. They are granted U.S. citizenship.

- China is now an ally of the United States.

1942: February 19, 1942: President Franklin D. Roosevelt, fearing Japanese immigrants or those with Japanese ancestry had taken part in planning the attack on Pearl Harbor, issued Executive Order 9066 forcing more than 120,000 Japanese Americans living on the West Coast into 10 internment camps in the U.S. According to the National Archives, approximately 70,000 of those targeted are U.S.

citizens, and no charges are made against any of them. The internees are denied the right to vote. Most lose their homes, businesses, and belongings, and are held prisoner until the war ends. Japanese Americans are confused and angry because German and Italian Americans are not treated the same way.

- Congress passes Public Law 503 to impose penal sanctions on anyone disobeying orders to carry out Executive Order 9066.
- Four Japanese Americans challenged the constitutionality of the Order and refused to comply: Fred Korematsu, Mitsuye Endo, Gordon Hirabayashi, and Minoru Yasui.
- Some internees are shot and killed at Poston and Manzanar relocation centers.
- Hearst newspapers vilify Japanese Americans and call for mass exclusion policy.
- California fires all Japanese Americans in the state's civil service.

1943: Incident at Topaz Relocation Center. Registration crisis leads to Tule Lake Relocation Center's designation as a segregation center.

- In addition to African Americans and Native Americans, the U.S. Army segregates Japanese Americans into separate units.
- Hawaiian Japanese Americans in the 100th Battalion are sent to Africa.
- China is an ally of the U.S. against Japan, so Congress repeals all Chinese exclusion laws, grants Chinese the right of naturalization and a very small immigration quota to Chinese (105 per year).
- Japanese American soldiers from Hawaii join the U.S. Army 100th Battalion in Europe.
- The U.S. Army drafts over 20% of Chinese men living in the United States.

1944: The primarily Japanese American U.S. Army 100th Battalion merges with the all-volunteer Asian Americans of Japanese descent 442nd Regimental Combat Team.

- Tule Lake was placed under martial law.
- Draft reinstated for Nisei.
- Draft resistance at Heart Mountain Relocation Center.
- December 18, 1944: The U.S. Supreme Court declared that loyal citizens of the United States, regardless of cultural descent, could not be detained without cause. The exclusion order is revoked.

1945: August 6: Atomic bomb dropped on Hiroshima, Japan, ushering in the nuclear age. The explosion immediately killed about 80,000 people and tens of thousands more would later die of radiation poisoning. President Harry Truman said that the use of the atomic bomb was intended to cut the war in the Pacific short, avoiding a U.S. invasion of Japan, and saving hundreds of thousands of American lives. His advisors said that conventional bombing of Japan, already in effect, followed up by a massive invasion of Japan would likely result in U.S. casualties of up to one million men.

- August 9, 1945: A second atomic bomb was dropped on Nagasaki killing about 40,000 people instantly and destroying a third of the city. Only recently have Japanese documents been discovered that the Imperial Japanese Army was never going to surrender, having forced all their men to fight to the death since the start of the war. All civilians were going to be mobilized and forced to fight with bamboo spears and satchel charges to act as suicide bombers against Allied tanks. The documents indicated their army was prepared to accept up to 28 million civilian deaths.
- August 15, 1945: Japanese Emperor Hirohito announced his country's surrender to the Japanese people in a radio broadcast.
- September 2, 1945: Japan formally surrenders, ending World War II.

- Korea gains independence from Japan.

- Under the War Brides Act, Asian wives, fiancées, and children of American servicemen are allowed entry into the U.S. (about 200,000 war brides come).

- The all-Japanese American 442nd Regimental Combat Team gains fame by becoming the most highly decorated unit in American history while their families are held as prisoners in their home country. They were awarded 18,143 decorations including 9,486 Purple Heart decorations.

1945-1946: The ten American concentration camps run by the War Relocation Authority close. Japanese Americans begin the process of resettlement largely on their own, being given only $25, and a one-way train ticket. Many feared leaving camp and rejoining society, as anti-Japanese sentiment was still rampant.

1946: The Philippine Trade Act granted non-quota immigrant status to Philippine citizens, their spouses and children who have resided in the U.S. for a continuous period of three years prior to November 30, 1941.

- The Luce–Celler Act grants naturalization opportunities to Filipino Americans and Indian Americans and re-established immigration from the Indian subcontinent and the Philippines.

- Wing F. Ong becomes first Asian American to be elected to state office in the Arizona House of Representatives.

- The Rescission Act deemed that U.S. Filipino WWII veterans did not engage in military service and therefore did not deserve full veteran benefits.

- May 22: The California Supreme Court affirms that a Filipino born in the Philippines during the Commonwealth is not an alien and is allowed to purchase real estate in California.

- July 4: The Philippines is given independence from the United States. U.S. citizenship offered to all Filipinos living in the United States, not just servicemen.

1947: An amendment to the 1945 War Brides Act allows the immigration of foreign wives, husbands, fiancés, and children of U.S. Army personnel; 6,000 Chinese women enter the United States as wives of Chinese American servicemen. This helps these veterans to feel a bit of equality with other veterans.

- Under the Japanese American Evacuation Claims Act, the U.S. government must compensate former internees for financial losses due to their forced evacuation during World War II (ten cents is returned for every dollar lost).
- Wataru "Wat" Misaka was drafted by the Basketball Association of America (BAA) in 1947, making him both the first non-white player and Asian American to play professional basketball in America.

1948: Olympic divers Vicki Draves and Sammy Lee became the first Asian Americans to win an Olympic gold medal for the United States.

- The U.S. Supreme Court finds unconstitutional a California law prohibiting interracial marriage.
- The Korean peninsula becomes separated into North and South Korea.

1949: U.S. breaks off diplomatic ties with newly formed People's Republic of China.

- The United States grants refugee status to 5,000 highly educated Chinese after China institutes a Communist government.
- This Central Intelligence Agency Act (CIA Act) encourages Chinese scientists, engineers, and physicists to enter the United States in furtherance of U.S. national security interests.

1950: The Chinese American population in U.S. is 150,005 out of 151,325,798. There are 122,707 Filipinos in the U.S.

- Korean War brides begin emigration to the U.S.

June 25, 1950: The Korean Conflict begins when North Korea invades South Korea following clashes along the border and rebellions in South Korea. North Korea was supported by China and the Soviet Union, while South Korea was supported by the United Nations, principally the United States. During this period, approximately 15,000 Koreans immigrated to the U.S.

1950-1964: Approximately 6,000 Korean students entered the U.S. Many became professionals such as medical doctors, lawyers, and professors.

1952: A clause in the Walter–McCarran Act was added to revoke the Asian Exclusion Act of 1924, nullifying all federal anti-Asian exclusion laws, and allowing all Asians to be naturalized. It also grants a small immigration quota to Japanese. A small number of Asians are also allowed to immigrate to the United States and given citizenship status.

1953: The Korean Conflict ends with the signing of the Mutual Defense Treaty reestablishing the status quo along the 38th parallel.

- The Refugee Relief Act offers unlimited immigrant visas to Chinese refugees.
- The University of Chicago Philippine Studies Program is established.

1954: The French Indochina War ends with the signing of the Geneva Conference Peace Accords; Vietnam is split into South and North Vietnam; Laos and Cambodia become independent.

- Peter Aduja is elected to the Territorial House of Representatives, becoming the first Filipino to be elected to public office in Hawaii and the United States.
- May 17: The U.S. Supreme Court unanimously rules in Brown v. Board of Education of Topeka, Kansas, that state-sanctioned segregation of public schools is illegal.

1955: Around this time, Chinese leaders and the American media start to portray Asians as the "model minority." They portray Chinese families as model households where there's respect for law and order as well as respect for parents and teachers. Others begin to point to blacks and Hispanics, saying that if they would only be more like Asians, they, too, would be successful. This totally ignored the different histories of systemic racism each group has experienced. Asians now feel a need to quietly keep studying and working hard because they are treated better than blacks or Hispanics. This is the beginning of "Yellow Privilege."

- James Wong Howe becomes the first Asian American to win an Academy Award (Best Cinematography) for *The Rose Tattoo*.

1956: California repeals its alien land laws.

- Bobby Balcena becomes the first Asian American to play in Major League Baseball, playing two games for the Cincinnati Redlegs.

1957: Miyoshi Umeki becomes the first Asian American to win the Academy Award for Best Supporting Actress, for *Sayonara*.

- January 3, 1957: Dalip Saund of California is sworn in as a U.S. Representative, becoming the first Asian American, first Indian American, and first Sikh to serve in Congress.

1959: The U.S. government institutes the "Confession Program" under which illegal aliens may change their immigration status by informing on other illegal aliens.

- August 21, 1959: Hawaii becomes the 50th U.S. state.
- August 24, 1959: Hiram L. Fong is sworn in as Hawaii's first U.S. Senator, becoming the first Asian American elected to the chamber.

1960: The Filipino population in the U.S. is 176,310.

- In Kimm v. Rosenberg, the high court rules that a Korean national should be deported for refusing to answer whether he is communist or not.

1962: Daniel K. Inouye of Hawaii elected for the US Senate; he wins reelection in 1968, 1974, 1980, 1986, 1992, 1998, 2004, and 2010

- Professional American Football player Roman Gabriel was the first Asian American to start as an NFL quarterback. He is half Filipino and half white.
- Spark Matsunaga becomes a U.S. congressman from Hawaii. He was a war hero and attorney who served as United States Senator for Hawaii from 1977 until his death in 1990.
- Wing Luke the first Asian American to hold elected office (Seattle City Council) in the State of Washington.
- The Kennedy Emergency Immigration Act (KEIA Act) permits 5,000 Chinese immigrants to enter the United States during the period of China's "Great Leap Forward" movement.
- Macel Wilson, Miss Hawaii, becomes the first Asian American and Filipino American to win the Miss USA Pageant.

1963: Rocky Fellers, a Filipino American boy band, is first Asian American to hit Billboard 100. "Killer Joe" reached No. 16 on the *Billboard Hot 100* in April 1963, No. 1 in both New York and Los Angeles, CA.

1964: Congress passes a Civil Rights Act of 1964, which prohibits discrimination of all kinds based on race, color, religion, or national origin. It also provides the federal government with the power to enforce desegregation. It also passes another Civil Rights Act in 1965.

- Senator Hiram Fong of Hawaii becomes first Asian American to run for President of the United States; he runs again in 1968.

1965: Immigration Law abolishes "national origins" as basis for allocating immigration quotas to various countries. Asian countries are on an equal footing with others for the first time in U.S. history.

- January 4, 1965: U.S. Representative Patsy Takemoto Mink of Hawaii became the first Asian American woman, and first woman of color, to serve in Congress.

- March 1965: Assistant Secretary of Labor, Daniel Patrick Moynihan, publishes "The Negro Family, the Case for National Action" where he places much of the blame for Black poverty on what he describes as the "tangle of pathology of the Black family." He admonishes them to rehabilitate their dysfunctional families in order to achieve economic and social assimilation.

- September 8, 1965: Filipino American Larry Itliong leads a five-year-long Delano Grape strike in California of 2000 Filipino American farmworkers that started a global grape boycott. Farmworker activist Cesar Chavez and Latino workers joined in, and the two unions ultimately form the United Farm Workers union.

- October 3, 1965: President Lyndon B. Johnson signs the Immigration and Nationality Act into law. Also known as the Hart-Celler Act, it puts an end to immigration policies based on ethnicity and race and quota systems, resulting in a wave of Asian immigrants who had previously been barred from entry. Thousands of Filipino medical and administrative professionals start coming in.

- President Johnson deploys the first U.S. military combat troops to South Vietnam to fight the Viet Cong and orders the bombing of Hanoi.

- A select group of Korean Americans, who had much higher socio-economic and educational attainment relative to the native-born US population, enters the country. They are unable to replicate their former status due to lack of familiarity with English and the American culture, so they turn to employment as small-business owners, opening shops in predominantly black communities.

1966: The term "model minority" is introduced by sociologist William Peterson in his January 9, 1966, article in *The New York Times Magazine* "Success Story, Japanese American Style."

1967: In a landmark civil rights decision of the U.S. Supreme Court in Loving v. Virginia ruled that laws banning interracial marriage violate the Equal Protection and Due Process Clauses of the Fourteenth Amendment to the U.S. Constitution.

1968: A coalition known as the Third World Liberation Front (TWLF) is formed between the Black Student Union and other student groups at San Francisco State University to lead a five-month-long strike on campus to demand a radical shift in admissions practices that mostly excluded nonwhite students and, in the curriculum, regarded as irrelevant to the lives of students of color.

- Yuji Ichioka is credited with coining the term "Asian American." He and student activist Emma Gee founded the Asian American Political Alliance, adopting the name to unify previously separate groups of ethnic Asian students. He taught the first Asian American Studies class at UCLA.

1969: At U.C. Berkeley, the Third World Liberation Front (TWLF) demand that the University acknowledge the histories of minorities of color. The three-month-long protests resulted in the creation of Black Studies in the Department of Ethnic Studies. In the following years, Asian American Studies, Chicano Studies, Native American Studies, and comparative Ethnic Studies programs start at U.C. Berkeley and the University of California at Los Angeles.

1970: The Chinese American population of the U.S. is 237,292 out of 179,323,175. The U.S. Filipino population is 343,060.

1972: President Marcos declared martial law in the Philippines, forcing many to seek political refugee status in the U.S.

- Frank Chin becomes the first Asian American to have a play (*The Chickencoop Chinaman*) produced on a major New York stage.

1973: Martial arts movie *Enter the Dragon* premieres, three weeks after its action star, Bruce Lee, dies from an allergic reaction to pain medication in Hong Kong.

1974: March Fong Eu is elected California's secretary of state. She was the first Chinese American to hold a constitutional office in California and the first woman to hold that office.

- Lau v. Nichols rules that school districts with children who speak little English must provide them with bilingual education.

- The Marcos regime in the Philippine enacted the Labor Export Program (LEP) to systematically export Filipino workers as commodities to work in other countries and use their remittances to finance the underdeveloped Philippine economy.

- Benjamin Menor Jr. becomes the first person of Filipino ancestry to be a State Supreme Court Judge in Hawaii and in the U.S.

- Thelma Buchholdt is elected to the Alaska House of Representatives becoming the first female Filipino American legislator in the U.S.

1975: The Vietnam War ends and over 130,000 refugees enter the U.S. from Vietnam, Kampuchea, and Laos. The post-Vietnam War era saw an increase in hostility against Southeast Asians. This makes all Asians in America uneasy because few whites have ever been able to distinguish one Asian group from another. Many Southeast Asians settled in Texas, where they started their own shrimping businesses. This resurrected the belief that immigrants were coming to steal white jobs. The Ku Klux Klan was quick to respond, setting Vietnamese shrimping boats on fire under the darkness of night.

- Thousands of Vietnamese "boat people" fled their country by sea following the collapse of the South Vietnamese government. Crowded into small vessels, they were prey to pirates, and many suffered dehydration, starvation, and drowning.

- April 26, 1975: After a minor traffic accident involving two motorists in New York's Chinatown, one white and one Chinese, a large crowd gathered in front of the Fifth Precinct. As police dispersed the crowd, they confronted a young architectural engineer, Peter Yew, and dragged him inside the precinct, where he was stripped and badly beaten. The incident brought long-simmering tensions between the Chinese community and police officers to the surface. A rally against police brutality at City Hall brought out 20,000 protesters and forced the closure of most Chinatown businesses. After weeks of public pressure, all charges were dropped against Peter Yew on July 2, and an important message had been delivered to city leaders: the Asian community would no longer be too timid to protest or fight for their rights.

- American physicist Samuel Ting wins the Nobel Prize in Physics.

- Eduardo Malapit is elected mayor of Kauai, Hawaii, as the first Filipino American mayor in the U.S.

1975-1994: After the fall of Phnom Penh to the communist Khmer Rouge regime in 1975, a few Cambodians were able to escape. Two million Cambodians were killed during their reign (one-quarter of the country's population). After the regime was overthrown in 1979, large waves of Cambodians begin immigrating to the U.S. as refugees. Between 1975 and 1994, nearly 158,000 Cambodians were admitted to the U.S.

1976: President Gerald Ford rescinds Executive Order 9066, 34 years after WWII.

- The Health Professions Educational Assistance Act reduced the influx of foreign doctors, nurses, and pharmacists. The Eilberg Act further restricted immigration of professionals.

1977: The Eilberg Act restricts immigration of professionals, reducing job opportunities for aliens. It required all immigrants entering the country under the professional preference part of the 1965 immigration legislation to have a job offer from an American employer. It also specially placed medical personnel under this act, which led to a decrease in the number of Filipino doctors who had been coming at a rate of over 700 a year. However, it did increase the number of nurses from the Philippines, as American hospitals were willing to offer jobs to foreign nurses.

- Raymond Townsend is drafted by the Warriors in the 1978 NBA draft, making him the first Filipino American to play professional basketball in the U.S.

- August 4, 1977: Elderly Filipino and Chinese tenants of the International Hotel in San Francisco are evicted to make way for a new development causing massive protests.

1978: The national convention of the Japanese American Citizens League adopts a resolution calling for redress and reparations for the internment of Japanese Americans.

- The migration of Vietnamese "boat people" becomes a humanitarian crisis when it peaks in 1978 and 1979 but continued into the early 1990s.

1979: Establishment of diplomatic relations between the People's Republic of China and the U.S. reunites members of long-separated Chinese American families.

- March 28, 1979: President Jimmy Carter proclaims a week in May as Asian/Pacific American Heritage Week. In 1990, President Bush broadens the observance to cover the month of May. In 1992, Congress passes a law permanently designating May as Asian/Pacific American Heritage Month. May is chosen in honor of the first official Japanese immigrant's arrival on May 7, 1843, and because May 10, 1869, marks the completion of the transcontinental railroad.

1980: Congress creates the Commission on Wartime Relocation and Internment of Civilians to investigate internment of Japanese Americans during WWII. In 1983, the report finds that Japanese American internment was not a national security necessity.

- The Socialist Republic of Vietnam and the United Nations High Commissioner for Refugees set up an Orderly Departure Program to enable Vietnamese to emigrate legally.
- There are 774,652 Filipinos in America.

1981: The Commission on Wartime Relocation and Internment of Civilians (set up by Congress) holds hearings across the country and concludes the internment was a "grave injustice" and that Executive Order 9066 resulted from "race prejudice, war hysteria, and a failure of political leadership."

- Approximately 120,000 Southeast Asian refugees arrive in the U.S.

1982: On June 23, Chinese American Vincent Chin dies four days after being beaten with a baseball bat by two white autoworkers in Detroit who blamed their unemployment on the rise of Japanese car imports. They were convicted of manslaughter in a plea deal and sentenced to three years' probation plus a $3,000 fine with no jail time. The Asian American community petitioned the U.S. Department of Justice to review the case and, eventually, one of the assailants is sentenced to 25 years in prison. Asian Americans begin to feel the power of speaking out and working together.

- Maya Lin's design selected for the Vietnam Veteran's Memorial.

1983: The National Committee for Japanese American Redress (NCJAR) asks the federal courts to authorize monetary compensation for World War II internees.

- Fred Korematsu, Min Yasui, and Gordon Hirabayashi file petitions to overturn their World War II convictions for violating the curfew and evacuation orders.

1984: Haing Somnang Ngor becomes the first Asian American to win the Academy Award for Best Supporting Actor, for *The Killing Fields*.

1985: Since 1976, more than 762,000 refugees from Southeast Asia have immigrated to the U.S.

- Irene Natividad is elected Chair of the National Women's Political Caucus, becoming the first Asian American woman to lead a national U.S. political organization.

1986: Gerald Tsai becomes the first Asian American CEO of a Fortune 500 company (The American Can Company).

- Immigration Reform and Control Act imposes civil and criminal penalties on employers who knowingly hire undocumented aliens.

- The Marcos regime in the Philippines collapses after decades of people's legal and underground resistance.

1987: First formal signing of the Proclamation of Asian Pacific American Heritage Week by the White House.

- The U.S. House of Representatives votes 243 to 141 to make an official apology to Japanese Americans and to pay each surviving internee $20,000 in reparations.

- *TIME Magazine* publishes a cover article entitled "The New Whiz Kids." Many Chinese Americans express a concern about the "model minority" stereotype.

1988: The U.S. Senate votes 69 to 27 to support redress for Japanese Americans, creating The Civil Liberties Act of 1988.

- The American Homecoming Act allows children in Vietnam born of American fathers to immigrate to the U.S.

- President Ronald Reagan signs Civil Liberties Act of 1988, apologizing for Japanese American internment during WWII and provides reparations of $20,000 to each victim.

1989: Immigration Nursing Relief Act allowed foreign nurses holding temporary work visas to become permanent residents. The H-1A visa is also created, which is a temporary visa for foreign nurses.

- The Chinese government deploys troops to suppress pro-democracy demonstrations in Beijing's Tiananmen Square.
- President George Bush signs into law an entitlement program to pay each surviving Japanese American internee $20,000.
- U.S. reaches agreement with Vietnam to allow political prisoners to emigrate to the U.S.
- Michael Chang becomes the first Asian American winner of a Grand Slam tennis tournament in men's singles, winning the French Open.
- Amy Tan's *The Joy Luck Club* marks the beginning of an explosion in Asian-American cultural production.

1990: The Chinese American population of the U.S. is 1,645,472 out of 248,709,873. There are 1,422,711 Filipinos in the U.S. Census results show Asian Americans to be the fastest-growing ethnic minority group in the U.S., with a 1990 population exceeding 7.2 million.

- The Immigration Act of 1990 creates a new preference system including family-sponsorship and employment-based diversity visas.

1992: Korean businesses looted and burned as a result of riots in Los Angeles due to outrage over Rodney King verdict. Between 2,000 to 2,500 Korean businesses are destroyed.

1993: Due to protests by Asian-American students, professors, and other activists, the University of California, Irvine, agrees to establish an Asian Studies program.

- Gary Locke is elected Governor of Washington, becoming first Asian American to be elected Governor of a mainland U.S. state.

- Dr. David Ho is named *TIME Magazine's* Man of the Year for his research into HIV/AIDS.

1994: California voters pass Proposition 187, which seeks to cut off health, education, and other social service benefits to undocumented immigrants. The Courts later deem it unconstitutional.

1996: The Illegal Immigrant Reform and Individual Responsibility Act (IIRIRA) moves to criminalize and deport U.S. Filipinos who are contract workers, immigrants, and U.S. citizens.

- Proposition 209, The California Civil Rights Initiative, passes the November ballot. The proposition seeks to end gender and racial preferences thus ending affirmative action.

1999: Eric Shinseki becomes the first Asian American four-star general and Chief of Staff of the United States Army.

2000: The Chinese American population of the U.S. is 2,879,636 out of 281,421,904. There are 1.8m Filipinos in the U.S.

- Angela Perez Baraquio Grey becomes the first Asian American to win the Miss America (2001) pageant.

- July 21, 2000: Japanese American Norman Mineta is sworn in by President Bill Clinton as the U.S. Secretary of Commerce, making him the first Asian American to serve in a presidential cabinet.

2002: The USA PATRIOT Act (Uniting and Strengthening America by Providing Appropriate Tools Required to Intercept and Obstruct Terrorism) and the Homeland Security Act dissolved the Immigration and Naturalization Service (INS) and established the Department of Homeland Security. Within the Department of Homeland Security, the government's immigration enforcement capacities were bolstered with the formation of ICE (Immigration and Customs Enforcement).

2009: Dr. Jim Yong Kim is appointed as President of Dartmouth College, becoming the first Asian American president of an Ivy League School.

- Congress proclaims October as Filipino American History Month.
- February 17, 2009: President Barack Obama signs the American Recovery and Reinvestment Act of 2009, creating the Filipino Veterans Equity Compensation Fund.

2010: Immigration from Asia surpasses immigration from Latin America. Many of these immigrants are recruited by American companies from college campuses in India, China, and South Korea.

- Daniel Inouye is sworn in as President Pro Tempore making him the highest-ranking Asian-American politician in American history.
- Jean Quan is elected as the first Asian American Mayor of Oakland, California. Quan is the first Asian American woman elected mayor of a major American city.
- Far East Movement becomes the first Asian-American music group to earn a No. 1 on the *Billboard Hot 100*, for "Like a G6."

2013: Nina Davuluri becomes the second Asian American and first Indian American to be crowned as Miss America. She is the second Asian American following Angela Perez Baraquio in 2000.

- Kevin Tsujihara becomes the first Asian-American CEO of a major Hollywood studio (Warner Bros Entertainment).

2015: Bobby Jindal, Governor of Louisiana, becomes the first Indian American to run for President of the United States.

2018: Aziz Ansari becomes the first Asian American to win a Golden Globe for acting in television. Director Jon M. Chu's *Crazy Rich Asians* breaks box office records, becoming North America's highest-earning romantic comedy in a decade.

2019: Jeremy Lin becomes the first Asian American NBA Champion.

2020: Awkwafina becomes the first Asian American to win the Golden Globe Award for best actress in the musical or comedy category, for *The Farewell.*

2020-21: A report released by the Center for the Study of Hate and Extremism at California State University, San Bernardino, examined hate crimes in sixteen of America's largest cities and found a 150% surge in anti-Asian hate crimes in 2020.

January 20, 2021: Kamala D. Harris is sworn in as the first female, first black and first Asian American vice president of the United States. She is the daughter of an Indian mother and Jamaican father.

Today, Asians still live in limbo in America, not quite being treated equal to whites but still allowed more freedoms than Blacks. Because we are mostly invisible on radio and television and in films, white Americans do not understand or want to interact with us. We are still the victims of stereotypes as unknowable foreigners and hard workers, never leaders, but we are still allowed more success than other minorities…if we behave.

This is why it's so important to teach Asian American history in schools. People in the United States need to understand the challenges and discrimination that we have faced, very similar to how they have learned about the backgrounds and contributions of African Americans, Hispanics, and other groups. As author and activist Helen Zia said, Asian Americans are not "missing in action"; they are "missing in history."

TIMELINE OF THE DEVELOPMENT
OF THE MODEL MINORITY MYTH

1871: The largest recorded mass lynching of seventeen Chinese occurs in Los Angeles.

1875 & 1882: The first U.S. law to restrict immigration, the Page Act of 1875, bans entry to the so-called "lewd and immoral" Chinese women. The 1882 Chinese Exclusion Act places a moratorium on incoming Chinese immigrants. These laws are the first of many policies born out of the false perception that Asians pose a threat to America's economy, health, and safety.

1890s: Some U.S. health officials blame the Chinese for causing diseases like the bubonic plague. Asians are vilified as the "yellow peril," an inscrutable race of mysterious others who would take over the Western world if not stopped.

1940s: China becomes a U.S. ally in WWII, but Under Executive Order 9066, more than 120,000 people—mostly Americans of Japanese descent—are imprisoned during the war. In December 1941, *Life* magazine runs a two-page pictorial entitled "How to tell Japs from the Chinese." It includes passages such as, "U.S. citizens have been demonstrating a distressing ignorance on the delicate question of how to tell a Chinese from a Jap. Innocent victims in cities all over the country are many of the 75,000 U.S. Chinese, whose homeland is our staunch ally."

1943: The U.S. repeals the Chinese Exclusion Act to counter Japanese wartime propaganda that points out American racism in an attempt to erode the country's alliance with China. Chinese Americans are recast as "good" Asians in contrast to the "bad" Japanese. At the end of the war, Japanese Americans are released from concentration camps with explicit and implicit instructions to assimilate into white society. The record of the 442nd Regimental Combat Team—a segregated, all-Japanese unit that suffered heavy casualties during WWII—is touted as a positive example of patriotism and used to help rehabilitate the image of Japanese Americans. Groups like the Japanese American Citizens League begin spreading the idea that Asian Americans are model citizens.

1950s-1960s: With the start of the Korean War, Congress passes the Emergency Detention Act, which gives the U.S. Attorney General the power to establish concentration camps for anyone who might be deemed a domestic threat. Chinese Americans are very aware that what was done to Japanese Americans ten years earlier could be done to them as well. The notion of "keeping one's head down and working hard" begins to be promoted.

The U.S. grants Japanese immigrant's nationalization as a gesture of gratitude toward the Japanese Americans who served their country and in the hopes of cultivating postwar Japan as an ally amid rising Cold War tensions. The U.S. engages in the Cold War and devastating hot wars in Korea, Vietnam, Cambodia, and Laos, claiming to fight communism and "bring democracy" to the rest of the world. But the growing civil rights and ethnic power movements put a spotlight on racism and discrimination at home. The liberal media, government officials, and their sympathetic allies start applauding Japanese Americans for how quickly they recovered from the concentration camps. They attribute their model citizen behavior to the Confucian culture, which emphasizes obedience and strong family values. This new recasting proves useful at a time when policymakers, social scientists, and journalists are agonizing about how to solve what they call the "Negro problem." They popularize the idea of protesting black and brown Americans as "problem minorities" and of the supposedly passive, hardworking Chinese and Japanese Americans as a "model minority." Some Asian Americans buy into this idea, like Hokubei Mainichi editor Howard Imazeki, who stirs up controversy with a 1963 editorial calling on Black Americans to "better themselves" before asking for equal rights.

1964: The Watts riot in the summer of 1964 and the growing demands of African Americans for economic equality, political rights, and an end to segregation in the South make white Americans uneasy.

1965: The Immigration and Nationality Act of 1965 ends national origins quotas, allowing more immigration from Asia and other non-European countries. But a new tier system gives preference to "skilled" immigrants with relatives already in the U.S., creating steep barriers to entry for poor and working-class immigrants.

Blacks are leading the civil rights movement, so policymakers use Japanese and Chinese Americans as examples of minorities that made it without being criminals or depending on welfare. Such comparisons between Asian Americans and Black Americans became much more explicit and common. Assistant Secretary of Labor, Daniel Patrick Moynihan, publishes "Report on the Black Family," where he places much of the blame for black poverty on what he describes as the "tangle of pathology of the black family." He admonishes them to rehabilitate their dysfunctional families in order to achieve economic and social assimilation.

1966: The term "model minority" is introduced by sociologist William Peterson in his January 9, 1966, article in The New York Times Magazine "Success Story, Japanese American Style." He asserts that Japanese Americans—despite facing intense racism, discrimination, and internment during WWII—achieved success in a way that other minority groups had not. He contrasts Japanese Americans with groups that he labels as "problem minorities," meaning those that failed to overcome the barriers placed on them by a racist majority.

In December 1966, a U.S. News and World Report article, "Success Story of One Minority Group in U.S." said: "At a time when it is being proposed that hundreds of billions be spend on uplifting Negroes and other minorities, the nation's 300,000 Chinese Americans are moving ahead on their own with no help from anyone else." This is a best example of how the myth was used against other minorities but also against Asians, saying that we don't need any help like social services programs, affirmative action, etc.

1960s-1980s: Many Asian Americans gain access to better housing, education, and jobs thanks to the Civil Rights Act, the overturning of restrictive housing covenants, and other achievements of black activists. But racist practices like redlining, predatory lending, and "broken windows" policing create and maintain additional barriers that disproportionately impact black and brown communities. Hidden beneath the veneer of Asian American "success" are stories of Southeast Asian refugees resettled in under-resourced and over-policed neighborhoods where they lack access to social services, of elderly residents of historic Chinatowns, Japantowns, and Manilatowns displaced from their homes by "urban renewal," and of Asian American youth navigating a crisis of addiction and suicide.

1988: After more than a decade of political lobbying—much of it focused on the patriotism of the 442nd Regimental Combat Team—the Japanese American redress movement culminates in the Civil Liberties Act of 1988, which grants a formal apology and payments of $20,000 to living survivors of WWII incarceration. The descendants of those who died before the bill's passage are excluded to avoid creating a precedent for reparations to black and Indigenous people.

1992: On April 29, riots erupt following the acquittal of four LAPD officers in the brutal beating of black motorist Rodney King. Korean-owned businesses sustain much of the damage, fueled by anger over a lenient sentence handed to convenience store owner Soon Ja Du for the killing of black teen Latasha Harlins, as well as tensions between black and Latinx South Central residents and Asian shopkeepers perceived as "middleman minorities." The LAPD largely ignores the violence in South Central LA to protect wealthier, whiter neighborhoods, while the mainstream media obscures the deeper, systemic problems behind the riots. Instead, it creates a sensationalized narrative of black and brown mobs attacking Korean immigrants. Politicians blame the riots on a "culture of dependency" and, in the aftermath, enact policies gutting the social welfare system, while investing heavily in prisons and policing.

1996: Congress passes the Antiterrorism and Effective Death Penalty Act (AEDPA) and the Illegal Immigration Reform and Immigrant Responsibility Act (IIRIRA) that allow immigrants to be deported for minor, nonviolent crimes, and previous convictions.

2000s-2010s: Thousands of Southeast Asian refugees are targeted for detention and deportation in the wake of AEDPA and IIRIRA. In Chinatowns across the country, luxury real estate developments displace many low-income residents and the businesses and institutions that serve them, triggering a housing crisis and increasing poverty for many Asian immigrants.

2014-2016: Chinese American NYPD officer Peter Liang kills Akai Gurley, an unarmed black man, a few months after the police murders of Mike Brown and Eric Garner that ignited #BlackLivesMatter protests across the country. In response to his 2016 indictment, thousands of Asian Americans rally in support of Liang, claiming he is a scapegoat for white officers who were never held accountable for similar shootings. The rallies are widely denounced as an example of the model minority myth in action—including by many Asian Americans—but pro-Liang and anti-Black sentiment remains in many Asian American communities. Meanwhile, a small but vocal group of Asian Americans align with white conservatives seeking to end affirmative action, joining a lawsuit, and filing federal complaints against Harvard University claiming their race-conscious admissions policy discriminates against Asian applicants in favor of black and Latinx applicants.

2020-2021: The murder of George Floyd by Minneapolis police officer Derek Chauvin sparks global protests. Many see the role of Hmong American officer Tou Thau, who did not act to stop Chauvin, as a symbol of Asian American complicity in anti-Black violence—which then becomes a call to action for Asians to stand with Black communities against white supremacy.

Verbal and physical attacks on Asian Americans surge during the COVID-19 pandemic, fueled by political rhetoric attributing the virus to China. According to the FBI, between 2020 and 2021 there was 167% increase in anti-Asian hate crimes[61] and a 339% increase from 2021 to 2022.[62] Amid viral videos of attacks on Asian elders and the murder of eight people in two Asian massage parlors in Atlanta in March 2021, some argue that Asian Americans should protect themselves through appeals to patriotism, while others say the violence shows how little protection the model minority myth truly provides.

---

[61] "New FBI Data Shows More Hate Crimes. These Groups Saw the Sharpest Rise." *The Marshall Project* (2023).

[62] J. Lvovsky, "2023: The year of the hate crimes," *Wooton Common Sense,* 5 May 2023.

HISTORIES OF TRIUMPH—AAPI
(Asian Americans and Pacific Islanders)
CONTRIBUTIONS TO AMERICA

When I was growing up, I was amazed to learn about George Washington Carver—how he was born into slavery but became the first African American to earn a Bachelor of Science degree and went on to develop more than 300 products from peanuts. But I wondered why I had not heard about any Asians. For too long, Asian immigrants have been viewed as "taking" from America without giving anything back. Well, it turns out that there are plenty of AAPIs who have contributed greatly to this country and the world! I have listed a few here, in alphabetical order, to remind readers that not only have we been a part of America, almost since its founding, but have also helped to make it what it is today.

CIVIL RIGHTS & SOCIAL JUSTICE

Chung, Cecilia: A transgender woman, Chung is one of the country's most important voices in anti-discrimination, transgender rights, and HIV/AIDS education.

Itliong, Larry: Labor organizer and union leader, in 1956 he formed the Filipino Farm Labor Union, which later merged with the National Farm Workers Association to become United Farm Workers, making major strides for agricultural workers, regardless of ethnicity.

Kochiyama, Yuri: After her internment camp during WWII in the U.S., her civil rights work extended to the Black, Latinx, Indigenous, and Asian American communities.

Lee, Mabel Ping-Hua: A champion of women's rights, particularly of the right to vote, she became the first Chinese woman to earn a doctorate in economics in the United States in 1921.

Nguyen, Amanda: She founded Rise, a nonprofit organization that supports sexual assault survivors, and was involved in drafting the Sexual Assault Survivors' Rights Act. For her work, Nguyen was nominated for a Nobel Peace Prize in 2018.

Tape, Mamie: After Mamie was denied admission to the all-white Spring Valley Primary School in 1884, her parents filed a lawsuit and won. The case resulted in one of the most important civil rights decisions.

DANCE

Abrera, Stella: First Filipina American principal ballerina (American Ballet Theatre) and now the artistic director of the Kaatsbaan Cultural Park Dance Theater.

Chaya, Masazumi: Japanese American dancer, choreographer, and associate artistic director of Alvin Ailey American Dance Theater.

Dang, Viet: Internationally known Hip-Hop dancer, dance teacher, and choreographer.

Dja, Devi: Known as the "Pavlova of the Orient," she choreographed and appeared, often unattributed, in films like *The Picture of Dorian Gray* (1945). She was the first Indonesian woman to become an American citizen in 1954.

D'umo, Napoleon & Tabitha (Nappytaps): Emmy Award-winning married choreographer best-known for the television shows *So You Think You Can Dance* and *America's Best Dance Crew.*

Generosa, Angelica: Principal dancer at Pacific Northwest Ballet.

Gilmour, Ailes: Japanese American dancer, pioneer of the American Modern Dance movement of the 1930s, and among the first members of Martha Graham's company.

Hanagami, Kyle: Japanese American choreographer and one of the most in-demand names in the Los Angeles dance industry.

Inaba, Carrie Ann: Japanese American TV personality, dancer, choreographer, actress, and singer, she is best known for ABC TV's *Dancing with the Stars*.

Ito, Michio: Acclaimed Japanese American director and choreographer.

Liang, Edwaard: Award-winning ballet dancer and choreographer.

Osato, Sono: The first Asian American dancer to travel the world with the Russian Ballet and star in a hit Broadway musical.

Pazcoguin, Georgina: Soloist with the New York City Ballet, she is known for challenging racism in ballet and for performing on Broadway.

Sato, Ruth: Dancer, musician promoter, and nightclub manager. She was the first Japanese chorus girl on Broadway, where she worked for 20 years.

Tayag, Phil (Philippe "SACBxY" Tayag): MTV VMA nominee for best choreography; this Filipino American has worked with Bruno Mars and the Superbowl with Beyonce and Coldplay.

Yuriko (Yuriko Amemiya): Danced principal roles with Martha Graham, founded Graham 2, played feature roles in the original Broadway productions of *The King and* I and *Flower Drum Song*, and restaged numerous Graham works.

EDUCATION

Kim, Jim Yong: The first Asian American president of an Ivy League school (Dartmouth College), Kim chaired the Department of Global Health and Social Medicine at Harvard Medical School, co-founded Partners In Health, and served as president of the World Bank. In 2013, he was named the world's 50th most powerful person by *Forbes Magazine*.

Matsuda, Fujio: The first Asian American president of a major U.S. university (University of Hawaii).

Tien, Chang-Lin: The first Asian American to lead a major research university (UC Berkeley). As chancellor, he was a leading supporter of affirmative action.

ENTERPRISE

Bhatia, Sabeer: In 1996, this Indian American businessman co-founded Windows Live Hotmail, which was later acquired by Microsoft for nearly $400 million and turned it into Microsoft Outlook.

Chai, Nelson: Investment banker and former CFO of the New York Stock Exchange.

Chang, Do Won: Born in South Korea, he founded the clothing store Forever 21, which grew to 600 stores with 30,000 employees by 2015.

Chen, Perry: Creator and principal founder of Kickstarter along with Charles Adler and Yancey Strickler.

Chen, Steven: In 2005, this Taiwanese American, along with Bangladeshi-German American Jawed Karim and Chad Hurley, founded YouTube.

Lee, Brian: Co-founder of Legalzoom.com, ShoeDazzle.com, and The Honest Company.

Ly, Eric Thich Vi: Entrepreneur and investor. Ly co-founded LinkedIn. He is currently the CEO and founder of Hub, a blockchain-based trust protocol.

Ngoy, Ted: Of Cambodian descent, he is known as "The Donut King" for building a doughnut shop empire.

Tsai, Gerald: He became the first Asian American CEO of a Fortune 500 company (The American Can Company) in 1986 and helped build Fidelity Investments into a powerhouse. After purchasing Primerica, he became the first Chinese American to lead a Dow Jones Industrials company.

Tsujihara, Kevin: The first Asian American CEO of a major Hollywood studio (Warner Bros Entertainment).

Yang, Jerry: Taiwanese American tech investor and co-founder of Yahoo, Yang has mentored and invested in numerous technology startups.

Yu, Gideon: The Korean American investor and executive became chairman of Bowers & Wilkins and co-owner of the San Francisco 49ers.

FASHION, BEAUTY & CULINARY ARTS

Baraquio, Angela Perez: Crowned Miss America 2001 as Miss Hawaii. She was the first Asian American and first Filipino American to win that pageant.

Broyles, Emma Leigh: The first Korean American and the first Miss Alaska to be crowned Miss America (2022).

Chen, Joyce: Chinese American chef, restaurateur, and author credited with popularizing authentic, northern-style Chinese cuisine in the U.S. and for pioneering the all-you-can-eat Chinese buffet concept. In 2014, the U.S. Postal Service issued a stamp in her honor.

Fashion Designers: Some of the most influential designers in New York's fashion industry in the 1980s and 1990s were Anna Sui,

Vivienne Tam, and Kimora Lee Simmons. Today, prominent Asian American designers include Prabal Gurung, Phillip Lim, Jason Wu, Derek Lam, Bibhu Mohapatra, Dao-Yi Chow, Carol Lim, and Humberto Leon.

Lee, Corey: The Korean American chef-owner was the first to receive three stars from the Michelin Guide for Benu, which was named among The World's 50 Best Restaurants. Lee is also a two-time James Beard Award winner, a former Food & Wine Best New Chef, and a Goodwill Ambassador to Seoul.

Wang, Alexander: The first Asian American creative director and head of a French haute couture house (Balenciaga, 2012-2015), as well as the recipient of the CFDA/Vogue Fashion Fund in 2008.

Wang, Vera Ellen: The youngest editor ever at *Vogue* magazine, she has designed for celebrities like Ariana Grande, Chelsea Clinton, Alicia Keys, Mariah Carey, Victoria Beckham, and Kim Kardashian. She was inducted into the U.S. Figure Skating Hall of Fame in 2009 for her contribution to the sport as a costume designer and was awarded the Council of Fashion Designers of America Lifetime Achievement Award in 2013. She placed 34th on the *Forbes* "America's Richest Self-Made Women 2018."

FILM & TELEVISION ARTS

Ahn, Philip: Widely regarded as the first Korean American film actor in Hollywood, he was one of the most recognizable character actors with over 180 film and television credits between 1935 and 1978.

Alcroft, Hayley Kiyoko: Singer, dancer, and actress who appeared in films like *Scooby-Doo!* (2009–2010) and TV series *CSI: Cyber* (2015–2016).

Ansari, Aziz: The first Asian American to win the Golden Globe for Best Actor—Television Series Musical or Comedy for *Master of None* in 2018.

Awkwafina (Nora Lum): Chinese Korean American rapper, actress, and comedian; she is the first woman of Asian descent to win a Golden Globe in any lead actress film category.

Chan, Jackie: Hong Kong film star, martial artist, director, producer, stuntman, and singer, Chan was the first Asian to host *Saturday Night Live* in 2000. He has appeared in over 150 films.

Cho, John: The first Asian American actor to be cast as a romantic lead in a sitcom and to star in a mainstream Hollywood thriller (*Searching*, 2018) for which he was nominated for the Independent Spirit Award for Best Male Lead.

Condor, Lana Therese: Vietnamese-born American actress who made her film debut in *X-Men: Apocalypse* (2016).

Eng, Dayyan: The first Asian American and only foreigner to be invited into the China Film Director's Guild and to have a film nominated for Best Picture at the Chinese academy awards.

Hiro, Kazu: The first Asian American to win the Academy Award for Best Makeup and Hairstyling (2019) after two nominations in 2006 and 2007.

Howe, James Wong: Earning 10 Academy Award nominations for Best Cinematography and winning twice (1955, 1963), he was named among the 10 most influential cinematographers by the International Cinematographers Guild.

Hsu, Stephanie: Nominated in 2023 for an Oscar for Best Performance by an Actress in a Supporting Role in *Everything Everywhere All at Once*.

Liu, Lucy: The first Asian American female to host *Saturday Night Live* (2000), she earned a Primetime Emmy Award nomination for Outstanding Supporting Actress (Comedy Series) and a Screen Actors

Guild Award nomination for Outstanding Performance by a Female Actor (Comedy Series).

Ngor, Haing S.: Of Cambodian descent, he is the only Asian to win an Academy Award for Best Supporting Actor (*The Killing Fields,* 1985), and only one of two non-professional actors to win an acting Oscar.

Nguyen, Dustin: Born in Saigon, he became a successful actor, director, writer, and martial artist. His most famous roles are in the movies *21 Jump Street* and *VIP.*

Oh, Sandra: The Canadian American actress of Korean descent has won two Golden Globe Awards and four Screen Actors Guild Awards. In 2019, *Time* magazine named her one of the 100 most influential people in the world.

Okazaki, Steven: The first Asian American to win the Academy Award for Best Documentary (Short Subject).

Quan, Ke Huy: Won the Oscar for Best Supporting Actor in *Everything Everywhere All at Once* in 2023.

Shum, Harry Jr.: Nominated for four Screen Actors Guild Awards for his performance in the TV series *Glee*, winning once. He also won The Male TV Star of 2018 in the E! People's Choice Awards for *Shadowhunters.*

Takei, George: Best known as Lieutenant Hikaru Sulu in the original *Star Trek* series, the actor is also a prominent LGBT rights advocate and political activist who has won awards for his work.

Tashima, Chris: The first Asian American to win the Academy Award for Best Live Action Short Film for *Visas and Virtue* in 1997.

Umeki, Miyoshi: The first Asian American to win the Academy Award for Best Supporting Actress (*Sayonara,* 1957), she was also a Tony Award- and Golden Globe-nominated actress and singer.

Wong, Anna May: Appearing in over 60 movies throughout her career since starting in 1922, she was the world's first major Asian American film star and the first Asian American to lead a U.S. television show in 1951.

Wong, Jadin: Appeared in several films, headlined nightclub shows, entertained U.S. troops during WWII, and appeared on Broadway in *The King* and I and *The World of Susie Wong*, before opening Jadin Wong Management that represented over 400 Asian and Asian-American performers.

Yang, Bowen: The first cast member on *Saturday Night Live* of full Asian descent and the first SNL featured player to be nominated for a Primetime Emmy Award (2021).

Yang, Janet: She became the first Asian American President of the Academy of Motion Picture Arts and Sciences in 2022.

Yeo, Gwendoline See-Hian: Actress, musician, and writer best known for her roles in *General Hospital, Desperate Housewives*, and *Broken Trail,* as well as for voice work in *Wolverine, X-Men*, and *Teenage Mutant Ninja Turtles.*

Yeoh, Michelle: After bursting onto international screens in the James Bond film *Tomorrow Never Dies,* followed by *Crouching Tiger, Hidden Dragon*, the Malaysian-born Yeoh became the first Asian to win an Oscar for Best Actress in a Leading Role for *Everything Everywhere All at Once* in 2023.

Yeun, Steven: The first Asian American to be nominated for the Academy Award for Best Actor for *Minari* (2021) and by the Screen Actors Guild for an Outstanding Performance by a Male Actor in a Leading Role.

Young, Cyrus "Cy": Chinese American special effects animator, best known for his work for The Walt Disney Company._

JOURNALISM & LITERATURE

Chin, Frank: The first Asian American to have a play produced on a major New York stage in 1972 and the founder of the Asian American Theater Workshop, which became the Asian American Theater Company in 1973.

Chun, Ella Kam Oon: The first female journalist of any ethnic background at *The Honolulu Advertiser* to break away from the "society" pages when she became a City Hall reporter (1937).

Chung, Connie: She became the first Asian American to anchor a U.S. major network newscast (CBS Evening News) in 1993, also anchoring and reporting for NBC, ABC, CNN, and MSNBC.

Guillermo, Emil: The first Asian American male and first Filipino American to host a national news broadcast (NPR's *All Things Considered*, 1989).

Kashiwahara, Ken: Groundbreaking network television anchor and reporter, he won two Emmy Awards (1986, 1988). In 1993, he was awarded a Lifetime Achievement Award by the Asian American Journalists Association.

Ku, Ah Jook: The third woman of Chinese descent to graduate from the University of Missouri School of Journalism in 1935 and the first Asian American reporter for the Associated Press in 1943.

Mukerji, Dhan Gopal: The first Indian American to win a Newbery Medal for *Gay Neck: The Story of a Pigeon* (1928).

WuDunn, Sheryl: The first Asian-American woman to be hired at the *New York Times* and to win a Pulitzer Prize for International Reporting (with her husband, Nicholas Kristof). The couple also received the Dayton Literary Peace Prize's 2009 Lifetime Achievement Award. In

2011, WuDunn was named by *Newsweek* as one of the "150 Women Who Shake the World."

Young, Al: He became the first Asian American U.S. mainland sportswriter in 1970; he was an award-winning journalist and editor at the *Boston Globe, USA Today*, the *New York Daily News, the New Haven Register,* and *Bridgeport Post-Telegram.*

MEDICINE

Chang, Min Cheuh: The Chinese American reproductive biologist helped develop the birth control pill. As a pioneer of in-vitro fertilization, he paved the way for "test-tube babies."

Ho, David: A Taiwanese American physician, he developed foundational research for the modern "cocktail" antiretroviral therapy.

Jaisohn, Philip: The first Korean to become an American citizen and the first Korean American to receive an American medical degree in 1892. He also championed the Korean independence movement and founded *Tongnip Sinmun*, the first Korean newspaper in Hangul.

Joshi, Anandi Gopalrao: Born in India, she was the first Hindu and first woman to receive a medical degree in the U.S. at 20 years old in 1886.

Kwak, Larry: Pioneer of breakthrough innovations in immunology and cancer vaccines, he was named one of *Time Maga*zine's "100 Most Influential People" in 2010.

Luzuriaga, Katherine: Filipino American physician and pediatric immunologist, who—with virologist Deborah Persaud—was recognized for work leading to the "functional cure" of an HIV-positive infant.

Sekiguchi, Eugene: The first Asian American president of the American Dental Association.

Tsai, Peter: In the 1990s, he invented the N95 respirator, which is 10 times more efficient than other masks. During the COVID-19 pandemic, Dr. Tsai came out of retirement to study the best way to sanitize and reuse them.

Vo-Dinh, Tuan: The Vietnamese American biomedical engineering professor at the Duke University Pratt School of Engineering has authored more than 200 publications in peer-reviewed scientific journals, received more than 20 awards, and holds more than 20 U.S. patents.

Wong-Staal, Flossie: Her work led to identifying HIV as the cause of AIDS and to determining that "drug cocktails" are a key to managing HIV. The most cited female scientist of the 1980s with almost 7,800 citations, she helped lay the groundwork for understanding infectious diseases like COVID-19.

MILITARY

Bass, JoAnne S.: The first Asian American to hold the senior enlisted position in the U.S. Air Force, as the 19th Chief Master Sergeant in 2020.

Cheung, Katherine Sui Fun: Inducted into the International Women in Aviation's Pioneer Hall of Fame, she was one of the first Chinese women to receive a private pilot license and the first to obtain an international flying license. During WWII, she served as a flight instructor in the U.S.

Chung-Hoon, Gordon: An admiral in the U.S. Navy during WWII, he received the Navy Cross and the Silver Star. Later, he was promoted to rear admiral, becoming the first Asian American flag officer of the United States Navy.

Cuddy, Susan Ahn: The first female gunnery officer in the U.S. Army during WWII, the first Asian American woman to work in naval intelligence as a codebreaker and become section chief in the National Security Agency.

Harris, Harry Jr.: He was the first Japanese American to lead U.S. Pacific Command and the highest-ranking Japanese American in the U.S. Navy during his time as commander.

Lee, Kurt Chew-Een: The first Asian American officer in the Marine Corps in 1944, Lee earned the Navy Cross in Korea in 1950.

Ohr, Fred: Highly decorated WWII ace fighter pilot credited with the destruction of six aircraft in the air and seventeen on the ground, ending his tour as the squadron's commanding officer.

Shinseki, Eric: The first Asian American four-star general, Chief of Staff of the U.S. Army, and United States Secretary of Veterans Affairs in 2009. He was awarded three Bronze Star Medals and two Purple Hearts. As of 2004, he is the highest-ranked Japanese American to have served in the U.S. Armed Forces.

MUSIC

Aiko, Jhené: Japanese, Creole, Dominican, and European R&B singer, she is a six-time Grammy-nominated artist and well-respected for her philanthropic endeavors.

Anderson, Brandon Paak: Grammy award-winner, singer, rapper, and half of Silk Sonic.

Aoki, Steve: One of the most prominent DJs in the industry, record producer, music programmer, and record executive—in 2012, Pollstar designated Aoki as the highest-grossing electronic dance music artist in North America.

Au-Yeung, Jin (MC Jin): First Asian American solo rapper to be signed to a major record label in the U.S.

Barcelona, Danny: Filipino American jazz drummer best known for his years with Louis Armstrong's All-Stars.

Bhasker, Jeff: Record producer, songwriter, and multi-instrumentalist, he was awarded the Grammy for Producer of the Year in 2016.

Chang, Lynn: Violin soloist and chamber musician, she is a founding member of the Boston Chamber Music Society and a faculty member at MIT; Boston University; the Boston Conservatory; and the New England Conservatory of Music.

Chen, Mei-Ann: Taiwanese American conductor is music director of the Chicago Sinfonietta and conductor laureate of the Memphis Symphony Orchestra.

Elliman, Yvonne Marianne: Singer, songwriter, and actress of Japanese and Irish descent who performed in the first stage cast of *Jesus Christ Superstar* and had a number of hits in the 1970s, including the US #1 "If I Can't Have You."

Han, Wu: Taiwanese American concert performer, recording artist, educator, and cultural entrepreneur of international prominence.

H.E.R. (Gabi Wilson): Of Filipino and Black descent has won four Grammy wins and 13 nominations.

Hiroshima: American band that incorporates Japanese instruments in its music. Hiroshima has sold over four million albums worldwide.

Ho, Daniel: Musician, composer, and producer, he has recorded 18 solo albums, some of which have won, or were nominated for, Grammy Awards.

Huang, Frank Xin: Chinese-born American violinist and teacher, he is concertmaster of the New York Philharmonic.

Iha, James Yoshinobu: Guitarist and co-founder of the Smashing Pumpkins.

Ikeda, Suzee: The first Asian American solo artist at Motown, best known for her work with Michael Jackson and The Temptations.

Iyer, Vijay: Award-winning Indian American composer, pianist, bandleader, producer, and writer whom the *New York Times* called a "social conscience, multimedia collaborator, system builder, rhapsodist, historical thinker, and multicultural gateway."

Jain, Sunny: Acclaimed Indian American dhol player, drummer, and Indo-jazz composer recognized as a leading voice in the burgeoning movement of South Asian-American jazz musicians.

Jones, Norah (Geethali Norah Jones Shankar): The singer, songwriter, and pianist has sold more than 50 million records, won nine Grammy Awards, and was ranked 60th on *Billboard* magazine's artists of the 2000s-decade chart.

Kim, Kathleen: Korean American operatic coloratura soprano.

Lam, Larissa: Chinese American singer, songwriter, talk-show host, music executive, filmmaker, and producer.

Lee, Dai-Keong: His Symphony No. 2 was runner-up for the 1952 Pulitzer Prize for Music.

Liang, Lei: Chinese-born American composer who was a winner of the Grawemeyer Award and a finalist for the Pulitzer Prize in Music.

Long, Zhou: Chinese American composer, winner of the 2011 Pulitzer Prize for Music.

Ma, Yo-Yo: Chinese American classical music prodigy. He began performing at the age of four, recorded more than ninety albums, received eighteen Grammy Awards, the Glenn Gould Prize, the National Medal of Arts, the Presidential Medal of Freedom, the Polar Music Prize, and was once named "Sexiest Classical Musician" by *People* magazine.

Maddala, Vivek: Four-time Emmy-winning composer for film, television, theater, and dance productions.

Ming, Lee Pui: Pianist, vocalist, and composer; she is one of the most notable figures in the Asian American jazz movement.

Liu, Rose: The first Chinese American artist to make it to top four on *The Voice of China* television series.

Ryan, James (Malay): Record producer, songwriter, and audio engineer, he is a Grammy Award winner for Best Urban Contemporary Album.

Mars, Bruno (Peter Gene Hernandez): Half Filipino and half Puerto Rican American pop star, the singer, songwriter, and producer is known for his showmanship and wide range of musical styles.

Meyers, Anne Akiko: The American violinist was the top-selling classical instrumentalist of 2014 on *Billboard's* traditional classical charts.

Miyamoto, Nobuko JoAnne: Japanese American folk singer, songwriter, activist in the Asian American Movement, and member of the band Yellow Pearl, whose album *Grain of Sand* is considered the first Asian American album in history.

Nagano, Kent George: Japanese American conductor who was Music Director of the Montreal Symphony Orchestra from 2006 to 2020 and has been Music Director of the Hamburg State Opera since 2015.

Panikkar, Sean: This operatic tenor has performed in many leading opera houses, including the Metropolitan Opera, Teatro alla Scala, and Carnegie Hall.

Pak, Jung-Ho: Artistic Director of the San Diego Symphony and of the New Haven Symphony Orchestra, of which he is now Conductor Emeritus, as well as Music Director of the Diablo Ballet and the NEXT Generation Chamber Orchestra.

Park, Jonathan Edgar (Dumbfoundead): One of the most prominent Asian American rappers in the U.S., known for his socially conscious lyrics.

Phan, Nicholas: Born to a Chinese Indonesian father and Greek American mother, he has been called "one of the world's most remarkable singers" by the *Boston Globe*. He has performed with the New York Philharmonic, the Los Angeles Philharmonic, the Philharmonia Orchestra, the San Francisco Symphony, and the Chicago Symphony Orchestra.

Quitevis, Richard (DJ Qbert): He was named America's Best DJ in 2010, DMC USA Champion in 1991 (solo), and DMC World Champion in 1992 and 1993.

Ramos, Hilario D. "Larry" Jr.: In 1963, he won a Grammy with The New Christy Minstrels.

Salonga, Lea: Nicknamed "Pride of the Philippines," she is known for her roles in musical theatre, for the singing voices of Disney's Jasmine and Mulan, and as a recording artist and television performer. Salonga was the first actress of Asian descent to play Éponine and Fantine in *Les Misérables* on Broadway.

Scherzinger, Nicole: Of Filipino, Native Hawaiian, Ukrainian, and Polish descent, the singer, songwriter, dancer, actress, and TV personality is the lead singer of the Pussycat Dolls, one of the best-selling girl groups of all time.

Shimozumi, Hana: Billed as "the Japanese Nightingale," she is best known for playing Yum Yum in Gilbert and Sullivan's *The Mikado* (1919).

Tin, Christopher Chiyan: Composer of art music and film and video game soundtracks, has won two Grammy Awards for his classical cross-over album *Calling All Dawns*.

Vernimo, Asia Nalani (Asia Cruise): The first artist of Asian descent to be signed to Hitz Committee/Jive Records.

Vu, Cuong: Vietnamese American jazz trumpeter. In addition to his own work as a bandleader, Vu was a member of the Pat Metheny Group.

White, Jerome Charles Jr. (Jero): The first Black enka singer in Japanese music history.

POLITICS & JUDICIARY

Ariyoshi, George: The first Asian American governor (Hawaii, 1974-1986).

Cao, Ánh Quang "Joseph": The first Vietnamese American to serve in Congress (Louisiana's 2nd Congressional District, 2009-2011).

Chang-Bloch, Julia: The first Asian American U.S. ambassador (Nepal, 1989-1993).

Cherian, Joy: The first Asian American and first Indian American Commissioner at the U.S. Equal Employment Opportunity Commission (1984).

Choy, Herbert: The first person of Korean ancestry to be admitted to the U.S. bar and the first Asian American federal court judge, appointed to the U.S. Court of Appeals for the Ninth Circuit in 1971.

Duckworth, Tammy: The first person born in Thailand and the first female double amputee to be elected to the U.S. Congress.

Harris, Kamala: The first Asian American, first African American, first female vice-president, and the highest-ranking female official in U.S. history.

Hirono, Mazie: The first Asian American female senator from Hawaii.

Inouye, Daniel: President Pro-Tempore of the Senate, he was the highest-ranking Asian American politician in U.S. history until the election of Vice President Kamala Harris in 2021.

Kim, Andy: Elected to Congress from central New Jersey in 2018, he was the first Democratic and second Korean American overall to serve in Congress.

Kim, Jay: The first Korean American elected to Congress in 1992 as a representative for portions of Orange County, California.

Locke, Gary: The first Asian American governor of a mainland U.S. state (Washington, 1997–2005); among other posts. He served as United States Secretary of Commerce (2009–2011).

Mineta, Norman: The first Asian American to hold a presidential cabinet post as the Secretary of Commerce during the Clinton administration. Under Bush, he was the longest-serving Secretary of Transportation in the department's history.

Moritsugu, Kenneth P.: The first Asian American to be named U.S. Surgeon General in 2006.

Nguyen, Jacqueline: The first Vietnamese American federal judge and first Asian American woman on the Federal Appellate Court.

Ong, Wing F.: The first Chinese American not born in the United States to be elected to the Arizona House of Representatives in 1946.

Saund, Dalip Singh: The first Asian American, the first Indian American, the first Sikh American, and the first member of a non-Abrahamic faith to be elected to the United States Congress.

Takemoto-Mink, Patsy: The first Asian American woman elected to Congress (Hawaii), and the first Asian American Democratic candidate for U.S. president. She served 24 years in congress.

Veloria, Velma R.: The first Filipino American and the first Asian American woman to be elected to the Washington House of Representatives (1993-2004).

RELIGION & SPIRITUALITY

Nhat Hanh, Thich: Spiritual leader who is globally known for his groundbreaking teachings on mindfulness, ethics, and peace that have been applied by politicians, business leaders, activists, and teachers.

Wang, Ignatius: The first Asian American to be appointed bishop of the Roman Catholic Church in 2002.

Warnick Buchdahl, Angela: The first Asian American rabbi and cantor, she was named by *Newsweek* and *The Daily Beast* as one of America's "Most Influential Rabbis."

SCIENCE & TECHNOLOGY

Bhatt, Ajay: In 1994, Bhatt and his team created Universal Series Bus (USB) technology. Bhatt agreed to have Intel make the technology open and royalty-free. "I don't do these things for money," he said.

Fong, Wallace: One of the first Asian American engineering students to graduate from UC Berkeley in 1923's who designed the original lighting for the Golden Gate Bridge, which opened on May 27, 1937.

Gong, Lue Gim: Known as "The Citrus Wizard," this Chinese American horticulturalist's impact on the agricultural industry won him widespread recognition, including the first Silver Wilder Medal to be awarded by the American Pomological Society.

Kaku, Michio: A third-generation Japanese American, whose parents were interned in WWII, Kaku is a theoretical physicist, activist, futurologist, and popular science writer. Among his many books are three New York Times best-sellers. He is a frequent and popular presence on radio and TV, with a large following on his own blog.

Tang, Ching Wan: With Steven Van Slyke, he invented the organic light-emitting diode (OLED) that produces a more vibrant display than LCD. Named on 84 patents, he was inducted into the National Inventors Hall of Fame in 2018.

Ting, Samuel C.C.: The first U.S.-born Asian American to win the Nobel Prize in Physics in 1976.

Wu, Chien-Shiung: Known as the "Queen of Nuclear Research," she was instrumental in developing atomic science, including the first atomic bomb. She received the inaugural Wolf Prize in Physics and was the first woman to serve as president of the American Physical Society.

Yang, Chen-Ning & Lee, Tsung-dao: Winners of the Nobel Prize in Physics in 1957. They became U.S. citizens in 1964 and 1962 respectively.

Yau, Shing-Tung: The first Asian American to be awarded the Fields Medal in 1982, the highest honors a mathematician can receive.

SPACE EXPLORATION

Chawla, Kalpana: Serving as a mission specialist and robotic arm operator, she became the first woman of Indian descent in space on the *Columbia* (1997). Sadly, Chawla died when the spacecraft disintegrated during its re-entry into the Earth's atmosphere in 2003.

Onizuka, Ellison: The first Asian American and the first person of Japanese origin in space on *Discovery* in 1985. In 1989, he died on the *Challenger*, which was destroyed seconds after launch.

Trinh, Eugene H.: The first Vietnamese American to travel into outer space and the second Vietnamese in space (after Phạm Tuân, Soyuz 37) on *Columbia STS-50.*

SPORTS & ATHLETICS

Achiu, Walter Tin Kit: The first East Asian to play in the National Football League (Dayton Triangles) and one of the first minority players in any major American professional sports league, preceding Jackie Robinson by 20 years.

Balcena, Bobby: The first player of Filipino ancestry to appear in a major league baseball game, playing two games for the Cincinnati Redlegs in 1956.

Chang, Michael: To this day, the only tennis player of Asian descent to win a men's singles Grand Slam event (1989).

Chin, Tiffany: The first Asian American U.S. figure skating national champion, two-time World bronze medalist (1985, 1986), and a two-time Skate America champion (1983, 1986). Chin finished first in all three phases of the competition at the 1985 U.S. Championships.

Cho, Rich: The first Asian American general manager of an NBA team (Portland Trail Blazers), he currently serves as VP of Basketball Strategy of the Memphis Grizzlies.

Chung, Eugene: The first Korean American to be drafted in the 1st round, he played offensive line (New England Patriots). As a coach, he won Super Bowl LII with the Eagles.

Gabriel, Roman: He became the first Asian American and Filipino American NFL quarterback in 1962, then went on to a 16-season professional career.

Kahanamoku, Duke: Nicknamed "The Big Kahuna," this five-time Olympic medalist in swimming also popularized surfing, which had been previously known only in Hawaii.

Koo, Younghoe: The first Asian American to lead the NFL in scoring in a season and to be named to the NFL Pro Bowl in 2020 as a placekicker.

Le, Thanh: Vietnamese American mixed martial artist and former ONE Featherweight World Champion, he competed in Legacy Fighting Alliance.

Lee, Sammy: The first Asian American male to win an Olympic gold medal for the U.S., the second Asian American to win a gold medal overall, and the first man to win back-to-back gold medals in Olympic platform diving in 1948.

Lin, Jeremy: His stellar play helped the Knicks make the 2012 playoffs, generating a phenomenon known as "Linsanity." One of the few Asian Americans to play in the NBA, he is first to win an NBA championship (2019).

Magpayo, Mike: Men's head coach at UC Riverside, he became the first Asian American to hold this position in NCAA Division I men's basketball in 2020.

Manalo Draves, Victoria: The first American woman to win two gold medals in diving and the first Asian American to win a gold medal in the Summer Olympics in 1948.

Mariota, Marcus Ardel Taulauniu: Quarterback for the Atlanta Falcons of the National Football League, he was the first Hawaii-born athlete to win the Heisman Trophy in 2014.

Misaka, Wataru: The first non-white player to play in the NBA in 1947.

Ng, Kimberly: The first Asian American general manager of an MLB team and the first female GM of a team in the Big Four leagues in North America. She is currently GM of the Miami Marlins and the highest-ranking female baseball executive.

Nguyen, Dat: The first Vietnamese American to play in and be recognized as an All-Pro in the NFL.

Nguyen, Lee: His fifteen-year career spanned the Netherlands, Vietnam, and the U.S. with over 250 matches in Major League Soccer.

Roberts, Dave: The first Asian American baseball manager to win the World Series in 2020. He played for five MLB teams and coached for the San Diego Padres before becoming the Dodgers' manager in 2016.

Shibutani, Alex Hideo & Maia: Winners of many Olympic, World Championships, and other competitions, in 1983, the sibling duo became the first ice dancers both of Asian descent to medal in team figure skating and ice dancing.

Spoelstra, Erik: The first Asian American head coach of the National Basketball Association (Miami Heat) in 2008.

Wakamatsu, Don: Japanese American drafted by the Cincinnati Reds, he became the first Asian American MLB manager in 2008.

Ward, Hines: Korean-born pro football player, he was voted MVP of Super Bowl XL. He is regarded as one of the best wide receivers and a key contributor to the Steelers' success during the 2000s.

Wie West, Michelle: Professional golfer who plays on the LPGA Tour, she won her first and only major at the 2014 U.S. Women's Open.

Woods, Tiger: The first Asian American to win the U.S. Amateur Championship in 1994. Woods' ancestry (¼ Chinese, ¼ Thai, ¼ African American, ⅛ white, and ⅛ Native American) also made him the first African American to achieve this feat. He is tied for first in PGA Tour wins, ranks second in men's major championships, and holds numerous golf records. Woods is widely regarded as one of the greatest golfers of all time and is one of the most famous athletes in modern history.

Yamaguchi, Kristine Tsuya: The first Asian American woman to win gold in a Winter Olympics (1992), two-time World champion (1991, 1992), and U.S. champion (1992). As a pair skater with Rudy Galindo, she is the 1988 World Junior champion and two-time national champion (1989, 1990). In 2005, she was inducted into the U.S. Olympic Hall of Fame.

VISUAL ARTS & ARCHITECTURE

Amino, Leo: Japanese American sculptor whose work is held at institutions like Carnegie Museum of Art and the Smithsonian American Art Museum.

Asawa, Ruth Aiko: Japanese American sculptor whose work is featured in collections at the Guggenheim and the Whitney Museum. In 2020, the U.S. Postal Service produced a series of ten commemorative stamps. She received the Honor Award from the Women's Caucus for the Arts, the Asian American Art Foundations Golden Ring Lifetime Achievement Award, and since 1982, San Francisco has declared February 12th to be "Ruth Asawa Day."

Bing, Bernice: Chinese American lesbian recipient of the National Women Caucus for the Arts Visual Arts Honor Award in 1996.

Butt, Ambreen: Pakistani American artist who received the inaugural James and Audrey Foster Prize from the Institute of Contemporary Art, the Brother Thomas Fellowship from the Boston Foundation, the Maud Morgan Prize from the Museum of Fine Arts, and an Artadia Award.

Chau, Karen Kai-Lan: Chinese American artist and creator of the children's TV series *Ni Hao, Kai-Lan* that was nominated for an Emmy award in 2010.

Chen, Hilo: Taiwanese-born American painter whose work is in major museum collections throughout the world including the Solomon R. Guggenheim Museum and the Taipei Fine Arts Museum.

Chen, Susan: Asian American recipient of the Hopper Prize and a Forbes "30 Under 30" honoree.

Chinn, Lenore: She is best known for her American realist paintings and her queer activism.

Gee, Yun: Chinese American modernist who is considered one of the most daring avant-garde painters of his time.

Chung, Tiffany: Vietnamese American, globally recognized, multimedia artist.

Hashmi, Zarina (Zarina): The Indian American artist became one of the most celebrated South Asian artists. Her works are in the permanent collections of the Museum of Modern Art, the Whitney Museum of American Art, the National Gallery of Art, and the Bibliothèque Nationale de France.

Ishigaki, Eitaro: The Japanese American artist was a founding member of the John Reed Club and a member of the Federal Art Project. In the 1930s, he was also involved in the Artists Congress and other WPA activities.

Kingman, Dong: A Chinese American watercolor master who won widespread critical acclaim. His works are included in over 50 public and private collections worldwide, including Metropolitan Museum of Art, Museum of Fine Arts, Brooklyn Museum, de Young Museum and Art Institute.

Kuniyoshi, Yasuo: Japanese American painter, photographer, and printmaker who was awarded the Guggenheim Fellowship, was an Honorary member of the National Institute of Arts and Letters, and the first president of the Artists Equity Association (NY Artists Equity Association). In 1948, he became the first living artist chosen to have a retrospective at the Whitney Museum.

Lai, Timothy: Of a Mexican American and Chinese heritage, Lai's paintings have been exhibited internationally. In 2021, Artsy named him a rising artist of the Asian diaspora in the United States.

Lee, Young Kwok: Chinese American activist, community organizer, photographer, journalist, and the unofficial Asian American Photographer Laureate. He called himself an "ABC from NYC...yielding a camera to slay injustices against APAs."

Lin, Maya Ying: Designer and sculptor, who achieved national recognition when she won a national competition to design the Vietnam Veterans Memorial in Washington, D.C. Lin has designed numerous memorials, public and private buildings, landscapes, and sculptures, including the Civil Rights Memorial in Montgomery, Alabama.

Liu, Hung: Chinese-born American contemporary artist, one of the first Chinese to establish a career in the United States.

Nakagawa, Osamu James: Japanese American photographer who received a Guggenheim Fellowship and awards from the cities of Higashikawa and Sagamihara in Japan, among others. He has exhibited internationally at venues including the Metropolitan Museum of Art, Tokyo Photographic Art Museum, Museum of Fine Arts in Houston, and Sakima Art Museum in Japan.

Nakashima, George Katsutoshi: Japanese American woodworker and architect, who was one of the leading innovators of 20th-century furniture design and a father of the American craft movement. In 1983, he accepted the Order of the Sacred Treasure, an honor bestowed by the Emperor of Japan and the Japanese government.

Ng, Jane: Chinese American 3D-environment artist, best known for her work on the *Firewatch: The Cave* and *Brütal Legend* video games.

Ng, Win "Winfred": Artist, entrepreneur, decorative designer, and co-founder of the groundbreaking San Francisco department store Taylor & Ng.

Noguchi, Isamu: One of the twentieth century's most important and critically acclaimed sculptors who also designed stage sets for Martha Graham and furniture pieces including the iconic Noguchi table.

Ouyang, Catalina: Sculptor, writer, and interdisciplinary artist who has received awards from the Foundation of Contemporary Arts, the Puffin Foundation, the Santo Foundation, Real Art Ways, and the Elizabeth Greenshields Foundation.

Paik, Nam June: Korean American who is considered the founder of video art and credited with the first use of the term "electronic superhighway" in 1974 to describe the future of telecommunications. His artwork and ideas were a major influence on late 20th-century art.

Pei, I.M.: World-famous Chinese American architect who designed some of the most iconic buildings (e.g., John F. Kennedy Memorial Library, Herbert F. Johnson Museum of Art, Rock & Roll Hall of Fame and Museum, the pyramid at the Musée du Louvre). In 1983, Pei won the Pritzker Prize, which is referred to as "the Nobel Prize of architecture."

Sekimachi, Kay: Recognized as a pioneer in using the loom to construct three-dimensional sculptural forms.

Shih, Stephanie H.: Taiwanese American ceramic artist whose work focused highlights how diverse members of a cultural diaspora can express both unique and shared memories about their heritage and life in the foreign land they call home.

Shimomura, Roger Yutaka: Showcased in the U.S., Japan, Canada, Mexico, and Israel, his art was awarded the First Kansas Master Artist Award in the Visual Arts, the Joan Mitchell Foundation Painting Award, and the Kansas Governor's Arts Award.

Sikander, Shahzia: Pakistani American artist and recipient of the South Asian Women's Creative Collective Achievement Award, a Commendation Award from the Mayor's Office (NYC), the Jennifer Howard Coleman Distinguished Lectureship and Residency, and the National Medal of Honor from the Government of Pakistan.

Suh, Do Ho: Korean sculptor and installation artist who won the Ho-Am Prize.

Syjuco, Stephanie: Filipino American conceptual artist and educator, whose work is in the San Francisco Museum of Modern Art, the di Rosa Center for Contemporary, and the Whitney Museum of American Art.

Takaezu, Toshiko: Japanese American ceramic artist, painter, sculptor, and educator. She received a McInerny Foundation Grant, Tiffany Foundation Grant, National Endowment for the Arts Fellowship, Watershed Legends Award, and Konjuhosho Award (2010). She was named a "Living Treasure of Hawaii" in 1987 and received the "National Living Treasure" award from the University of North Carolina in 1994. Her work is in many museum collections including The Metropolitan Museum of Art and the Smithsonian.

Takamori, Akio: Japanese American ceramic sculptor who received the Flintridge Foundation Award for Visual Artists, the Virginia A. Groot Award, and several National Endowment for the Arts Visual Artists Fellowship Grants.

Tam, Kenneth: He works in video, sculpture, and photography and has had solo exhibitions at the Minneapolis Institute of Art, the MIT List Center for Visual Arts, the Commonwealth and Council (LA), and the Night Gallery (LA).

Tam, Reuben: American landscape painter, educator, poet, and graphic artist. His paintings are featured in many famous museums.

Tamotzu, Chuzo: Self-taught painter whose art is held in the collections of the Metropolitan Museum, Hirshhorn Museum and Sculpture Garden, and the New Mexico Museum of Art.

Tsai, Wen-Ying: Chinese American pioneer cybernetic sculptor and kinetic artist. As one of the first Chinese-born artists to achieve international recognition in the 1960s, Tsai was an inspiration to generations of Chinese artists around the world.

Wang, Jennifer Sheena "Jen": American cartoonist, writer, and co-founder/organizer of the Comic Arts LA festival.

Wing T. Chao, Wing T: A Disney Imagineer for 37 years, he led the design of Disney parks, hotels, and cruise ships. In recognition of his contributions, he was named a Disney Legend in 2019.

Wong, Martin: Chinese American painter, whose work explored multiple ethnic/racial identities, demonstrated multilingualism, and celebrated his queer sexuality.

Wong, Tyrus: Chinese-born American painter, animator, calligrapher, muralist, ceramicist, lithographer, and kite maker, as well as a set designer and storyboard artist. One of the most influential Asian-American artists of the 20th century, Wong was the lead illustrator on Disney's 1942 film *Bambi*.

Wu, Frank: Science fiction and fantasy artist who won the Hugo Award for Best Fan Artist four times (2004, 2006, 2007, 2009).

Xie, Xiaoze: Chinese American visual artist and professor, his work explores the ephemeral nature of time, history, and cultural memory.

Yachen, Wang: Chinese Asian modern artist whose work has been offered at auction multiple times with winning bids of as much as $598,440.

Yamasaki, Minoru: His work with an influential architecture firm kept him and his family out of internment camps during WWII. He established his own firm in 1949 and designed the Pacific Science Center and the World Trade Center (NY). He was one of the most prominent architects of the 20th century.

Yoon, Meejin: The Korean American became the first female head of the department of architecture at MIT in 2014. She designed the Collier Memorial at MIT and the White Noise/White Light installation for the 2004 Athens—Olympics.